I hope you didn't actually pay good money for this worthless book — I mean, that would be really stupid!

Sam Venable
Project Graduation
11/19/09

I'd rather be ugly than stuppid

... and other deep thoughts

Other books by Sam Venable

An Island Unto Itself

A Handful of Thumbs and Two Left Feet

Two or Three Degrees Off Plumb

One Size Fits All and Other Holiday Myths

From Ridgetops to Riverbottoms: A Celebration of the Outdoor Life In Tennessee

I'd rather be ugly than stuppid

... and other deep thoughts

by Sam Venable

Cartoons by R. Daniel Proctor

🏛 The Knoxville News-Sentinel

Cover design by R. Daniel Proctor
Front cover photograph by Clay Owen
Back cover photograph by Margaret Bentlage
Book design and layout by Jacquelyn Brown and Rey Pineda
Editing by Jacquelyn Brown and Susan Alexander

For Kay Fine, who always came through in the clutch.

Contents

IX. Clothes break the man

Foreword

Sam Venable writes about all sorts of "thingamajigs" and can come up with brilliant quotations such as, "I'd rather be ugly than stupid."

Sam obviously liked that phrase so much that he decided to misspell it and use it as the title for this book, which is another entertaining collection of columns from his (and mine, for that matter) favorite newspaper.

Sam also likes to say things such as, "I am not making this up," because he writes on the most unusual topics. His writing style has made him a favorite of our readers for more than 25 years.

This is the fourth introduction I have written for Sam, and I hope I have the opportunity to do more in the future. Every newspaper should be blessed to have among its staff someone as talented and caring as a Sam Venable. Yes, caring. He volunteers much of his time to help charitable organizations in the area, including the Helen Ross McNabb Mental Health Center, Volunteer Ministry Center, Habitat for Humanity, and the Empty Stocking Fund.

One of his friends, Jake Vest, says Sam is an ambassador to the regular folks out there. That fittingly describes Sam and explains his popularity among our readers.

Vest, who draws the comic "That's Jake," adds that Sam is what's missing in a lot of newspapers. "Some of them have potential Sams, but they aren't allowed to be what they can because they are misguided by the directionally impaired. It's good that he is as he is. It's good that you let him be that way."

One thing an editor should know is not to mess with something that does not need any tinkering. And that, of course, is Sam Venable. I know you will enjoy reading Sam's latest collection—or else you wouldn't have bought it. If the book was a gift, read it anyway.

In closing, before Sam walks off with all the credit, I want to say a special thanks to three News-Sentinel staffers for their help in putting this book together. They are Jacquelyn Brown, the newspaper's public service director, who saw to it that the project got completed; Dan Proctor, The News-Sentinel's art director, whose cartoons illustrate Sam's columns, and Rey Pineda, a News-Sentinel artist who spent many hours getting this project pulled together.

Harry Moskos, Editor
The Knoxville News-Sentinel
August 27, 1996

Preface

Dear fellow writer:

How do I know you're a writer? You have to be. Writers are the only people who ever glance at a preface, let alone actually read it. The paying customers always skip over this part of a book and go immediately to the main event.

Can't say that I blame them, of course. As you and I both know, the only thing that takes place in the preface is a bit of waxed eloquence about what drove the author to write a book in the first place. Most readers couldn't care less.

But now that we have a minute, let me ask a few questions:

Does it ever worry you that readers, who are intelligent enough to hold down real jobs, will some day catch onto the hoax we writers have been pulling all these years? When do you think readers will realize writers haven't discovered any more Great Truths and unlocked any more Great Secrets than anyone else? When will it dawn on them that the only job skill writers have perfected is being able to look at the mundane events that occur in everybody's life and then crack a few lame jokes and one-liners about them?

Even worse: Do you ever cringe in fear that someone who *really* knows the language arts–like maybe one of your old English teachers from junior high–will suddenly show up and ask, in a very loud voice, "Hey! Whatever gave this goof the idea he's a writer? Who does he think he's fooling? Just look at this theme he turned in! It's gibberish! Not the first footnote!"

Lord knows I've tried to come clean. I have confided to close friends that the only difference between writers and non-writers is that writers charge for the goods they deliver, while non-writers give it away for free. Those same close friends are usually quick to point out that prostitutes follow an identical vocational agenda.

Oh, well. We've kept the secret safe so far; maybe we can keep it going awhile longer. Cross your fingers, seal your lips, put on your best learned face, and go back to the word processor. Give 'em everything you've got, partner.

And remember: Never let on that deep down inside, you're stuppid.

Mum's the word,

Sam Venable
August 19, 1996

CHAPTER ONE

I'd rather be ugly than stuppid

Ask anyone who's crazy enough to write newspaper columns for a living and you'll get the same answer: The hardest part is coming up with an idea.

Fortunately, there are enough dumb things going on Out There, many by our own doing, to keep us in fresh material.

Often, it's a feast-or-famine situation. Just when the idea lake has dried down to its last few precious drops, along comes a deluge of blunders, goofs and gaffes and fills it to overflowing once more.

Listen! Wasn't that a rumble of thunder off in the distance? Yes!

You'll have to excuse me. I've got to run outside and play in the rain.

Double jeopardy

June 8, 1995

I've been reading a new book about the CIA's most infamous spy, and one thought keeps coming to my mind: How do double agents keep their stories straight?

The book, by David Wise, is called "Nightmover." It's about Aldrich Ames, the traitor who sold super-sensitive secrets to the Russians, ultimately causing the death of 10 CIA operatives inside the former USSR. Ames was arrested in February 1994. Two months later, he was sentenced to life in prison.

It's amazing enough that Ames worked as a well-paid double agent for the Ruskies for nine years, right under the noses of his bosses in Washington. You'd think someone would notice when a government employee earning $50,000 a year suddenly buys a $540,000 house, starts driving a Jaguar and blows $30,000 a month on credit cards. Then again, maybe they mistook him for a congressman.

But what I find most astounding is how people like Ames are able to keep up with the lies, half-truths, falsehoods, prevarications and other forms of fiction essential to the spy trade. Their own name, for instance.

Let's say you're an ordinary guy named Bill Jones. You're walking down the street one day and someone shouts, "Bill! How are you doing?" You look up and see a man you went to high school with 20 years ago.

You recognize his face, but can't recall his name. So you wind up stammering about how hot the weather has been lately or how great it was back in '75 when the football team whipped Hooterville.

But if you are a spy engaged in double agent shenanigans at the moment, you've got to know not to even respond when someone says, "Hi, Bill," because you're going by Jim Smith. Unless, of course, it's someone, like maybe your brother-in-law, who knows you are a spy and that your real, honest-to-gosh name is Bill.

Too bad. By that time, you have ducked into an alley and run off or shot the guy dead with a silencer-equipped pistol. Either way, it's a social embarrassment.

But that's simple compared with the mind-numbing process of trying to cover your tracks on a daily basis. It surely boils down to a never-ending game of "Who's On First."

For instance, let's say you have been stealing sensitive information from the McGruder file and passing it to enemy agents. Everything has gone smoothly for months. Then one morning your boss walks up and asks, "What have you learned from the McGruder file?"

"The McSuitor file?" you reply coolly. "I haven't seen it."

"No, not McSuitor. McGRUDER. I gave it to you yesterday. We talked about how those wingdigits might have been planted inside the wall of the agency as listening devices."

"Oh, yes, the McGruder file. I gave it to Filestone."

"No you didn't. Filestone gave it to me to give to you."

"Right. But I gave it back to him."

"How could you? He got on a plane for Spain as soon as he handed the file to me."

"A plane for Spain? He told me he was taking a train to Fort Wayne."

"Filestone never travels by train. It gives him a pain. You oughta know that."

"Of course I do. Silly me. It wasn't Filestone after all. It was Fieldstand."

"Fieldstand died last year."

"Ah-hah! And that explains why the file is missing!"

This presents a dilemma for your boss, who's not sure whether you are: (1) a bumbling nincompoop who ought to be fired, (2) a double agent for the enemy, or (3) a plant from the human resources division who's spying to see how effectively he manages his department. Mentally calling it a draw, you both retire to your respective offices and take a long, nervous pull of Maalox.

The double agent business is not for me, thank you. I have enough trouble trying to remember what's on the grocery list.

I'd rather be ugly than stuppid

August 7, 1994

I f you can relate to this incident, you have my deepest sympathy: Company was coming for supper, and I needed to finish mowing the grass. The time was drawing nigh. About five minutes before the job was done, my mower coughed and started losing power. I am familiar with that symptom; it means the lawnmower is running out of gasoline. I killed the engine and unscrewed the gas tank cap, just to make certain that was the problem.

It was.

No sweat. The fuel can wasn't more than 40 feet away. I walked over, picked it up, brought it to the mower, refueled and carried the can back to where it stays.

I returned to the mower and started to pull the cord. That's when I noticed I hadn't replaced the gas tank cap.

I looked around the mower. The cap wasn't there.

I walked to the fuel can and looked. Nothing.

I went back to the lawnmower and moved it forward a few inches, on the chance it had rolled over the cap. Nice try, but to no avail.

I went back again to the fuel can and picked it up, hoping I had left the cap under there.

I had not.

Please understand. Everything transpired within the span of 60 seconds. It wasn't like I'd gone inside the house before refueling the mower, or made a phone call, or fixed a snack. Nothing of the kind. I had walked directly from lawnmower A, through garage door B, out to fuel can C, and back. And yet the hateful gas tank cap, which I had removed only seconds earlier, was nowhere to be found.

My blood pressure was galloping along by then, but I was intrigued enough by the mystery to keep from coming unglued. I walked several yards downhill from the mower and searched in the grass, thinking perhaps it had rolled away. No dice. The gas tank cap had flat-out disappeared.

I retraced my steps for a third time. Searched both places again. Still nothing.

On the fourth-by-gosh-trip back to the fuel can, my eyes caught something on the back of a shelf in the garage. There was the @#$%! cap, right where I, in a state of total absent-mindedness, had placed it.

Aaaaarrrgh!

How can this happen? How can I be holding an object in my hands, set it aside for .00005-second, and then not have a clue where it is?

I do it all the time. Just now, on my desk, I unearthed two notes I had carried from home a couple of days ago. I distinctly remember bringing these notes to the office. I distinctly remember looking at them that morning. And I distinctly remember tearing my desk and briefcase apart in a vain attempt to find them later that afternoon.

In fact, it wasn't until right now—when I was inspecting an obscure envelope for some photographic negatives—that they fluttered out of hiding. Obviously, I had stuck them into the envelope when my mind was on a planet 150 million miles away.

This makes me doubly angry because it's so absolutely, positively senseless to set something aside and, half an eyeblink later, have no recollection whatsoever of having done it.

If there was an alarm that flashed red lights and screamed, "Idiot! Idiot! Idiot!" every time I was about to perform this trick, I'd buy one and install it immediately. Assuming I could find my screwdriver.

I don't know about you, but I'd rather be ugly than stuppid.

A parable

October 4, 1994

Today's sermon is taken from the book of Venob, Chapter II, verses 1-17:

1. In the city beside quiet waters dwelled contented people, given to hard labor and simple pleasures. And yet some among them began to grow restless.

2. "Throughout all our days, we have worked with diligence in our fields and in our shops," they made loud lamentations, "and yet we receive no great reward. If we had but a savior, one who could lead us into the land that flows freely with milk and honey!"

3. And, lo, it came to pass that a stranger, as tall as pine and with hair more silver than the finest chalice, approached the gates of the city. And his name was Jacob the Butcher.

4. "Hear me, ye leaders of the people," he sayeth. "I have come from the land of Maynardvillia, where I, along with my father and my brother, have prospered greatly in the accumulation of shekels. Abide and put thy trust in me."

5. A few of the elders and chief priests were unmoved. "Jacob the Butcher knoweth not our ways, and we knoweth not his," they admonished. "As it is written, 'Hard labor and simple pleasures are riches unto themselves.' " But their words fell upon deaf ears, and they were pushed aside.

6. And thus did the people hail Jacob the Butcher as their savior and did thrust their shekels into his hand. "Build for us a golden altar," they beseeched him, "so that we also may accumulate great riches."

7. And Jacob the Butcher built a tower, as round and bright and shiny as the sun. And people came from foreign lands to worship. Many were their festivals and feasts. The fatted calf was killed and good wine was poured. There was singing and dancing in the streets.

8. But, lo, at dawn after the last festival, there came a great weeping and wailing and gnashing of teeth. "Jacob the Butcher hath tricked us!" the people cried. "We have not become rich! Our shekels are gone! We owe debts as high as any mountain! Woe is

us!" And they cast Jacob the Butcher into prison.

9. A great remorse then fell upon the city beside quiet waters. "Never again shall we be tricked by strangers!" sayeth the people. "Verily, we shall return to hard labor and simple pleasures and covet not our neighbors' riches."

10. But soon, more among them began to grow restless. And they said, "Our labors make us weary. If we had but a savior, one who could lead us into the land that flows freely with milk and honey!"

11. And, lo, it came to pass that a stranger, short of stature and wearing small garlands of finest silk around his neck, approached the gates of the city. And his name was Chris the Whittler.

12. "Hear me, ye leaders of the people," he sayeth. "I have come from the land of Athens, where I, along with my fellow men, have prospered greatly in the writing of scrolls. Abide and put thy trust in me."

13. Again, some of the elders and chief priests were unmoved. "Chris the Whittler knoweth not our ways, and we knoweth not his," they admonished. But yet again, their words fell upon deaf ears, and they were pushed aside.

14. And thus did the people of the city beside quiet waters welcome Chris the Whittler into their camp and did heap favor and high praise upon him. And they joined their shekels with his shekels and built a great temple. And there was singing and dancing in the streets.

15. But, lo, it soon came to pass that Chris the Whittler abandoned the city beside quiet waters and fled to a foreign land, taking his shekels with him. And the people of the city stood in bewilderment. And they whispered quietly among themselves to hide their shame. And some of the elders and chief priests also stood by, weeping at the destruction around them.

16. Finally, one of the people spoke. "Fear not," sayeth he. "We shall find for ourselves another savior, one who will lead us into the land that flows freely with milk and honey!"

17. And they picked up rods and stones and smote him.

Going nekkid

July 12, 1992

This is National Nude Day. If you're one of those fun-loving, festive folks who celebrates every holiday, feel free to unlatch your Levis and run nekkid.

Please understand that I mean "nekkid" in this regard. Not "naked." Nekkid is a state of mind as well as body. Southerners go nekkid. Yankees, mannequins and cadavers go naked.

The Naturist Society of Oshkosh, Wis., sponsors this event "to promote acceptance of the body and understanding of the nude recreation movement as a natural solution to many problems of modern living."

Fine by me. I learned long ago to accept my body. Had to. No one else would. Still, I am a bit confused about how nudity can solve the "problems of modern living."

I guess a lot depends on what your particular problem happens to be.

If you live in Duluth, Minn., and it's the middle of February and one of your most maddening problems of modern living is driving through seven-foot snowdrifts en route to the office, going nekkid—or naked, since, after all, we're talking about Duluth—won't solve a thing. It will, however, get you arrested, freeing you of worry about snowdrifts, seven-foot or otherwise, for a good 11 months and 29 days.

I also have some questions about the role of nudism in recreation. With one very distinct exception, ahem, I can think of few forms of rest and relaxation that lend themselves favorably to buck nekkidness.

Fishing? Not a good choice. Too many sharp objects flying through the air.

Golf? Only if all shots stay out of the rough.

Chess, checkers, card games? Excellent, provided you avoid vinyl chairs, especially those exposed to direct sunlight.

Hunting? Out of the question. Wading through briars is torture enough with thick pants.

Hockey? Hmmm. At least it would give spectators something to watch besides the fights.

Gardening? Iffy at best, particularly if there's a Weed Eater nearby.

Of course, there's always swimming. Any grown-up from this part of the country who did not go jaybird during his/her youth is either a liar or totally void of adventure. But, alas, once you cross that great chasm into adulthood, jaybirding must be approached with a high degree of respect for local custom.

Back in the early '70s, I took a lawyer friend trout fishing deep inside the Cherokee National Forest. He was, as we say, "not from around here."

We separated on the stream. An hour or so later I started searching for the guy and, finding his clothes piled neatly upon a rock, came to the shocking revelation he no longer was fishing.

At that precise moment, a huge, pearly white set of gorilla buns boiled to the surface in mid-stream. When his head bobbed up seconds later, I shouted some words of advice: "You can't do that in this neck of the woods!"

"How come?" he yelled back.

I let out a pig squeal. "Does the word 'Deliverance' ring a bell?"

Yes, it did. And I was amazed how fast a fellow could get dressed when properly motivated.

Bring on the cane

June 28, 1994

Now that Michael Fay has returned to the United States, it's only a matter of time before he becomes a million-aire. Not that he hasn't put up with some pain for his reward. Fay is the Ohio teenager who was caned in Singapore for spray-painting cars.

Fay insists he didn't commit the crime but was forced into making a confession. He swears that during interrogation proce-dures, the Singapore police jerked him around by the hair and struck him with their fists.

Maybe. Maybe not. By the time young Fay finishes the Oprah-Phil-Geraldo circuit and completes a book and co-authors a movie script, perhaps we shall know.

The more I think about this case, though, the more I truly believe there are people who deserve an occasional taste of the rattan.

Inconsiderate drivers, for instance.

You know the kind. They stack up in line at a red light but won't allow someone in the turn lane to cross in front of them. Or else they stubbornly refuse to let motorists from an on-ramp blend into interstate traffic.

Who else is in desperate need of the cane? How about those fungal forms of life who hog two places in a parking lot?

Check out the asphalt anywhere. I promise you'll see some jerk's vehicle— usually new and shiny—sitting squarely in the midst of two slots.

If these people want to take extra precautions against dents and dings, fine; let them park in left field, far away from the masses. But if they insist on crowding everyone else out of their way, it's Bun Warmer City.

Visit the nearest grocery store and you'll find yet another batch of dolts who beg for a switching. The aisle-jammers.

No matter how many other people are behind them, they park their carts smack-dab in the middle of an aisle and start wandering aimlessly from side to side, comparing prices and checking labels.

The solution? Four strokes for each instance when another shopper has to move their cart.

Come to think of it, supermarkets offer a treasure trove of potential canees. The woman who waits until her groceries are tallied and bagged before she gets out her checkbook definitely belongs on this list. So does the guy who works his way to the cash register, stands there until the last item has been rung up and then—"Oops! Holy @#$%! Where's the guava paste?"—has to dash back to Aisle 14.

I dare not omit the pinheads at fast food joints, either. I know you've seen them in action.

They walk into, say, a McDonald's, and the line is 10 people deep. They take a place and stand there—hands in pockets, eyes in the air, brain in neutral—for the next 15 minutes as the customers in front are served.

Finally, it's their turn. And what happens?

"Hmmm," they say, eyes suddenly glued to the overhead menu, as if it only appeared to them that very moment. "I really don't know what I'll have today. A hamburger? Naaaa. A fish sandwich? Maybe. Let's see now . . ."

It is the patriotic duty of anyone behind these dolts to cane them immediately.

All in favor say "aye."

My cowardly dog

March 15, 1994

Ken-L Ration recently gave awards for canine bravery, and for the seventh straight year, my dog didn't win. Not that she had a ghost of a chance of making the short list. The only award Goldie will ever win is Wuss of the Universe.

Goldie, a lovable English setter, is a great pet. She is relatively well-behaved. Our family adores her. But in matters of bravery, she makes the Cowardly Lion look like a Teenage Mutant Ninja Turtle.

Oh, she puts on a good show. Under the right conditions, Goldie can fluff her fur and bark and act like she's going to kick some serious butt. But it's 100-percent theatrics. "The right conditions" means whatever she's barking at is attached to a short, stout leash.

You know how even the most timid dogs become courageous on

their own turf? Not Goldie. Your place or hers, she will invariably retreat.

Two summers ago, a friend from Nashville spent the night at our house. She brought along a smallish pooch of yip-yip lineage. You've seen the kind before: a $10 hairpiece on four legs that yammers ceaselessly, two octaves above your basic "bow-wow."

Anyhow, this dog bounced out of the car and began sniffing and anointing various shrubs. Seeing a foe she outweighed by 30 pounds, Goldie raised her hackles, barked furiously, and charged in to challenge the pip-squeak.

"Yip-yip!" said the pip-squeak.

"Holy @#$%!" Goldie screamed in English setterese. She turned tail and, I am not making this up, RAN AWAY FROM HOME! She did not return until after the pip-squeak left.

Not long ago—ask my wife if you don't believe me—a German shepherd puppy wandered into our yard and sent Goldie slinking into her dog house. Note I said "puppy." We are not talking Rin Tin Tin.

Didn't matter. Goldie cowered inside her box for the 10 minutes that the puppy poked around our yard. Only after the younger dog ambled down the hill did Goldie come sprinting out to chase the infidel from her midst.

Still, the least of her problems is other dogs. Some months ago, the Whites, who live behind us, acquired a large, hairy cat. When it wandered into our yard one day, I watched the following encounter with my own baby blues:

Goldie, who apparently had never seen this cat before, ran toward it at full cry. Her display was quite convincing; for once, she even fooled me. The cat arched its back and hissed. Goldie skidded to a stop. She stared at the cat for a moment and then turned toward me with the most pathetic, Oh-Lord-what-have-I-gotten-myself-into-now? expression I've ever seen on a dog's face. I think the fact I was convulsing with laughter actually hurt her feelings.

Clearly the champion, the cat turned and walked defiantly back to the chainlink fence that separates our yards. Goldie didn't so much as flinch.

Ever since, Goldie has ignored the cat. Unless it's on the

White's side of the fence, of course, in which case she paces like a tiger and barks menacingly.

If the Ken-L Ration people depended upon Goldies of the world for bravery, they'd go broke inside of 24 hours.

Enough PMS to go around

June 11, 1991

As one who believes foursquare in the principle of equal rights for men and women, I say it's time to legitimize PMS for everyone.

The way things stand now, only people of the female persuasion are privy to this excuse. They grow irritable and irrational several days a month, and it's OK for them to blame their behavior on premenstrual syndrome.

You think I'm kidding? Look what happened the other day in Fairfax, Va.

A woman named Geraldine Richter had been arrested for DWI. According to State Trooper S.M. Lunsford, Richter also used vulgar language and kicked him.

In court, Richter admitted she had been drinking. Four glasses of wine, she said. That might explain why she registered 0.13 on a Breathalyzer test—.03 higher than many states consider to be an indicator of drunkenness.

But, the woman and her attorney argued, it was neither the hooch nor the devil that made her do it. It was the PMS.

A gynecologist, whom the defense paid $1,000 for expert testimony, said Richter's behavior was similar to anyone suffering from PMS. The disorder was described as an assortment of physical and emotional reactions, including fatigue, depression and irritability, just before the start of the menstrual cycle.

It worked. Fairfax General District Judge Robert Smith declared Richter not guilty.

This isn't the first time PMS has been used as an excuse in court. Last January in Pittsburgh, a woman accused of beating, choking and stabbing an elderly patient at a nursing home cited PMS as one of several extenuating circumstances.

There's more. I quote from a 1984 article in Psychology Today magazine:

"In 1980 and again in 1981, the British courts set free two women who had been charged with murder. In each case, the charge was reduced to manslaughter because, it was argued, premenstrual syndrome had lessened the women's responsibility for their actions."

Fine. But what about something for us men? Can't we have a designated two or three days per month when we fly off the handle? And get away with it, I mean?

Nobody's perfect. Men have moods too.

There are days when our biorhythms are off and we're out of synch with the rest of the world. From the moment we get out of bed until we slide back between the sheets, we are cranky and fussy and prone to cat-and-dog tirades at the slightest provocation.

But what happens if this behavior gets us into trouble? We either get a good chewing out or a punch in the nose or 11 months, 29 days, that's what.

I am not a student of laws. But I'm willing to bet that if your average Joe Bubba tossed back four barley sodas, weaved in and out of traffic, got stopped by the law, blew a .13, gave the cop a good cussing and kicked him in the shins—and then asked the judge for mercy because of cyclical irritability—court would be adjourned until the laughter died down.

But we can always hope for a change in attitudes. Call it PMS: Pushy Male Syndrome. Or CJS: Callous Jerk Situation.

The name really doesn't matter. All we ask is our fair shake.

Easy as pie

August 2, 1992

The next time I'm in the mood for blackberry cobbler, I'm going to contact deputies with the Knox County Sheriff's Department. They'll know where the sweetest, juiciest berries are found.

At least they ought to know. After spending several days tripping lightly through the briars and brambles of our region, these people should be on a first-name basis with berry bushes from Forks of the River to Dixie Lee Junction.

This important knowledge was gained last week when deputies raided two patches of marijuana.

The first, near Buffat Mill Road and Love's Creek, yielded 243 plants. According to a spokesman for the sheriff's department, this was a relatively young operation. Most of the wacky weed was in seedling stage, although some stalks ranged upwards of six feet.

But the second—off Kingston Pike, just west of Cedar Bluff Road—was blue ribbon material. Deputies hacked down 86 mature plants, most in the 10- to 12-foot variety.

Assuming all 329 of these plants had made it to maturity, and assuming they brought top dollar on the street, they were worth a total of $600,000, deputies estimated.

In both instances, officers were tipped by blackberry pickers. These gentlefolk were strolling through the garneymuckle, merrily filling their little tin pails with nature's finest nectar, when they wandered into mini-plantations of The Stuff.

Such discoveries bring several observations to mind.

First, it is abundantly clear that the sheriff's department needs to organize a Blackberry Beat. If amateur pickers—who are more watchful of hornets' nests and poison ivy than dope—can ferret out patches of puff plants, just think what full-time officers can do! And if this venture is successful, the territory can be broadened. The Strawberry Beat bears watching, as does the Corn Beat, the Cherry Beat, the Okra Beat and, naturally, the Beet Beat.

Second, one must assume there is a botanical link between yields of blackberries and marijuana. Cross-pollination, perhaps.

You take the flower of your standard, prickly, chigger-infested East Tennessee blackberry and fertilize it with pollen from Maui Wowie, and you wind up with a thornless, laid-back berry that wants to make love, not war.

Third, perhaps the secret to eradicating dope growers is to cultivate blackberries on every square inch of available land in the county and then encourage citizens to pick them.

Ever better, plow money into research to find a blackberry strain that bears fruit throughout the year. That way, pickers will be combing the hills and hollows in December as well as July.

Not only will this greatly increase the likelihood of more marijuana discoveries, it will also saturate the consumer market with millions of pints of freshly picked fruit.

Who knows? Blackberry cobbler might wind up replacing pumpkin pie on Thanksgiving Day tables throughout the United States.

Except at the Bill Clinton house, of course, where they chew blackberries, but don't swallow.

In the wake of St. Nick

December 26, 1995

'T is the day after Christmas
And all through this place,
It looks like the site
Of a big NASCAR race.

There's pushing and shoving
And bumps from the start.
They call it "Exchange Day"
Down at the Wal-Mart.

The line stretches 'cross
Twenty aisles, maybe more.
It looks like 10,000
Are crammed in this store.

They're back with the presents,
Once hand-picked with care;
Mostly hideous garments
They never would wear.

There's Fred with a necktie
That's purple and green.
Perhaps it's as ugly
As he's ever seen.

(You'd never have known it
On Christmas Day morn,
When he thanked Aunt Matilda
And said it'd be worn.)

Next Judy's in line
With a sweater so large,
It would cover the stern
Of a grain-hauling barge.

"Doesn't quite fit me,"
She laughs to the clerk,
Who's already bored
And quite tired of this work.

Behind her is Betty
With 3-year-old Bill,
Bringing back socks, coaster sets
And Dad's drill.

Then Frank with a suitcase
And Patty with soap,
Plus Sandy with mittens
And Herb with some rope.

Next Sue with a doll
That is missing an arm,
And Jennifer's clock
With non-working alarm.

Daniel has blue jeans
That sag past the knees,
Plus Evelyn's 19-pound
Gift pack of cheese.

Can't forget little Larry
With boots, size 11.
And Helen with perfume
That stinks to high heaven.

They all come to Wal-Mart
With junk others bought.
Then go spend the money
On something THEY want!

More people show up
With the presents they got.
The line now snakes out
To the front parking lot.

They bring bicycles, tricycles,
Books, games and toys,
That all were rejected
By girls and by boys.

"This dolly won't do,"
One tired momma laments.
"She HAD to have Barbie."
(What Mom needs is some sense.)

"Same with us," moans one dad
From the back of the line.
"A ball just won't bounce
"If some jock did not sign."

"This shirt, I discovered,"
Adds a woman named Mabel.
"Simply won't fit
"If it has the wrong label."

No problem, of course,
To exchange and take back.
These gifts will be routed
To another store's rack.

And then in two weeks
The commercials will say,
"Be sure to shop here
"For Valentine's Day!"

Where the sun doesn't shine

August 30, 1994

I'll be the first to confess relative ignorance in matters of illegal drugs. I'm too old to know any better. The drug of choice for my rushing-toward-retirement generation comes in bottles and cans and is heavily taxed by the government. The only place it is sold under the table is a dry county.

Thus, you can imagine my surprise a few days ago when I was perusing a North Carolina newspaper—I was on vacation at the beach, sipping a malt beverage, now that I think of it—and happened upon a story about a crackdown on crack houses. It listed the names of the folks arrested, location of the houses, street value of the drugs, cash recovered, blah-blah, 10-4 over and out.

But down in the fine print, it told how one suspect was carrying his cache. When the cops patted him down, they found $20 worth of crack cocaine in a most unusual area. It was wrapped in plastic and attached—how do I say this politely?—to a part of the human anatomy found only on males.

The first thing I did upon returning to Knoxville was ask one of our police reporters how large $20 worth of crack cocaine actually is. Are we talking about a thimble or a 5-pound sack of Kennebec potatoes? Neither seemed like a pleasant arrangement, particularly if held in place by rubber bands or—*yeee-iii!*—duct tape, but I was curious nonetheless.

Turns out $20 worth is quite concealable. Not much more than a few aspirin. Even so, I would greatly prefer a shirt pocket.

Next, I telephoned the cop shop to see if this mode of transportation was as common in Knoxville as it apparently is in North Carolina.

Goodness yes, narcotics investigator Mike Perrin told me; where had I been all these years? He said druggies have discovered any number of places to hide their goods. The ol' where-there's-a-will-there's-a-way routine.

Not necessarily the men either. Women often sneak the stuff into their bras and hair buns. Some are even more inventive.

Officer Perrin described several recent Knoxville cases in which women had stashed their cra. . ., er, drugs inside a pill bottle and then—how'd I get into this?—deposited the entire inventory in a region of the human anatomy found only on females.

I daresay either case presents some rather unusual sales techniques, not to mention contortions, down at the street corner, but that's neither here nor there. Based on what I could glean from the cops, buyers and sellers don't mind the inconvenience.

Smugglers have always been a resourceful lot. Back in the bootleg whiskey days, it was nothing for a souped-up car to be equipped with twin tanks: one for gasoline, one for white lightning. You better believe illicit liquids have been hidden in everything from fruit jars to hot water bottles, garden hoses to paint cans, coffee pots to milk buckets.

But you also better believe if Zeb approached Caleb out in Hootin' Holler and requested a pint of 'shine, and Caleb prepared to produce it in the manner of today's male drug smugglers, there would've been an awful fight.

Male mothers

December 18, 1994

In his new movie, "Junior," Arnold Schwarzenegger behaves in a most un-Schwarzeneggerish manner. He doesn't blast, zap, terminate, bomb, shoot, beat, kick, stomp, whip, cripple, kill or maim anyone.

Instead, he has a baby.

The plot goes something like this: Schwarzenegger plays Dr. Alex Hesse, a medical researcher who is working on a drug to prevent miscarriages. The FDA won't let him test it on a woman, so Hesse volunteers his own body. A fertilized egg is planted in his abdomen with the idea that it'll break down after he conducts his experiments. But before you can say nuthin'-means-lovin'-like-somethin'-from-the-oven, Hesse finds himself smitten with the idea of being a mother and decides to have the baby—by Cesarean, I should point out, before men everywhere scream in agony.

THERE ARE MANY REASONS WHY MEN SHOULD NOT HAVE BABIES...

RUINING THEIR FIGURE IS NOT ONE OF THEM.

This is nothing new for Hollywood. In 1978, Billy Crystal starred in a similar flick called "Rabbit Test." Five years earlier, Marcello Mastroianni wore maternity clothes in "A Slightly Pregnant Man."

But in real life? Naaa. Even if science did make it possible for men to play a larger role in the baby-making process, I doubt many of us would accept the offer. We know a good thing when we see it.

In the first place, we're too impatient: "It's gonna take nine months? You gotta be kidding! Look, if we can't wrap this project up by the middle of next week, just count me out."

In the second place, we're wimps. As a maleperson myownself, I can testify that men do not handle pain well. In any uncomfortable situation, we whine and moan, ever louder, until a femaleperson finally pays attention and comes to our assistance. If men had done all the baby bearing since the dawn of creation, I guarantee the world's population would number in the tens of thousands, not billions.

One more: For the life of me, I cannot imagine a bunch of men at a baby shower, oohing and aahing over diapers and blankets. Sure, we'd throw showers, but we'd buy more practical gifts for the soon-to-be-born. Like bowling balls, spinning reels, baseball bats, power tools and subscriptions to Field & Stream.

There's also the problem of all the secondary decisions that need to be made once The Deed is done.

You think husbands and wives argue over routine household chores now? Imagine what it'd be like when it comes to deciding who carries the wee one to term: "Aw, c'mon, Gladys. I know it's my turn to have a baby, but the office softball league starts in six months. How can I bat if the kid covers the strike zone?"

It's far better to nip this crazy notion in the bud. Leave male pregnancy where it belongs. In the movies.

God knew what he was doing when he made males and females and gave them distinct physiological differences—like the funny-looking thing that sticks out in front of a man.

You know, a beer gut.

Treasure in the trunk

September 8, 1994

T he next time I shop for a used car, I'm not going to kick the tires or look under the hood. I won't even take it for a test drive.

I will, however, check the trunk. Thoroughly. Maybe there's another car with $896,518 hidden in the trunk, and I want to be the person who finds it.

That's what happened recently in Campbell County. A deputy blue-lighted a car for speeding, grew suspicious as he questioned the driver, got permission to search and—*sha-zam!*—found the loot inside a hidden compartment in the trunk.

The driver, identified as 36-year-old George Franklin Lao of Miami, posted a $750 cash bond and walked away. Deputies said Lao denied any knowledge of the money. The last they saw of him, he was making a telephone call from a booth near the jail.

Far be it from me to speculate, but authorities think this incident could possibly, ahem, be drug-related. If so, I can only imagine how the conversation began: "It's me. George. Heh-heh, you'll never believe what just happened . . ."

Obviously, somebody, some place, knows where the loot came from. If this person doesn't make a claim in three weeks—don't hold your breath—it'll be split, 80-20, between the Campbell County Sheriff's Department and the Drug Enforcement Administration.

In the meantime, you never know when, or where, another car full of money might turn up.

I made a spot check of Knoxville automobile dealers. None of them had ever discovered $896,518 inside a trade-in, but what they had found was strange enough. Such as:

"Just about anything you can imagine," said Paul Siler of Reeder Chevrolet. "Yard tools, stadium seats, sunglasses, sometimes a gun. Once, we even found a small amount of marijuana. We always try to contact the former owner, but in the case of the marijuana we pitched it into the trash. We figured whoever it belonged to didn't want to hear from us."

Dope isn't the only thing former owners would just as soon forget.

Danny Ballinger of Beaty Chevrolet found a pair of panties and some used condoms in one car. Buzz Carrol of Lance Cunningham Ford remembered a blowup doll. Joe Wendelken from Clayton Volvo recalled "a picture of a guy with his girlfriend doing bad things." And Phil Clapp from Burgin Dodge uncovered a divorce decree.

"I telephoned the customer and told him about it," said Clapp. "He told me, 'Hell with it! Don't bring that thing up again!' "

Pocket change is pretty common, of course. A few dimes and

quarters most of the time. Which would take an eternity to add up to $896,518.

"Once we did find $21 worth of change under a seat," said Ken Nobinger of Neill Sandler Ford. "We called the guy, and he came back for it."

In any event, you better believe this case has changed my perspective on used automobiles. The next time I see a car commercial on TV and the salesman screams, "Folks, this baby is loaded!" I'm going to sit up and pay very close attention.

Makeovers for everyone

October 10, 1995

General Mills is giving Betty Crocker a facelift. Again. The company recently announced it is changing the appearance of its 75-year-old fictional queen of homemaking.

Betty has had eight images since she was created in 1921. Her last makeover occurred in 1986. That's when she acquired a red business suit and a bow tie. The company gave no hint about what Betty will be wearing this time around, but it did say her face will reflect a "multi-ethnic" background.

I am not joking. These wizards of marketing are going to take photos of dozens of women and digitally "morph" them into a new, '90s Betty who will reflect the diverse face of America.

Nothing wrong with that in theory. But practical application is another matter. How in the name of common sense can one person accurately represent this country's myriad ethnic roots?

She's only got two eyes. What color you suppose they'll have after the makeover—a greenish, brownish shade of blue?

As for hair, the mind boggles. Perhaps it will be a neat coif that accurately reflects her curly, straight, short, long, blonde, brunette, red, black locks. With just a touch of gray.

But who am I to argue with a jillion-dollar cake company? If they want to dump Betty's ingredients into a blender and create a new recipe, more power to 'em.

Who knows? Mayhaps other companies should follow suit. I prowled the aisles at a grocery store the other night and noticed quite a few corporate images that might be considered candidates for a '90s makeover. Among them:

- Chef Boyardee—In these lean and mean times, those jowls have gotta go.

- Green Giant—Put some clothes on this goof; fig leaves went out in Genesis.

- Quaker—Lose the Barbara Bush hair. And make him nondenominational.

- Mrs. Paul and Mrs. Smith—Aren't these women secure enough in themselves to use their own first names? Works for Sara Lee.

- Dr. Scholl—What kind of doctor is he in the first place? Did he get his degree from one of those diploma mills?

- Red Baron—Would you get on an airplane if a pilot from World War I was at the controls? I rest my case.

- Prince Albert, Sir Walter Raleigh, King Edward, Dutch Masters—Perhaps these geezers haven't noticed how many chicks Joe Camel attracts with his slick looks and cool clothes.

- Orville Redenbacher—Now that the real Orville has gone to that big corn patch in the sky, what about toning down his geekiness a level or two? Maybe "morph" him with the Brawny paper towel man.

- Mr. Clean—No changes needed whatsoever. He's perfect. With his chrome dome hair style and earring, this guy is Mister Modern American.

Go on and say it

October 30, 1994

There's an old hillbilly joke about cussing that reminds me of the town in New Jersey that recently passed an anti-swearing ordinance.

Seems there was this 6-year-old boy who cursed a blue streak. No matter how many licks of the paddle he received, no matter how many times he had to stand in the corner, no matter how often he had to write "I will not cuss in school," Johnny's bad habit continued.

The teacher decided to try positive reinforcement. She knew Johnny liked animals, so she promised if he'd go five straight days without an oath, she would buy him a pet.

Bingo. The boy's lips were pure, and he was rewarded with a rabbit. It stayed in a cage in the back of the room and became the focus of much attention.

What the teacher didn't realize, though, was that the rabbit was pregnant. One day, there was a commotion back there amongst the desks.

She asked, "Is something wrong, Johnny?"

"I reckon the (bleep) there is!" he shouted back. "This (bleeping) excuse for a (bleeping) rabbit you gave me is fallin' apart!"

OK, so it's a corny story. But it's been around for years, and I guarantee it'll still be with us long after the ordinance in Raritan, N.J., is ground into judicial dust.

In case you missed the story, Raritan's council passed the rule earlier this month. It forbids "noisy, rude or indecent behavior by using profane, vulgar or indecent language, by making insulting remarks or comments to others." Violators face a fine of $500 and

90 days in the clink.

The story made a big splash in newspapers all around the country. Based on what I read, Raritan's residents were split about the measure. Such as:

"I'm not saying I want a cop on every corner with a bar of soap in his pocket to wash your mouth out," said Brad Honigsberg. "But I do think cursing in public should be banned. People can't seem to do it voluntarily, so it's up to lawmakers."

"What were (council members) thinking?" countered Bree Dougherty. "The days of 'Leave It to Beaver' and 'American Bandstand' are long gone. The council should be more worried about how to protect citizens from crime and how to keep property taxes low."

I'm no lawyer, but I predict this regulation will evaporate the instant someone challenges it in court. Even though the tongue of America could stand a few strokes of Ivory—on street corners, in schools, on TV, in the movies, wherever—freedom of speech is far too precious to abandon, even if that same speech is sprinkled with a few @#$%!'s and %$#@!'s.

Indeed, there are times when an emphasized, perfectly placed cussword is needed to drive home a point.

If Admiral David Farragut had shouted, "Phooey on the torpedoes!" he'd have become a naval nobody, and the town of Farragut would be known by a different name.

And for the life of me, I can't imagine Harry Truman giving anybody, or anything, heck.

Very naughty and not nice

December 2, 1994

You know the world has slipped several degrees off plumb when Santa Claus gets a death threat.

That's what happened last December at a Colorado shopping mall, and it forced officials to create a high-security area to protect the jolly ol' elf this year.

At the Aurora Mall near Denver, Santa greets kiddies at the end of a trail that winds through a forest of twinkling trees. It may look like a peaceful Yuletide scene, but the layout was designed to prevent the kook who sent threatening messages from following through on the deed.

The threats, mailed and faxed to the mall, called Claus an "impostor" and included statements such as "he will be history along with anybody that gets in my way" and "time is running out on that fatso."

Wow. Talk about somebody who's been big-time naughty.

Mall officials took the threats seriously. They turned the evidence over to postal authorities and the FBI, but a case was never made. As Postal Service inspector John Freeman told reporters, "It was my impression the person was looking for attention and probably got too much. Quite frankly, we don't have any clues."

I also suspect, and dearly want to believe, this was a foolish prank, someone's very sick, very warped idea of a joke. Otherwise, what we have here is the most tormented soul in all of humankind:

"He sees me when I'm sleeping, does he? And he knows when I'm awake! He thinks I better watch out and better not pout! I'll give him something to cry about! Ah-ha-ha-ha-ha!"

But you never know. There seems to be a bumper crop of weir-does these days, which is why we have metal detectors in schools and three layers of protective seals on bottles of aspirin.

If this trend continues, taking Junior to see Santa will require security clearance from the CIA. Or else Claus will sit behind a pane of bulletproof glass and talk to the youngsters through a metal grid—the same arrangement used in all-night filling stations and prison visitation areas—while his elves monitor the negotiations closely, their little hands gripping concealed Uzis.

Indeed, this situation has the potential to balloon into all-out Christmas chaos. Given such a hostile environment, do you think Santa will continue to slide down chimneys unprotected? Not a chance.

At the very least, he'll want a sworn, notarized statement from homeowners pledging there are no burglar alarms to scare the bejesus out of him while he works, no guard dogs to rip his red suit to shreds, no booby-trapped canisters of Mace to send him screaming into the night. Plus a document from the local health department attesting that the milk and cookies left for him are free of bacteria.

If you think that's bad, wait till you see the legal papers Santa will insist parents sign in advance, holding him blameless for wrong sizes, models and colors, as well as any absence of batteries and sheets of instructions.

Beat the Christmas rush, folks. Hire your lawyer today.

Flat hats and goofy gowns

May 14, 1996

It's that time of year when people dress up in weird costumes and celebrate, and I'm not talkin' Halloween or New Year's Eve.

This is the season for graduations, a rite of spring practiced from kindergartens to colleges all over the nation. In the next few days, untold millions of graduates will walk down the aisle in honor of this custom, and it's high time somebody tells these poor folks what to expect.

First, they're going to have to wear a cap and gown that makes them look goofy.

If you weigh 452 pounds and have no neck whatsoever, a graduation gown will not hide your shame. Instead, you will look like a sumo wrestler draped with a tent. If you are a humanoid beanpole, the gown will do just the opposite. Imagine a black pipe cleaner.

The cap is worse. That's because it is supposed to be worn directly on top of the head.

"Supposed" is the key word here. Today's students, who think every head covering should be slung low and backward—like a baseball cap with the bill toward the rear—are not accustomed to something perched so high on their noggins. Thus, they often pin it on incorrectly, giving the distinct impression a black, flat airfoil is stuck in their hair.

Alas, even wearing the mortarboard correctly offers no relief. Students are so afraid it'll fall off when Principal Crabmore hands them a diploma, they wind up walking like stilts, stiff-legged and stiff-backed, afraid to so much as blink.

But blink they must because all they can see is a blinding burst of flashes and strobe lights as 576 sets of parents attempt to capture The Moment.

In order to capture The Moment, however, these parents must attract the attention of their own personal graduate. Thus, they stand on their tippy-toes, frantically waving a program and flailing their arms, as if trying to coordinate the simultaneous landings of two dozen 747s.

It never works, of course. Instead of capturing The Moment, they wind up with an underexposed sea of tiny, bleary faces that all look the same because they have just endured The Speech.

The Speech has been given at every graduation ceremony since the Middle Ages and contains one or more of the following words: opportunities, horizons, frontiers, crossroads, challenges and dreams. Since it is not on the final exam, however, no one is required to listen.

Then there is this matter of applause.

During a typical graduation ceremony, everyone in the house

will applaud approximately 3,582 times to honor the valedictori-
an(s), class officers, class sponsors, scholarship winners, top athletes, band members and cheerleaders.

It would simplify the process, not to mention carve a good 30
minutes from the schedule, if the notion of please-hold-applause-
until-all-the-names-have-been-announced was followed. But that
never works because the moment the person in charge says,
"Please hold your applause until all the name have been
announced," this is a signal for 576 sets of parents to begin clap-
ping.

So remember, graduates, as you stand on the horizon of this
challenging new frontier: Don't forget to turn your cap and gown
back in.

Famous last words

May 23, 1993

T he people at the National Archives in Washington gave us
a chuckle the other day when they released more of former President Richard Nixon's secret Watergate tapes.

One of them contained what has to be the worst miscalculation
of American attitudes in the history of 20th century politics. It was
uttered in the Oval Office by the president on June 21, 1972, when
he and chief of staff H.R. Haldeman were discussing political fall-
out from the botched break-in.

Said Nixon: "I don't think you're going to see a great, great
uproar in the country about a Republican committee trying to bug
the Democratic headquarters."

Bummer of a call, Mr. Forced-To-Resign-From-Office.

Still, we shouldn't be too hard on Richard Nixon just because
he suffered chronic foot-in-mouth disease. We all have spoken
words, intentional or accidental, we'd sorely love to reel back in.

In Nixon's case, though, he was dumb enough to have installed
a tape recorder. Now, instead of slowly rotting in the dusty pages of
a history book, his crude quotes will be replayed jillions of times

until the year 10,001.

Earlier presidents were a lot luckier. They may well have swallowed their feet on occasion, but because the hidden microphone had not been invented, they didn't have to suffer the consequences.

Just think what might have happened—*might,* I reiterate—if the tape recorders had been rolling when—

■ Abe Lincoln sat down to write his Gettysburg address: "Rats! Another cemetery to dedicate! What's with my staff, anyway? They think I've got nothing more important to do than freeze my buns off in the middle of some field and talk about a bunch of dead soldiers? Geeze! How do I begin this stupid thing? Maybe something like, 'Eighty-seven years ago' . . . "

■ John Tyler ascended to the presidency after William Henry Harrison died from complications of a cold he caught during his inauguration 30 days earlier: "I told the old coot to wear a raincoat, but would he listen to his vice president? Nooooo!"

■ Thomas Jefferson received word that his special envoys had completed the Louisiana Purchase for $15 million: "Wait a minute! You're telling me these guys plunked down 15 big ones for a few rivers and some land? What were those fools thinking? That money grows on trees? *Aii-yii-yii!* I can just see me trying to sell this thing to Congress!"

■ George Washington retired to his tent after reviewing troops at Valley Forge: "Gripe, gripe! That's all I ever hear anymore! What did those clowns expect when they signed up—a tropical holiday? Sure, it's cold! Sure, the food's no good! Sure, we're nearly out of gunpowder and bullets! But that's life in the military! Oh, while you're up, steward, a little more wine, please. And don't pile so many blankets on my bed tonight. I toss and turn like crazy when I sweat."

CHAPTER TWO

People do the weirdest things

People are fun to write about. No matter who they are or where they live, they've always got a story to tell. All you've gotta do is ask.

The frustrating part is knowing that on any given day, there are so many, many people stories that go untold.

It's a little like fishing. No matter how many times you cast, you can never cover all the water. And even when you do manage to reel in a good one, you can't help but think about the others that got away.

Go get your rod and tackle box, though. The boat's about to leave the dock.

Uncle Sam wants you

July 23, 1993

P aul Trammell knew things were changing in Uncle Sam's armed forces. But until a few days ago, when he plucked an official envelope from his West Knoxville mailbox, he didn't realize just how radical the shift had been.

The letter was from the United States Marine Corps. Which is no great surprise. Trammell gets quite a bit of mail from the Marines. He's a retired colonel with 28 years of active duty and three wars on his record. Indeed, he looks forward to letters from the Marines—especially those containing a monthly token of respect for all his years of dedicated service.

But when he opened the flap on this particular missive and read its contents, Trammell almost passed out. From laughter.

He was being offered the chief of staff position at Sixth District headquarters in New Orleans.

Paul Trammell is 74 years old.

"If they need me as chief of staff down there, we must be in serious trouble," he said. "I've been retired since just after the present commandant of the Marines received his commission!"

Actually, the letter offered Trammell a choice of assignments. If he didn't want to go to New Orleans, he could have applied for a post at Camp Lejeune, N.C., or Camp Pendleton, Calif.

Thank you just the same.

"If I can't be commanding general," said Trammell, "I ain't takin' any of them."

Yes, of course, it was a snafu. One of those grand and glorious military mistakes. Someone is probably being chewed out for it as I type these words.

"I called the phone number listed in the letter and found out what happened," said Trammell, still relishing the humor of the mix-up. "From what I gathered talking to the sergeant on duty, I wasn't the only retired officer who got this thing. It was supposed to have gone out to all colonels in active reserve. Instead, someone got the wrong distribution list and it went out to 'all colonels.'

"That poor sergeant. He told me he'd been hearing from old folks from all over the country all day. Some of them said they were crippled and couldn't understand why the Marines wanted them back in service. This thing's probably not real funny to the people on the other end, but me and my friends have gotten some great laughs out of it."

A graduate of Knoxville High School, Trammell hitchhiked to Nashville to enlist in the Marines in 1940. He rose through the ranks, earned his commission and saw duty in World War II, Korea and Vietnam.

He retired from the military in 1968 and spent six years with the Thiokol Corp. In 1974, he retired for good and has been enjoying life ever since.

Said Josephine Trammell, his wife of 50 years: "I told Paul if the Marines planned on bringing him back to active duty, they were gonna have to issue him a new wife. I've already served my time."

If the shoe fits, hide it

February 25, 1993

The Case of the Missing Shoe has been solved, and both parties involved are exceedingly glad. Herman Gettelfinger is glad to have his 4-year-old, size 10½, black loafer back on his right foot, and Cathy McNeal is glad she has an answer to a most-puzzling question. But most of all, Cathy is glad her husband was along on her cruise to San Juan. Otherwise, things might be difficult to explain. For everyone.

Let's start at the beginning and see why:

Gettelfinger, president of Knoxville's Kelso Oil Co., went to Florida a few days ago to watch the Daytona 500. After the race, he and several buddies boarded a Delta flight for the trip back home. Among the luggage he checked was a folding suit bag.

"It was late when we arrived in Knoxville," said Gettelfinger. "I was too tired to unpack, so I just went to bed. When I got home from work the next day and started putting things up, I discovered this hole in my suit bag."

Actually, the hole was the second discovery Gettelfinger made. The first, and much more distressing, was that a shoe was missing.

"Those were the most comfortable loafers I've ever worn," he said. "I wouldn't take anything for them. If you've ever had a good pair of shoes, you know what I'm talking about. But there I was, with a left shoe and a hole in my bag. The right one must have fallen out somewhere. It was long gone."

Then again, maybe not.

Gettelfinger's daughter, Julie, is a Delta flight attendant, stationed in Atlanta. He telephoned her for suggestions, and she recommended the airline's lost-and-found department. Gettelfinger made the call, gave a description and figured he'd never see the shoe again.

In fact, several days did pass with no word of success.

"But when I got home the other day, there was a message from Delta. A woman in Maryville had found my shoe—in her luggage. Talk about surprised! Try explaining that to your wife!"

Gettelfinger wasn't the only surprised person. Cathy McNeal did quite a double take herself when she opened her own suit bag, started to extract her husband's brown shoes and came up with a size 10½, right-footed, black loafer.

"I knew there had to be an answer to this crazy thing," said McNeal, who works in the optical department of Sam's Wholesale Club. "So I called Delta in Atlanta."

You can pretty much take it from there.

The next day, Gettelfinger drove to McNeal's office to retrieve his shoe and compare notes. It seems McNeal and her husband, Jack, were on the same Atlanta-to-Knoxville flight as Gettelfinger.

The McNeals had come from Puerto Rico, Gettelfinger from Orlando.

Apparently, when their bags were being loaded onto the Knoxville-bound airplane, Gettelfinger's shoe squirted out the hole in his suit bag and was picked up a baggage handler, who tucked it into the next available piece of luggage and moved it on down the line.

Now, about the bra and panties . . .

An Amanda for all seasons

February 2, 1992

I'm giving you fair warning right now. This column will be confusing as heck. My advice is to find a pencil and a piece of paper and keep notes as we move along. I'll try to go slowly.

This saga involves a class of 4-year-olds at Ridgeview Baptist Learning Center, 6125 Lacy Road. These kids are what's known as "pre-kindergartners." Meaning they are being prepared for kindergarten, which will prepare them for pre-school, which will prepare them for first grade. I think.

The educational system wasn't nearly so complicated when I started school. None of this "pre-anything" business. I went straight from the sitting-around-the-house-eating-graham-crackers-and-milk stage to first grade, which damaged my psyche and caused me to write confusing columns like this one.

Anyhow, there are six children in this class. They are being taught by Katherine Smithwick. This is Old Lady Smithwick's—we always called our teachers "Old Lady Welch" or "Old Lady Vesser," but maybe pre-whatever students of the '90s refrain from using the crude term—first year of teaching at the learning center.

And, at this point, she says it has been a very difficult experience.

Difficult? With six kids who are 4 years old? How difficult can that be?

"Well, for one thing, it's hard to get their attention," Smithwick replied. "I have to call out the entire name just to get someone to turn around and listen."

"You mean to tell me," I asked, "that 4-year-old kids are so rowdy you have to shout their middle names and everything?"

"Oh, no. They're not rowdy at all," Smithwick corrected me. "It's just that they all have the same name."

Correction. Not ALL of them.

One child, Bryan Peterson, has the dual distinctions of being the only: (a) boy and (b) Bryan.

All the rest are girls. And they're all Amandas.

The easy Amandas are Amanda Ashe and Amanda Hines. Things get more complex when Amanda Jean Burgin, Amanda Jean Smith and Amanda Jane Berry walk through the door.

"The only thing I can figure is, Amanda was a very popular girls' name back in 1987," said Smithwick.

As with any unique situation, this one has its minuses and pluses.

On the down side, there's the matter of discipline. Whenever Smithwick wants to know who tore up the coloring paper or who left cookie crumbs or who didn't flush, the answer is unanimous: "Amanda did it!"

"But it sure has been easy teaching everyone to write their names," Smithwick said with a laugh. "All I've had to do is put a giant AMANDA on the blackboard!"

Southern exposure

August 20, 1992

I'm happy to report that the Southernization of Katy Koontz and Steven Friedlander is progressing nicely. They have purchased a home in Knoxville. They have learned to use a lawn mower. They are growing a garden and have even built a compost pile. They have become proficient with the barbecue grill—after discovering the source of fire, or "far," as we say it around here.

"Neither Steve or I smoke," Katy was explaining to me. "The

first time we tried to use the grill, we had to scrounge some match-es from our neighbors."

When Katy and her husband moved to Knoxville four years ago, the length and breadth of their experiences with daily life in (a) the South and (b) a midsized town would barely have filled a thimble.

Katy was raised in suburban Philadelphia but spent most of her adult life amid the concrete and steel of Boston and New York. Steven, bless his sheltered soul, came straight out of Manhattan. Thus, when they migrated to Tennessee, the degree of culture shock they experienced was measurable on the Richter scale.

I learned about their tribulations in a hilarious piece Katy wrote two years ago for Woman magazine. In it, she marveled at newfound luxuries like walk-in closets, free laundry delivery and inexpensive restaurants. The fact that eateries don't stay open all night around here was a testy issue, as was Knoxvillians' cavalier attitude about precise timekeeping. She wrote, "In Knoxville, no one really knows what time it is. It just doesn't matter if it's 2:43 or 2:46."

Good girl, Katy. You're catching on.

But the crown jewel was her description of Steven's introduc-tion to the concept of land.

"One evening I heard terrible splashing sounds coming from the downstairs bathroom. I ran to confront the disaster and found my husband holding an overturned bag of potting soil above the toilet and spilling dirt all over the toilet and the floor."

She asked in disbelief, "What are you doing?"

"I was trying to flush the leftover dirt down the toilet, and the bag got away from me," Steven replied.

"Dumping it on the grass had never occurred to him," said Katy. "The man had never had grass to dump dirt on before."

That occurred when Katy and Steven lived in an apartment. Now that they're comfortably ensconced in a house, he can scatter dirt to his heart's content. He can even get down on his hands and knees and play in the garden.

"You should see our tomato plants," she said. "One of them is huge. We have named it Damien.

"Oh, and when we first moved into the house, Steven would just walk out to the garage and stand there and stare. It was larger than an entire apartment he once had in New York!"

Rome was not built in a day, of course. Katy tells me neither she nor Steven has bought a gun. And it'll still be awhile before either of them can twang out a good, "Hale far! How'yew folks gettin' 'long?" when they run into friends.

But I have faith. These thangs take time.

Elvis lives!

April 21, 1994

Elvis Presley is neither dead nor happily munching doughnuts at a pastry shop in Michigan. He lives in West Knox County, watches UT football games, travels on a motorcycle and sends postcards to friends all over the country.

At least that's the impression you get after a session with Lee Durand, who has been officially named "World's Greatest Elvis Fan."

Durand, a retired advertising executive, recently beat several hundred other applicants in an essay contest sponsored by Hasbro Inc., maker of the Elvis doll series.

"I'm alive and Elvis is too," says Durand. "I just can't find him at the moment."

After a quick glance at the "Velvet Elvis Memorial Shrine" in Durand's Fox Den Village

home, you'd swear The King maintains permanent residence. There are Elvis dolls, Elvis hats, Elvis stickers, Elvis posters, Elvis pennants, Elvis clothes.

Ah, yes; the clothes. That's what started everything.

"It was back in the late '70s, when all the Elvis sightings began," said Durand. "I was visiting a son in Chicago. He told me about a store that was selling Elvis pants. Said I had to go see them.

"I went by the place, and they had one pair left—size 28. On a lark, I bought them. Somebody had to buy them! I wear size 36, so my wife had to sew a wedge in the back so I could put them on."

There was no stopping him after that.

"It was strictly tongue-in-cheek," says Durand, "but now, it's taken on a life of its own."

Durand bought a Honda motorcycle—the "Elvis Mobile"—and plastered it with Elvis stickers. He started collecting "Where's Elvis?" memorabilia. He decorated the rear of his travel trailer with a sign that asks "Where's Elvis?" When motorists pass, they see another sign reading, "In here!"

"That really gets a lot of attention on the road," Durand said. "Truckers honk, and people roll alongside and take pictures."

But perhaps Durand's most fun-filled endeavor has been in the field of communications. Routinely, he signs Elvis postcards and mails them to friends around the country. "I'll put something like, 'A hunka-hunka burnin' love to you' and send a whole batch to someone in another city. He drops them in the mail for me. That way, the postmarks don't always come from Knoxville."

Durand even has a personalized Elvis stamp, a computer-designed knockoff of the Presley stamp issued by the U.S. Postal Service. Durand sticks one on his letters—along with the official postage.

"Mine is a good copy of the Elvis stamp, except I'm a lot uglier."

Durand's family has gotten caught up in the fun too.

"My son Brian works as a computer programmer for the Chicago Art Institute. Some of the greatest masterpieces in the world hang there. But do you know what's hanging in Brian's office and people are all the time asking to see? His giant velvet Elvis painting."

Thankyouvurrymuuuch.

Never a dull moment

April 10, 1994

Mark Downing was scheduled to fly from Knoxville to Syracuse, N.Y., a few days ago. Several hours before takeoff, his flight was canceled. He was not upset.

"It's just as well," he said with a laugh. "I hadn't packed my surgical gloves."

The way Downing's travel arrangements have unfolded lately, he might also want to pack a rabbit's foot, a four-leaf clover and a jug of Madame LeRoux's lucky elixir. Just in case.

Downing is an energy economist for Lockheed Martin Energy Systems in Oak Ridge. A couple of weeks ago, he was scheduled to fly from Brainerd, Minn., to Minneapolis, thence to Winnipeg.

Snow and ice interrupted the first leg of that journey. He had to rent a car and drive—"slide" is a more accurate term—the 150-mile distance. Amazingly, he arrived in only three hours.

Then he was off to Hawaii for a conference. At the conclusion, he boarded a jumbo jet in Honolulu for the trip to Knoxville, preparing himself for a siege of crossword puzzles, napping and pecking on his laptop computer, all the while enjoying elbow-to-elbow pleasure of 300 fellow passengers.

"About one hour into the flight, the captain asked if there was a doctor on board," said Downing. "A little while later, he repeated the message."

By virtue of his Ph.D., Mark is officially known as "Dr. Downing." And, at 6-feet, 4-inches, he'd grown weary of holding his knees above his ears. So he got up and wandered rearward where there seemed to be a disturbance.

"A woman had gone into labor," he said. "She was sitting in the middle of a wide row."

Downing carried her to the galley. Based on his Keystone Cops description of the situation, the airline should have charged admission.

"It was sorta like, 'Excuse me, sir, I'm sorry my foot is on your arm and my leg is in your face, but I'm trying to help this woman.'"

Voila! A physician did appear; he'd been asleep when the captain's appeals were made. A registered nurse also was on board. Between them, Downing and flight attendants, the woman was made as comfortable as one can be (1) during labor (2) in an airplane galley (3) six miles above the Pacific Ocean.

"I don't know where she was from," he related. "We never got into that. She did say she'd been to visit her husband, who was on business in Hawaii. Since she was only seven months along, she assumed it was safe to travel."

Although the woman had begun to dilate, birth appeared not to be imminent. The pilot, woman and doctor conferred and decided to proceed toward Atlanta, as planned, instead of making an emergency landing in Los Angeles.

Unfortunately, I must leave the conclusion hanging. When the plane touched down in Georgia, an ambulance was waiting. Passengers remained seated while a team of emergency technicians boarded. They loaded the woman into a wheelchair and vanished.

"At least," Downing observed, "it kept the flight from being boring."

Homegrown nicknames

April 7, 1992

I t doesn't take a genius to realize Knoxville's hayseed era is history. Hardly a day goes by around here without news of an interstate sniping, a drug-gang shooting, pipe bomb experimentation in high school or elementary kiddies packing heat into class.

Still—heaven be blessed—this isn't New York City, where organized criminals have a nasty habit of littering the sidewalks with their competitors' brains. And in that regard, let's pray Knoxville and New York never meet. They probably won't because Knoxville lacks one of the most important ingredients for organized crime.

Our crooks don't have scary nicknames.

I thought of this the other day when New York mobster John

Gotti was convicted of racketeering and murder and sentenced to life in prison.

Gotti was nailed primarily through testimony from one of his underlings, Salvatore "Sammy Bull" Gravano. Even though he admitted to 19 murders himself, Gravano sung like a tenor before the jury and tied almost everything back to his boss. It took jurors little time to cry, "Guilty!"

Quite understandable. When a guy named "Sammy Bull" is talking, you're going to sit up and pay attention. Likewise if he goes by "Scar Face" or "Machine Gun" or "Meathook" or any of the other ferocious nicknames big-city gangsters might adopt.

You don't find names like that here in River City. Just to make sure, I called Bobby Hubbs, an information officer for the Organized Crime Unit of the Knoxville Police Department and asked him for a rundown.

Who goes by what on the sinister streets of our town? Consider some of these for-real names—

■ Cornbread: What's his M.O., a whack across the noggin with a sack of meal?

■ Duckie, Pookie and Little Billy: Sounds like the perfect combination for a jazz trio.

■ Flat Top: I have this mental image of Eddie Haskel saying, "Gee, Mr. Cleaver! That certainly is a handsome wallet. Would you mind handing it over?"

■ Bubba: Must be thousands of 'em.

■ Skinny: Unless he totes a fat .44, no problem.

■ Big R: Wasn't there a popular fishing plug by the same name a few years ago?

■ Fat Sam: No comment.

■ Chili: No. 1 suspect for shoplifting around fast food establishments.

■ Wonder Woman: Who came up with this name—satisfied customers?

■ Soapy and Stinky: If these guys worked as a team, they could clean up the town.

Make no mistake. Crime is crime, whether it's in the heart of the Bronx or the corner of Henley and Clinch. A knife in the face is just as menacing. A bullet will kill you just as dead.

And please understand that Knoxville police also keep tabs on "Moose," "Lurch," "Snapp," "Bam-Bam" and others who may have earned their titles the Manhattan way.

But having walked the streets of both cities, I feel much safer here in K- Town.

So does Bubba.

Big Red

May 29, 1994

When Army Air Force Tech. Sgt. Howard Weaver and his fellow crewmen began their D-Day assault, they gave German forces a dose of the Red Ass.

Literally.

"That was the name of our B-24," said Weaver, who lives in Karns. "Almost all the airplanes had a nickname back then. Our crew came up with 'Red Ass' when we were in training together in Denver.

"We found an artist to paint it. He drew a bright red mule sitting on a bomb, and the words 'Red Ass.' I don't know how much we paid for the job, but I remember we divided it up between ourselves."

I bring you this nugget of military information to set the record straight. As America prepares to commemorate the 50th anniversary of the D-Day invasion, I thought it would be fitting to officially give the Red Ass its proper place in history.

You see, according to the Army, the Red Ass never existed. At least not by that name.

Yes, the airplane and crew are well-documented. They were attached to the 446th Bomb Group, 704th Squadron. They led the 8th Air Force on D-Day. The Army published several photographs of this particular B-24 and the men who flew it.

But the name was always censored by darkroom technicians. Protocol, you understand.

"In every picture from the Army, 'Red Ass' was blotted out," said Weaver, who served as the aircraft's flight engineer. "We didn't mean for it to be obscene, but I guess someone figured it wasn't appropriate."

Actually, there were four Red Asses over an 11-month period.

"We flew the first Red Ass from the United States to England and made our first mission in it," said Weaver. "The next day, another crew took it up and got shot down. We got two more B-24s and named them Red Ass, but we lost them and their crews too. Our last Red Ass was still flying when I got discharged, but I understand it cracked up on landing a little while later."

When it came his time for discharge, 30 combat missions were required, Weaver said. He made 28 of them with his original crew.

"Every now and then, one of 'em would fill in with another crew. By the time they reached 30, I still had two to go. I made them with another crew and got out.

"Our whole crew survived the war. There are five of us still living."

Although Allied ground forces were under horrendous fire on D-Day, Weaver remembers the air war as far less intense.

"All of our missions were scary, but some were worse than others. Once over Berlin, we were in heavy flak for 37 minutes. Another time, there were 78 shrapnel holes in the plane when we landed."

Weaver worked at Oak Ridge after military service and later compiled 33 years in industrial engineering at Robertshaw. He retired in 1984.

Oh, yes—and his high-altitude experiences ended with the Red Ass: "I've never been in a plane since the war."

Blunders in the blizzard

March 26, 1993

The guy had every reason to be concerned. He had a freezer full of meat but, thanks to the Blizzard of '93, no electricity. So he called Knox County's Emergency Operations Center in the City County Building to seek advice.

"Someone told him to take everything outside, into the cold," said Knoxville information officer Mike Cohen. "He said OK and hung up."

About an hour later, the man called back.

"He said he'd tried and tried, but he just couldn't shove that freezer through the door."

Hoo-boy . . .

Now that the worst snowstorm in 100 years is officially history, staffers in the emergency office have had time to breathe a sigh of relief and compare notes. Of the hundreds upon hundreds of telephone calls these people fielded during the wintry ordeal, some of them were, shall we say, less than well-thought-out.

Such as the man who called the center and asked, in all seriousness, "How will I know when the power's back on?"

Well, sir, it's like this: If you walk to the wall and flip the switch and the light bulb over your head illuminates, your power is back on. If not, your power is still out. Unless, of course—and we don't mean to confuse the issue—the bulb has burned out. In that case, forget it. With 17 inches of snow outside, you won't be able to drive to the store for a replacement.

Then there was the woman who wanted to know why her microwave wasn't functioning.

"Is your electricity off?" the emergency worker asked.

"Yes," she answered.

"Well, that explains it."

"No, no, you don't understand," the woman insisted. "My regular oven is out, but my microwave should still be working. Shouldn't it?"

But if you thought her misunderstanding of Electrical Engineering 111 was bad, consider the woman who demanded to know why her power was still off when a car had just driven past her house and its headlights were burning brightly.

Concern over animals also figured in a number of requests, Cohen noted.

"One woman wanted us to help put her goat inside the house so it could stay warm. We told her we were more worried about cold human beings at that point."

And then there was The Flaming Gerbil. I am not making this up. Neither is Mike Cohen.

"This guy put a lighted candle in his gerbil cage to keep it warm. The gerbil knocked the candle over, which set the bedding material, and the gerbil, on fire. When the man jerked the cage open, everything fell onto his carpet and started it burning, too. The gerbil died, but fortunately, the fire was put out with minimal damage."

And you think you had problems?

Potentate of the pumpkin

October 6, 1994

Throughout time, the masters of sculpture have worked in a wide variety of media. Michelangelo sculpted "David" from marble. Frederic Remington's "Bronco Buster" was modeled in clay, then cast into bronze. Gutzon Borglum dynamited a mountain of granite to begin "Mount Rushmore."

Pat Cotter selected something altogether different for his opus. He created "Big Ol' Jack-O'-Lantern" from a pumpkin.

"I'm tellin' you, it was a big one," says Cotter. "It weighed between 250 and 300 pounds. That thing was so big, I was able to carve three separate faces on it."

Alas, this masterpiece didn't last for long. None of them ever do.

"I've heard of a wax treatment you can put on a jack-o'-lantern that's supposed to keep it fresh, but I doubt it'll work," says the longtime Clinton resident and unquestioned potentate of the pumpkin. "People tell me they've stuck my jack-o'-lanterns in the freezer and kept 'em till Halloween night, but they ruin real quick after that. Once you cut a punkin, it's pretty much over with."

Cotter should know. For years, he's been picking up pumpkins, opening his Case pocketknife and breathing life into jack-o'-lanterns by the multiplied thousands.

"There's no tellin' how many I've carved in all," he said in response to my query. "I do over a hundred in a typical Halloween season."

Gouging eyes, a nose and some snaggle teeth into the hide of a pumpkin is no big deal.

Just ask any kid with a kitchen knife. But sculpting a detailed, three-dimensional face is graduate school stuff that never fails to attract a crowd.

"I've always been a whittler," said Cotter, a teacher who runs Anderson County's alternative school. "Back when I was growing up on my grandpaw's farm near Chattanooga, everybody carried a knife. We were always making toys—tops, slip whistles, flips, that sort of thing.

"Later on, I started carving faces into walking sticks and making little mountain characters.

"Once at a folk festival, a bunch of kids were standing around watching me work.

"There happened to be a punkin nearby, so I got it and started carving a jack-o'-lantern. I was surprised how many of these children had never done that sort of thing.

"That little batch of kids grew to be 20, then 50, then over 100. So every year, I've been carving more and more.

"Actually, you can use most any kind of fruit," he added.

"I like to start kids out on apples. They can use a plastic knife and not hurt themselves, but still learn how to create a 3-D effect."

Listen up, kids. Pay close attention to what Mr. Cotter is saying to you.

This is one of the few times you can play with your food and not get fussed at by your parents.

Taking the cure

October 9, 1992

Take it from Doc Randall: Laughter is good medicine. But if you've already tried the chuckles and something still ails you, a slug of his tonic might be the answer.

Just listen to this unsolicited testimonial, straight from the good doctor's mailbag: "My husband has a wooden leg. He took a dose of your Rootin' Tootin' Tonic last week. Now, he has to carry a hatchet around with him to keep the sprouts chopped off."

Or this one: "Grandmaw took Rootin' Tootin' Tonic for years. She died last week at 103. In childbirth. Fortunately, we were able to save the baby."

And if that's not enough to make you plunk down $2 for a bottle, Doc will give you a testimonial of his very own: "My wife used to have bad breath. But after drinking Rootin' Tootin' Tonic, her breath is so fresh, she'll put her mouth up against anybody's!"

Actually, you shouldn't get Doc Randall started. Asking him any question is like pulling the cord on a chain saw: "This tonic contains ginseng, kerosene and benzene. Good for onions, bunions, corns and nubbins. Guaranteed not to rip or tear. Cures neuritis, oritis and the meanest ritis of all—arthuritis. Made from the choicest roots and herbs taken from the north side of the hill when the moon is full and the sap's going down."

"Doc" Randall Hoard, traveling medicine man and cornpone comedian, has been entertaining audiences with that sort of patter since 1949. He's a regular at the Fall Homecoming at the Museum of Appalachia in Norris.

Hoard lives in Hawkins County. He works in quality control at the International Playing Card and Label Co. in Rogersville. Twelve to 15 times a year, though, he becomes Doc Randall. With his frumpy clothes, silver goatee (the real stuff), old-timey glasses, warm smile and steady stream of one-liners, he never fails to keep 'em laughing. His act has played on "Hee Haw" and was featured in a BBC documentary on Southern Appalachia.

"I love performing for the youngsters," he said. "That's how I got started with this. A teacher asked me to put on a little program for some of her students.

"I'd always been interested in the old-time traveling medicine shows. And when I was growing up, we still used a horse and buggy. So it was kind of a natural thing to do."

Kids used to be a part of the show, in fact. When Hoard's two children (now grown with youngsters of their own) were little, they were included in the cast.

"I'd wrap my son in chains," Hoard said with a laugh. "Then he'd take a dose of Rootin' Tootin' Tonic and break out of them. That ended one day, though, when he asked his momma, 'When is Daddy gonna stop makin' me act crazy?' "

In the early years of performing, Hoard used honest-to-gosh horsepower to pull his buggy to an engagement. As the back roads became more crowded, he switched to internal combustion.

These days, his century-old wagon comes in on the back of a truck. But once the buggy and makeshift stage are in place and Doc steps out in his tattered suit and derby, it's the 1890s all over again.

"Traveling medicine shows began in England in the 16th century," said Hoard. "They played an important role in the early days of this country. Doctors and nurses were in short supply, and there wasn't much money.

"Most of the traveling doctors were good with herbs and could make some pretty decent medicine. Of course, some of 'em used a lot of alcohol too. When the Food and Drug Administration came in, that was the end."

Just in case you were wondering, Doc's Rootin' Tootin' Tonic is harmless—spring water, sassafras tea, honey. With, of course, the obligatory "secret ingredients."

Does it work?

Says Doc Randall: "Shore! It's guaranteed to cure what ails you or your money back.

"If you can catch me."

My hero

September 29, 1991

I wish it were hoax! I wish it were ruse!
Please tell me they're wrong 'bout the death of Doc Seuss!

All over the world on this oh-so-sad day,
The parents are trying to find the best way,
To gather their kiddies and tell them, "Gosh darn!
"Our great riddle-rhymer has just bought the farm!"

My mother first read me the works of the Seuss.
I liked him much better than Old Lady Goose.
I laughed at his ziffles and zonkers and zids,
And happily passed him along to my kids.

When dark rolled around and the time came for bed,
They knew without asking which book would be read.
I chose Doctor Seuss for his riotous fiction,
And also the way that he handled his diction.

With poems and drawings on jillions of pages,
He entertained wee ones all down through the ages.
He taught them to think and to laugh and explore,
And always the youngsters would shout out for more.

His words were quite simple—and sometimes made up;
He could whiffle a Whuffle or dobble a Dupp.
Then just when you thought he had hopped back in line,
He would jiggle or joggle the prose one more time.

He weaved and he bobbed, and you never knew next,
What joys would be found in a new batch of text.
The pen of this poetic genius was fertile,
It drew Thidwick and Horton and Lorax and Yertle,
The Cat in the Hat and Miss Gertrude McFuzz,
(Plus green eggs and ham—the worst meal ever was),
Bartholomew Cubbins and nasty old Grinch,
Whose cruel Christmas antics can still make us flinch.

But now Doctor Seuss, like the other great sages,
Is gone from this orb; he belongs to the ages.
We'll miss his sharp wit and his keen observations,
And promise to quote him on many occasions.

I've never quite understood creation's plan.
But I'm thankful God gave us this kind, gentle man.
Hats off to my hero, Doc Seuss, 87,
Who no doubt is writing fun stories in heaven.

His books and his pictures sure touched all our lives,
Giving millions of Baby Boom husbands and wives:
The chance to forget about hassles of biz,
The chance to unwind from the fuss and the fizz,
The chance to read whimsy as funny as whiz,
The chance to be little again with our kids.

Wedding bell blues

October 25, 1990

Given their respective professions—he's an anesthesiolo-
gist; she's an anesthetist—you couldn't blame Don and
Karen Pearson if they wrote off their wedding ceremony
as a dream that started out bad and kept getting worse.

"It was smooth at the start," said Karen. "We were going to
have the wedding at our house. It was a beautiful day. The florist

had come and gone. Everything was perfect."

That's when Murphy's Law kicked in.

They should have known something was amiss when the photographer showed up with a freshly bashed-in car. Seems he'd had a wreck on the way. But he was OK, and it was time for "Here Comes the Bride" to begin playing.

"The photographer took three or four pictures and his camera broke," Karen continued. "He thought it was a dead battery, so we stopped while he drove to Kmart for a new one."

After everyone waited 15 to 20 anxious minutes, the cameraman returned and fumbled with his equipment once more. It didn't take long for him to realize the battery wasn't to blame. Instead, the camera itself was broken.

"I told him we'd wait till he got his backup camera ready," said Karen. "He told me he didn't have a backup camera."

Karen went inside and found her own camera and a 24-exposure roll of film. The photographer agreed to take snapshots.

The wedding began again.

"About the time we started saying our vows, this big black Labrador retriever from up the street came running into the yard," Don said. "Daisy's a sweet dog. We play with her a lot, but we didn't want to play right then. She started sniffing at Karen's dress. I was afraid any minute she'd jump up on her."

Don's sister, Melissa Long, came to the rescue by taking matters into hand. Literally.

"Melissa was holding my bouquet," Karen said. "She started swatting Daisy with the flowers and finally ran her off. The preacher was trying to keep things under control, but he was really getting tickled."

Karen and Don had written their own ceremony. It started with the words, "We are gathered here amid the beauty of nature." But by the time the I-do's were done, nature had lost a lot of its luster.

"I started to put a ring on Don's finger, and a yellow jacket landed on him," said Karen. "Thank goodness, we were able to swat it away."

That's when Daisy, ever the determined Daisy, re-entered the scene. If nobody would throw her a stick, she'd bring one of her own.

"She must have dragged it off the woodpile," Karen said. "It wasn't really a stick. It was a log! She brought it over to us and put it down and waited for someone to throw it. I thought about stopping the ceremony and taking her home, but we went on with it."

Bride, groom and preacher managed to sidestep Daisy long enough to conclude the ceremony. Then everyone repaired to the table for a taste of wedding cake and champagne.

"The place was swarming with yellow jackets," said Karen. "Don swatted at one of them, and this time he got stung."

At long last the ordeal ended, and the happy couple took off for Asheville, N.C.

"Once we got away, things went according to plan," Don said.

Too bad. After that kind of buildup, how could a honeymoon be exciting?

CHAPTER THREE

I am not
making this up

Every entry in this chapter contains the same six words: "I am not making this up."

Newspaper columnists often use these words when we are writing about an extraordinarily bizarre topic. It helps us separate the worst of the chaff from the wheat.

Then again—as more than one editor has pointed out to me—if columnists wouldn't pull peoples' legs on occasion, there would be no need for clarification and amplification when we are, in fact, telling the unvarnished truth.

Naaa. I like it better this way.

Home repairs in outer space

September 27, 1994

E very homeowner who ever picked up a hammer, a saw or a screwdriver can sympathize with the government over the loss of its weather satellite.

Sympathize in theory, I should say. When we klutzes botch a job, it only costs us a new piece of paneling. In the case of the weather satellite, the bill came to $77 million.

I am not making this up. A 12-member investigating committee in Washington just released a report about it the other day.

The satellite was called NOAA-13. It was launched from California's Vandenberg Air Force Base on Aug. 9, 1993. For two weeks, everything worked fine. Then the entire system shorted out.

How come? Because a 1¼-inch screw extended too far.

The screw apparently penetrated some insulation and made contact with a metal plate. This resulted in instant french fry city and another piece of expensive litter Up There.

WHEN HE'S NOT BUILDING SATELLITES FOR NASA, JIM ENJOYS FURNITURE REFINISHING.

If there is a silver lining to this dreary cloud, the investigating committee did say significant design changes have been made for future satellite projects, incorporating several important alternatives for reduction of electrical malfunctions.

In other words, they're going to use a shorter screw.

Not that it'll do any good. In situations like this, Murphy's Law invariably rears its ugly head. You can book it.

The guy installing the new screw will say to himself, "Hmmm. This isn't what we normally use. It's too short. Somebody musta made a mistake. I'll just rummage around in my tool box and find a longer one."

Or else he'll be attaching the new screw just before lunch break: "Hang on, guys. I'll be with you in a second. I've just got to screw this baby down reeeeealll tight."

We home-repair bumpkins know all about these mistakes. No matter how carefully we plan, no matter how closely we measure, no matter how accurately we count, something will always be off.

I don't care what the laws of physics and botany say to the contrary, I have seen seasoned pine boards shrink three-eighths of an inch within five seconds after being cut. And in a feat that defies every principle of metallurgy, I, with my own peepers, have watched a small tack bore completely through a 2-by-4, pierce a layer of sheet rock, and extend three inches into the adjoining room. I know you have seen these miracles yourself.

By necessity, we amateurs have developed a number of "recovery procedures" to overcome our mistakes. I guarantee you that 95 percent of the homes in America contain do-it-yourself coverups that violate every canon of the construction trades.

Maybe Uncle Sam oughta give this option a try too.

Agreed, a weather satellite wrapped in duct tape and bound with Super Glue might not be a thing of beauty. But what the heck. It sure beats $77 million down the tube.

Trouble in the classroom

September 16, 1993

Good morning, class. Today's topic is the sad state of the American edukat. . .edduca. . .edgeuk. . .uh, the sad state of skools in this countery.

As you may have read in recent news reports, half of American adults are now classified as "functionally illiterate."

We know this to be true because the government says so. The government in this case is the U.S. Department of Education, which has just released the results of a humongous, four-year, Gawd-only-knows-how-much-it-cost study.

The official findings: "We don't know. However, we have formed an interdisciplinary committee and expect a definitive report, complete with primary recommendations, secondary recommendations and alternatives, some of which may or may not be viable, in, approximately, 12 to 24 months."

Just kidding. What the Education Department really said—while wringing its hands and crying, "Woe is us!" or is it, "Woe are we!"?—was that 90 million American adults cannot perform routine mental tasks like adding, subtracting, multiplying, spelling and writing.

(Frankly, I don't see why the government is so peeved. Since those 90 million adults can't work a simple math problem, they don't realize how much of their paycheck is regularly siphoned off by Washington. Instead of complaining, the feds oughta thank their lucky stars this little secret stays on the QT. But I digress.)

This is a staggering problem, for sure. It's bad enough that American school kids are more fluent in MTV than their ABCs. But it's hard to blame them when the educators themselves are on permanent lunch break.

The Tennessee Department of Education—I am not making this up—recently mailed erroneous essay questionnaires to 435 top-notch high school seniors.

The text began by noting that "all Tennessee, like Caesar's Gual, is divided into three parts." It went on to discuss Nathaniel Hawthorne's classic book, "The Scarlett Letter."

Hoo-boy. What boneheads.

As embarrassed Department of Education officials are now admitting, the words "Gaul" and "Scarlet" were misspelled. The department has pledged to send out another batch of error-free questions. My hunch is the new ones will be inspected, word-for-word, sentence-by-sentence, like an English term paper from 1922.

Oh, well; we can always hope for better days ahead. At least the signs are encouraging.

For the first time in years, scores on both the American College Test (ACT) exam and the Scholastic Aptitude Test (SAT) have improved. Neither showed immense gain, but any improvement beats the traditional pattern of steady decline.

Who knows? Maybe this means today's students, who will enter that vast wasteland of adulthood in a few more flips of the calendar, actually have the smarts required to function as literate people.

If not, I say we line 'em all up and cut their guals into three parts.

Moist methodology

September 7, 1993

The members of my generation have witnessed a vast array of medical, scientific and technological breakthroughs during our almost-50-something years: Salk polio vaccines, exploration of outer space, personal computers, cellular telephones, microwave ovens, steam engines and VCRs, just to name a few.

(OK, you caught me. I tossed in one blooper to see if you were reading closely. You and I both know that microwave ovens were invented in 1767 by Thomas Alva Westinghouse and played a significant role in producing hot, high-fat meals for colonial soldiers during the decisive Battle of Dinty Moore.)

But none of these great advances can hold a flame to the development of a battery that runs on urine.

I am not making this up. It was announced last week in California. Three inventors—Nelson Camus, Edgar Aguayo and Ismael Valle—brought a prototype of their battery to a trade show in Pasadena.

The details are sketchy at this point. All the inventors will say is that their battery uses a lithium compound, activated by human tinkle.

Again, I reiterate, this is true. Your favorite morning newspaper even carried a story about it a few days ago. In a demonstration for photographers, Camus dribbled a few drops—from a syringe, thankfully—into the battery mixture, causing a small light bulb to illuminate. Camus, an electrical engineer, believes further refinement of the process will enable the battery to run an entire household.

Could be. But not everyone in the scientific world is impressed.

Gary Henriksen, a chemist who directs battery research at the Argonne National Laboratory, said the whole thing was "off the wall"—a comment that begs smart aleck response, but in the name of decency I shall remain mute. Robert Osteryoung, an electrochemist at North Carolina State University in Raleigh, noted that "without more information, it would be impossible to determine if there is anything here or not."

Such is the plight of pioneers in any field. When the Wright brothers announced they had conquered the sky, lots of people enjoyed a hearty belly laugh. Then again, the Wright brothers had sense enough to use gasoline in their flying machine. If they had taken the moist approach, aviation science would still be in its infancy and the delights of in-flight dining would be unknown to the culinary world.

For the moment, though, let us keep our fingers crossed that this new battery pans out. Think of the money we'll save!

I don't know about your home, but we always need fresh batteries around the Venob Estate. Walkman, flashlight, camera—if it needs batteries, too bad; they're always dead. Every now and then do I remember to buy one of those 12-packs, but invariably, it'll be down to one or two when I need four.

No problem with this new baby. If I understand the process, all you gotta do is duck into the john and remedy two problems at once.

I foresee tremendous economic advantages, as well. Sales of bottled water, soft drinks, beer and other liquids will surely increase to meet the demands of power generation. ("One more round, please, Mister Bartender. I've got a lot of office work to do tonight, and I want to make sure the ol' computer stays charged.")

Yes, this new process will call for some adjustments. If you're having a dinner party and the lights start to go dim, everyone in the room will know you've ignored some very important home maintenance. On the other hand, this type of electrical crisis should be easier to solve than crawling into a remote storage closet to change a fuse.

In any event, all we can do now is wait. Camus and his buddies are courting investors to bankroll additional research and development. They figure it'll take at least $5 million to put their wee-wee wonders on the market.

Too bad Thomas Alva Westinghouse himself isn't still around to touch for a few bucks. But you never know. He might tell 'em their grandiose plan is all wet.

He's got a nose for research

October 15, 1991

I thought I traveled some bizarre academic paths when I was in college.

Who else do you know who racked up three hours of credit for studying splints, snakebite treatment and other first aid techniques he had learned in the Boy Scouts?

And who else wrote an essay about a friend's sexual encounters for a sociology report?

I got A's in both of those classes, thank you.

But I must wave the white flag. Or handkerchief, as the case may be. I have met my match and bow to a superior force. Up at the University of Wisconsin-Madison, there's a researcher who can really sniff out an offbeat assignment.

He is asking people to describe their nose-picking habits. I am not making this up.

Dr. James Jefferson, a university psychiatrist who specializes in compulsive behavior, wants to know more about this time-honored skill. He has sent questionnaires to 1,000 Wisconsin residents to learn the tricks of their trade.

According to news dispatches from Madison, one question on Jefferson's form asks, "How much time do you spend picking your nose?"

Respondents can choose from answers ranging from "less than one minute per day" to "more than two hours."

There's more: "What finger do you use when picking your nose?"

The good doctor digs more deeply into this sensitive area, but I'll leave it to your rich imagination to determine specifically what he asks. In the event your rich imagination fails, check with any 6-year-old.

There's a very good reason for this study, Jefferson says. He wants to know if nose-picking is merely a harmless habit or the sign of severe psychological distress.

(Psychological distress, my foot. Anybody who spends two hours a day clawing around Up There surely has physiological stress, as well, not the least of which is a set of nostrils that look like exhaust pipes on a D-9 Cat. But I digress.)

In all fairness to this guy, he hasn't dreamed up a $150,000 grant application for the project. Quite the contrary. Jefferson expects to spend no more than $200. Which, he told reporters, "is not much to get into a totally untapped area."

And if his investigation can help unlock secrets about human behavior, so much the better. For all I know, Jefferson and his colleagues might be holding vast scientific knowledge on the tips of their fingers.

I just wish this project had come up years ago, back when I had a boss who, shall we say, "delved" on a regular basis.

I swear this is true. The guy would call you into his office to discuss a story, and for half the conversation he'd be exploring the cortex of his brain. The other half, he'd inspect his work. I consider myself strong of stomach, but there were several episodes when I was sorely tempted to throw up.

So study on, Doc. If your research will educate us about these knuckle-hiders—particularly how to avoid them—more power to you. And once you finish the definitive book on nose-picking, there's a multitude of associated research to tackle.

Speaking strictly from a personal point of view, gas-making, bottom-scratching and toe-itching have always been a source of utter fascination.

All-cotton politics

June 7, 1994

Oh, dear me! I'm afraid we taught our Taiwanese brothers and sisters too many lessons in politics.

If you've been following international news, you've surely seen stories and video broadcasts of the slugfests that have broken out at the Taiwan National Assembly in Taipei. These fights have erupted almost daily. It's because the 402-member group can't reach an agreement about constitutional changes.

Last week, delegates got into a humongous brawl over the issue of quorum size. I saw this one on television.

The legislators began by shouting. Then they shook fists in

each others' faces. I don't speak Taiwanese, but no interpreter was necessary since expressions like, "Oh yeah, you (whatever)!" and "You can kiss my (whatever)" tend to be international in nature.

Anyhow, someone uncorked one of those expressions, and delegates started punching with a fervor normally restricted to hockey games, family reunions and disagreements in church.

Tempers remained calm for a couple of days. Then they flared once more. Over underpants this time.

I am not making this up. According to an Associated Press report of the action, assemblywoman Kuo Su-chun made fun of opposition lawmaker Su Chih-yang because her undies showed when she sat down.

Ms. Su responded by slapping Ms. Kuo upside the head, and the hair-pulling began in earnest. Before it ended, four women were injured and a fifth had to be hospitalized because of high blood pressure.

Wow. Do you suppose this discord has its roots in Knoxville's Sister City program from the late 1970s?

That's when Knoxville joined hands with Kaohsiung, Taiwan. Each city sent groups of citizens to open lines of communications, establish business relations and exchange culture with one another. Perhaps someone from Knoxville gave the Taiwanese a history book that described how we used to settle differences.

Like what happened in 1954 when H.G. Loy, the no-nonsense principal of Central High School, kicked three boys off the football team for vandalism. Their parents appealed to the school board. Tempers flared at that meeting, and before you could say, "i before e except after c," Loy and school board member Jeff Cate were going at it. The suspensions were upheld, by the way.

And then in 1956, Knoxville city councilman and one-time mayor Cas Walker duked it out with fellow council member J.S. Cooper. This particular fight was captured by photographers and made newspapers around the world.

Craig Griffith, a spokesman for Mayor Victor Ashe, tells me that although no exchanges have occurred between the two towns in years, Knoxville and Kaohsiung officially remain sister cities. That being the case, I say we dispatch several of our people to Taiwan on a peacemaking mission. Quickly, before more blood is shed.

And tell 'em whatever they do, don't show their underpants.

For that special couple

July 18, 1993

Don't be surprised to read this in a wedding story some day: "The bride wore a white satin gown, trimmed in Alencon lace and Schiffli embroidery. Her veil was held by a Juliet cap encrusted with beads and pearls. In one hand, she carried a bouquet of tuberoses, stephanotis, white roses and baby's breath, atop a prayer book from her great-grandmother's wedding in 1907. In the other hand, she held a DeWalt professional 3/8-inch VSR power drill with 4.5-amp motor and textured grip handle."

Oh, perhaps things won't go that far. The bride might not be carrying a power drill at all. Maybe it'll be a 10-inch Weed Eater with 3-amp motor and Twist 'n Edge accessory. Or a Stanley five-piece combination wrench set. In any case, you may rest assured weddings will never be the same, now that Home Depot has gone into the marriage business.

I am not making this up. I just got off the telephone with Sandi Hubbard, who works at the special services desk of the Home Depot outlet on Kingston Pike. She said the idea for a bridal registry came from the company's home office in Atlanta.

"The reception has been very good," said Hubbard, who checked her records and found 11 couples currently listed. "It makes sense these days. A lot of people don't have money to spend on a big fancy present for their friends. Plus, the people getting married aren't always interested in getting a bunch of china and crystal they'll never use. They want something more practical."

Such as?

"Houseplants, plant pots, trimmers, tool boxes, drills, screwdrivers, hammers, vise-grips, pliers, mini-blinds, wallpaper and closet organizers," Hubbard replied. "Anything you might need to set up housekeeping. One couple even had a tool shower. They racked up."

The system works like a traditional bridal registry in gift shops and department stores: The couple comes in, signs up, takes a spin through the aisles, finds potential gifts and records everything on a clipboard. Their friends look over the wish list and select an item in their respective price range.

Sniff, sniff. Just the thought moistens these sentimental ol' eyes.

But even if this isn't what comes to mind when one thinks of a marriage, what's wrong with it? Quite the contrary; why not expand the concept to sporting goods stores, restaurants, super-markets, theaters?

I guarantee a bride and groom who enjoy hiking, for example, will get more use out of new boots than a place-setting of silver-ware that'll spend the next 40 years, tarnished, in the dark recess-es of a dining room drawer.

It even appeals to someone who got married Back Then.

"My husband and I will celebrate our 25th anniversary next year," said Hubbard. "I've already told our friends to forget all that silver stuff. I want Rubbermaid."

Getting picky over hickeys

January 23, 1993

A medical supply company in southern California has informed its employees they will be sent home, without pay, if they show up for work with a visible hickey.

The company—Clinicas de Salud Del Pueblo, Inc., located in Imperial County, near the Mexican border—believes hickeys look unprofessional.

I am not making this up. According to a news story I read the other day, several Clinicas de Salud customers complained about having to do business with hickeyed employees.

Could be. I can just imagine, say, some distinguished purchasing agent from a hospital looking over a selection of syringes held by a sales clerk who was hickeyfied the night before: "Yes, I believe this 50-c.c. model is what we—*Aaaack! Is that pizza on your neck?!?!*"

So the company's personnel department ruled that a hickey not covered by a shirt collar, a turtleneck sweater or makeup is grounds for temporary dismissal. In other words, stay gone till it's gone.

I suppose we should stop here and make certain everyone in class understands what a hickey is:

Occasionally, when people are in the heat of passion, they gnaw and suck on the neck of their partner. Or else they think that's what they're supposed to do in the heat of passion. Don't ask me why, for Pete's sake, since the neck is somewhat removed from the main event, if you catch my drift. For all I know, it's why President Bill Clinton chews on his lower lip all the time.

Whatever the reason, this causes a huge blood blister to erupt. Sorta like what happens when a door slams on your finger.

Ironically, people tend to say the same thing in either situation, albeit with different emphasis.

In the heat of passion, both the hickee and hickor might scream, "Aeeeeii! Ohhh, @#$%!"

The same "Aeeeeii! Ohhh, @#$%!" is often screamed when a door slams on your finger, but it denotes a radically opposite emotion. And since I'm about to break out in a cold sweat, let's move on to the problems faced by employees of Clinicas de Salud who have been told to hit the road because of their neck decorations.

Should these people:

1. File a civil-rights lawsuit?
2. Charge unfair labor practices?
3. Set up informational pickets?
4. Go on strike?
5. Move to East Tennessee?

The correct answer, of course, is No. 5.

These employees should relocate because hickey display is not considered an occupational offense around here. Quite the contrary, it is the red, purple and blue badge of courage.

Based on the degree of skin damage I have seen in and around Knoxville, we live in a hotbed of hickeydom. Our hickeys are worn with pride. What's more, they say something professionally positive about the establishment.

This is particularly true of restaurants serving breakfast.

Trust me on this matter. If you walk into a squeaky clean eatery and are greeted by a perky college sophomore who just stepped off the cover of Seventeen magazine, and she smiles and says, "Welcome to McBreakfast; may I take your order, please?" you will wind up with a doughy biscuit and a piece of mystery meat heated under the guidance of a Japanese computer.

Conversely, if you walk into a joint that smells like burned grease and come face-to-face with a waitress wearing a beehive hairdo, a quarter-inch layer of makeup, tattoos on her knuckles that spell out "Love Hurts" and a trio of hickeys stacked up like saucers under her chin, and she clicks her gum and barks, "What fer ye, honey?" brace yourself for a fried-egg-and-gravy banquet cooked in a black iron skillet.

Afterwards, when you stagger out in cholesterolic ecstasy, be careful not to let the door slam on your finger.

He simply had to go

October 29, 1993

The state of Florida, which lost jillions of dollars this year after a series of tourist murders, has sent another negative message to would-be guests: Stay away if you need to go to the bathroom.

That's the only conclusion I can reach after reading the sad story of a German visitor who was jailed for 10 months because he desperately had to do Number One.

I am not making this up. Johann Grzeganek, 24, was arrested last January when his airplane landed in Fort Lauderdale.

Grzeganek apparently had been drinking on board and was suddenly smitten with the urge to relieve the buildup of fluids. An argument with a flight attendant ensued and during the exchange, she misunderstood his urgency as a bomb threat.

Specifically, Grzeganek said his bladder was "going to explode." When the attendant ordered him to sit down, he replied, "No, no, no, the roof would go." And before you could say, "This is your captain speaking," he was under arrest on four counts of interfering with a flight crew and concealing a bomb.

Grzeganek couldn't make a $100,000 bond, so he cooled his heels, not to mention his bladder, in federal prison until his case came up last week. He

pleaded guilty to interference, and U.S. District Judge Norman Roettger sentenced him to time served. The judge also dropped the bomb charge and told prosecutors it was "a disgrace" Grzeganek had been behind bars so long.

Grzeganek eventually hopped a plane to Germany, and, I assume, refused to even sip his complimentary cola during the journey.

Can't say that I blame him. Nor would I be surprised to learn Grzeganek has started selling his own line of travel supplies—bullet-proof vests and chamber pots, for instance—to European tourists headed for Florida.

But the most important item would be a list of English expressions for those little emergencies when there's not a great deal of time for conversational pleasantries. Given the danger of international terrorism, it's easy to see how the flight attendant mistook Grzeganek's reference to his distended bladder as a bomb threat. One should never use words like "explode" or "blow" or "blast" in these situations.

I've been there myownself. In Japan several summers ago, I finished a mega-coffee breakfast one morning and started to leave the restaurant when I was similarly smitten with fluid buildup. I exited to the restroom and—*yikes!*—discovered a cleaning woman, busily at work.

I duck-walked out of the facility, waited several eternal minutes, and then returned. She was still working. She looked at me—I'm sure there was stark terror in my eyes by that time—gestured to a nearby porcelain device and said, "dozo," which is Japanese for "please."

I know little of Japanese customs. But I sincerely hope she meant for me to relieve the buildup immediately. Apparently so, for it did not lead to a 10-month stay in a Japanese prison.

Then again, we weren't at 32,000 feet, and I didn't breathe a word about an impending explosion.

Hazards to humanity

August 11, 1991

Perhaps all the fuss over gun control isn't necessary.
　　If the events of recent weeks are any indication, Americans have discovered several new ways to wreak havoc upon one another, and they can do it without having to pull a trigger.

The stories you are about to read are absolutely true. The names have not been changed to protect anyone. I have taken every detail straight off the news wires. So look over your shoulder and make certain nobody is creeping up on you, and then let's check out the latest in mayhem.

First was the case of Addie Davis, a Nashville woman who reached for a six-pack instead of a six-gun when someone broke into her home. The 85-year-old Davis told police she heard a noise and went to investigate. She found a man who had smashed a window and climbed in.

The prowler cut himself in the process. But that didn't stop him from grabbing the little ol' lady and pulling her to the floor. Davis groped around momentarily, found a six-pack—you never know when you'll be on the floor and need a quick brewski—and started flailing.

"She wore his head out," police officer Scott Sulfridge told reporters later.

Kenneth D. Huggins, 24, was charged with burglary. Last I heard, he was recovering from wounds to his head and neck, not to mention his pride, in the Nashville city jail.

And then there was the Fatal Feline Fracas in Tempe, Ariz. According to Associated Press dispatches, Edward Lee Treaster, 21, got into a spat with his roommate, David Little.

I don't know what the argument was about, but apparently one word led to another and before you could say "no hitting below the belt," Treaster grabbed the closest object and hurled it at Little's face.

A cat.

Treaster threw kitty with such force, the poor thing was killed. Little's injuries weren't nearly so severe. He was treated and released at a Tempe hospital and apparently suffered no ill-effects. Except for a sudden craving to chase mice and slap at balls of yarn.

Police charged Treaster with a variety of offenses, including assault, cruelty to animals and making threats. His was being held in lieu of $1,000 bond at the Maricopa County jail.

And finally, there was the story out of Babylon, N.Y., regarding the nastiest missiles ever known to mankind. True, these projectiles were not unleashed with felonious intent. But big deal. Try soothing the nerves of the people who were standing nearby when the awful things hit.

I am talking about three-foot lengths of frozen human urine. I am not making this up. Neither is the Federal Aviation Administration.

FAA officials were trying to determine which flight the stuff fell from because it was apparent an airplane's bathroom defroster was not working properly. The chunks smashed a car window and snapped tree limbs—in addition to scaring residents to the point of moistness themselves.

The moral of these three stories is clear.

Unless we act quickly and decisively, these weapons will surely fall into the wrong hands.

Ban six-packs, cats and frozen urine now. Tomorrow may be too late.

A politically correct Christmas

December 13, 1994

A shopping mall in Evansville, Ind., has taken political correctness to record holiday heights by hiring a female Santa.

Not as Mrs. Claus, you understand. We are talking about a woman to be the jolly ol' fat man—I mean, the nutritionally dysfunctional person himself, er, itself.

I am not making this up. Officials at Eastland Mall would not identify the woman but did acknowledge her existence after some of the children waiting in line smelled a rat. Not from lumpy padding and a fake beard, either. Based on what I read about the incident, all the kids and their parents had to do was listen to this Santa's ho-ho-ho to realize the person inside the red suit was of the female persuasion.

Cassie Gilliam, the mall's marketing director, would not elaborate, except to say the mall was an "equal opportunity employer."

Fine. If that's the way the forced-diversity people want it, I say give it to them, right straight down the line. Like this:

Reindeer will no longer have exclusive access to the sleigh.

The team selected to transport Santa Claus shall hereafter include representatives from throughout the animal kingdom, including insects, fish, birds, reptiles, amphibians, as well as mammals.

When it is the mammals' turn to nominate a potential member, equal consideration must be given to rodents, ungulates, primates, marsupials, carnivores, cetaceans and other orders.

Oh, yes. The region formerly known as "Rudolph's red nose" will be rotated among the various external organs of one team member, who may select a hue from wave lengths within the color spectrum.

Next, out with the evergreen Christmas tree.

Deciduous trees—including oaks, hickories, poplars, elms, ashes, maples, willows and dogwoods—have feelings too. So do shrubs, lichens, mosses, ferns and weeds, not to mention algae and fungi.

Indeed, the term "Christmas tree" is insensitive, in and of itself. Thus, the new title shall be "winter botanical selection." No plant may serve a second term until the honor has been at least offered to every other member of the kingdom.

Elves? Surely you jest. That cruel description went out with sweatshops. The new name shall be "height-impaired holiday co-workers."

Oops. Scratch that. How uncaring of me to single out the height-impaired. The corps of holiday co-workers should be open to persons of all shapes and sizes—height-enhanced, waist-advanced, hair-deprived or wart-intense.

Finally, no longer will Christmas presents be restricted to "good little boys and girls."

As anyone with any degree of diversity training knows, measures of relative "goodness" among human beings were formulated by white men and, therefore, are fraught with bias and must be purged.

Hereafter, all children, regardless of their behavior during the previous 12 months, are eligible to receive packages from Santa Claus.

Whomever he, or she, may be.

CHAPTER FOUR

Political incorrectness and other government fun

People who work for the government are tough. They have to be because they get bashed from all corners.

In any given situation, politicians, bureaucrats and government employees fall under one of two categories: (1) lazy bums who make a career sitting on their cobwebbed butts or (2) intrusive nitpickers who specialize in tormenting the rest of us with their insistence on crossed t's and dotted i's.

My opinion?

More power to them. May they prosper among us.

Without folks from the government to pick on, I'd have to quit this job and go find honest work.

Crimes against nature

August 11, 1992

I n Venob's Great Excuse Book for Avoiding Household Chores, there is a special chapter dedicated to yard work. It lists six reasons for not mowing the lawn.

1. The grass is too wet.
2. The grass is too dry.
3. It looks like rain.
4. It's too hot.
5. It's too cold.
6. The skojamflagit whipingdoodle on the intake manifibulator is broken, and it'll be three weeks before the repair shop can get a new one.

But now, thanks to the Environmental Protection Agency, there's a brand new excuse for not cranking up the lawn mower. The weed cutter, the chain saw and the leaf blower too.

These machines create too much air pollution and contribute significantly to the greenhouse effect. Honest. According to EPA statistics—after living here in the land of TVAisms, you know to believe the federal government explicitly when numbers are involved—a lawn mower can spew as many hydrocarbons into the air as a modern car. Chain saws and weed whackers are worse. That's why EPA administrator William Reilly recently announced a bold plan to clean up America's lawn mowers.

Any day now, I expect platoons of federal lawn mower police to charge across the backyards of America, bayonets fixed, and bring the full force of the law down upon miscreant homeowners who would dare send this great country coughing and hacking to its grave. Of course, these ministers of justice will arrive in caravans of hydrocarbon-spewing cars and trucks, but who's worried about details?

I don't know where this is going to end. We all worry about the environment and, as politicians love to say, we want to do "the right thing." But what is it?

Buy an old-time, non-motorized push mower? Not a bad idea if your yard is the size of a postage stamp, or else you can donate four days per week to mowing.

A cow? Saaay, there's a good alternative! Not only will a cow clip the grass, it will also provide you with lots of fresh, whole milk. The EPA will get upset again, however, because cows, collectively, create jillions of tons of methane gas when they belch. But don't worry about it. You won't be around long enough for legal action because all that whole milk from the cow, plus the free butter and cheese, will clog your arteries faster than six tubes of Crazy Glue.

Wait a minute. Isn't goat's milk lower in cholesterol than cow juice? Just turn a few of these beasts loose in the backyard. And then call your lawyer and tell him to be ready to defend you against the city codes police.

Face it. There is no solution. This is merely a fun game of frustration the government loves to play when it tires of tax regulations. My advice is to bulldoze your yard pancake flat, cover it with a layer of concrete and paint it green.

And be sure to follow EPA guidelines carefully when cleaning the paint brush.

Nudity exposed!

May 3, 1992

When Knox County commissioners approved an anti-nudity ordinance earlier this year, I was tempted to pick it apart, phrase by phrase. It would have been great fun to tease our elected officials for their high-brow attempts to define the physical condition we know as "buck nekkidness."

In other words, hee-hee, make 'em the butt of their own joke.

I refrained from this childish pursuit, though, because I thought it would be too simple. Surely any fool could sit down at a word processor and produce reams of wisecracks about such gibberish as "fully opaque covering of any part of the nipple and areola" when everybody from Kodak to Friendsville knows it means pasties.

But when I read about a similar law in Florida, I realized how lucky we are to have legal authorities in East Tennessee who can describe buck nekkidness without exhausting a dictionary.

A few days ago, St. Johns County, Fla., adopted a complex law prohibiting nudity at its beaches, bars and restaurants. I haven't read the entire ordinance, but for all I know, it could be placed page-to-page along Highway 1 and reach from St. Augustine to Miami.

In this tome, the definition of "buttocks" alone runs 136 words. If you don't know your rump from a rowboat, take careful notes:

"Buttocks—The area at the rear of the human body which lies between two imaginary lines running parallel to the ground when a person is standing, the first or top of such line drawn at the top of the cleavage of the nates (i.e., the prominence formed by the muscles running from the back of the hip to the back of the leg) and the second or bottom line drawn at the lowest visible point of this cleavage or the lowest point of the curvature of the fleshy protuberance, whichever is lower, and between two imaginary lines on each side of the body, which lines are perpendicular to the ground and to the horizontal lines described above, and which perpendicular lines are drawn through the point at which each nate meets the outer side of each leg."

There is method to this madness. Jim Sisco, the county law director who drafted the law, told me it came from a recent federal court ruling.

"But if I had it to do over again, I wouldn't have used that wording," he said. "I've been hearing from news media all over the world since this thing took effect. I've been quoted from Australia to Israel to Canada."

I asked Sisco to share some of the best one-liners he'd heard about the law.

"I'm not going to repeat any of them," he replied. "At first, they were funny. But by now, I'm kinda tired of them."

Sisco, who's been the county's legal adviser for 10 years, said even though the buttocks law has made headlines around the world, it's not the most controversial one during his tenure.

"You should have seen it a few years ago when we banned alcohol on the beaches and started charging for admission to our beaches. That really set the locals off."

I should say so. They probably told Sisco to kiss the lowest point of the curvature of their fleshy protuberances.

Dedicated to his job

August 26, 1994

There's a big stink in Washington right now because Secretary of Agriculture Mike Espy went to a football game and called it work.

According to documents obtained by the Associated Press through the Freedom of Information Act, Espy accepted four free tickets to the Super Bowl and then billed the government $849 for travel, lodging and meals. The secretary claimed the trip as official business because at half-

time, there was a 30-second tribute to Smoky the Bear, the fire-fighting mascot of the U.S. Forest Service, which is one of the agencies under his jurisdiction.

Makes perfect sense to me. As one who considers himself somewhat skilled in the creative art of expense-account writing, I tip my hat to this guy. In fact, I don't see why Espy doesn't dedicate the next five months to attending football games on behalf of the Agriculture Department. There's a world of official business that needs looking into.

For starters, he can check out the hot dogs.

Hot dogs are made from beef and pork. Beef and pork come from cows and hogs. Cows and hogs are raised by farmers. Farmers are the responsibility of the Agriculture Department. Clearly, it is of paramount importance for the secretary of agriculture to be on hand when hundreds of thousands of hot dogs are ingested at football stadiums around America.

See how simple government work can be when you shuck it right down to the cob?

The buns need inspection too. Are we talking plain white bread from American heartland flour? Or whole wheat? With sesame seeds, mayhaps? And what about the mustard, catsup, onions, relish and mayo, all of which are manufactured from farm products? Are they Grade-A?

These are questions only a well-trained, well-traveled—not to mention well-fed—agriculture secretary can answer.

I also expect Espy to take a long look at stadium seating.

Chairs, bleachers and benches are made from wood, which comes from trees, which grow in forests, which are regulated by the U.S. Forest Service. Perhaps he could become the first cabinet member in history to perform The Wave from coast to coast.

Any agriculture secretary worth his weight in walnut would want to inspect these seating facilities for overall lumber quality, incidence of heart rot, insect damage and wildfire scars. When he gets back to Washington, he can calculate how much the logging operations that produced this wood—plus milling, transportation, sales and construction—contributed to the gross national product.

Since artificial surfaces are being phased out around the country, there's plenty of work on the football field itself. Was wear-resistant grass sown? Has sufficient fertilizer been applied? Water schedule OK? Have USDA-approved pesticides been used? If so, were directions followed to the letter?

True, watching that much football at taxpayer expense could get risky. That's why Espy oughta pay attention to what they say in the huddle.

Watch out for the sack.

Professor Venob's lessons

March 7, 1996

A ttention, students. Since this is a presidential election year and you will be assigned tons of boring term papers on dreary subjects involving the American political process when you'd rather be goofing off in the sunshine, Professor Venob is happy to offer his vast insight.

You can trust Professor Venob. He took Political Science 111 three times before finally emerging with a D-; thus, he is more than qualified to comment authoritatively on this complex subject. Feel free to quote liberally from this text as you prepare your themes and essays. Heck, just run a photocopy of the thing, scribble your name on top, and go have fun. As Professor Venob says, "A little learning goes a long way."

Today's lesson centers on that unique American institution, the Electoral College.

The Electoral College is a school for wannabe politicians. It is located in the State of Confusion, just outside Washington, D.C.

You think it costs a lot of money to attend a state university like, say, UT? Hah! The Electoral College is even more pricey than Vanderbilt. Professor Venob has never seen an exact breakdown on tuition—it's one of those if-you-have-to-ask-you-can't-afford-it situations—but he knows it runs into the millions of dollars.

Most people, even politicians, can't afford so much as one semester at the Electoral College. There are exceptions, of course. Steve Forbes is rich enough to buy the whole dadblamed campus. But for the most part, politicians attend the Electoral College on borrowed money. Then, after they get into office and learn how to milk the system, they can pay off their student loans and still pocket a bundle.

What sort of subjects are taught at the Electoral College? Public relations, mostly. That's what politics is all about in America these days.

The Electoral College offers a broad curriculum in such highly specialized fields as Slogan Making, Credit Taking, Blame Deflection and Spin Doctoring. Students with even a glimmer of hope of being elected must pass these courses in the top 1 percent of their class.

Why? Because politics is such a competitive field these days, just like business.

Years ago, a cornball slogan on the order of "I Like Ike" was good enough for two trips to the White House. But this isn't your father's politics anymore. You've gotta strike a vein nobody has touched and mine the dickens out of it. Lamar Alexander dreamed up that plaid shirt scheme during his undergraduate days at the Electoral College. Some folks said it was goofy, but it got him elected twice as governor of Tennessee and just might usher him into the Big House in 2000.

Why the concentration on public relations at the Electoral College? Simple. There's no need to waste students' valuable time on stupid courses like economics, geography, public health, environmental sciences and other piffle; that's what the state universities are for.

But lest you get envious and wish you could attend the Electoral College, let me remind you of one serious drawback.

They ain't had a decent football team in the history of the school.

Toes tell all

August 5, 1994

W rite down this name: Veronica Nacchio. Commit it to memory. By the time the next presidential election rolls around, you might be hearing it a lot. Wouldn't surprise me to see CNN start airing the Nacchio Toe Poll, sponsored by Dr. Scholl's insoles and deodorant powder.

All this is possible if Veronica perfects her political foot-watching skills.

Nacchio's a former college teacher who lives in West Knoxville. She also serves as an election official. On election day this year, she was stationed in the gymnasium of Cedar Bluff Middle School, assisting South Cedar Bluff voters as they processed into the booth. She was looking down a lot.

"I like to watch peoples' feet when they're casting their ballots," she told me. "It's a real study in personalities."

Nacchio said human behavior has always interested her. During the years she taught biology in New Jersey, she began noticing a pattern among students in the classroom.

"It doesn't take long before you can determine which ones have studied and which ones have not," she said. "Just watch their body language. If they're prepared for class, they're a lot more relaxed. Many times I would ask a question and know in advance whether the student could answer it correctly."

So what does this have to do with election tootsies?

For one thing, the beat of the feet said a lot about the mood of the voter.

"Look at that person over there," Nacchio whispered to me,

pointing to a set of woman's legs—I think they were a woman's; these days, you never know—protruding below the curtain.

"See how at ease she is? I'll bet that person knows exactly who she's voting for. She's probably taken the time to study the ballot and knows all the issues. It won't take her long to finish."

We turned to a different section of the gym and Veronica spotted another set of legs. Female again. But they did not appear relaxed. Instead, the person was poised on the balls of her feet.

"Could be one of two things," Nacchio observed. "She's either tense about her choice of candidate or else she's very short."

As they say around the election commission, Nacchio's findings are exceedingly preliminary. There are innumerable bugs to be exterminated.

"I wonder—does this mean Republican?" she said, pointing her toes outward. "Or is it Democrat? Then again, if one foot is pointed outward and the other inward, does it mean independent? It's going to take some work."

"Have you seen any knocking knees?" I asked.

"Not yet," Nacchio replied. "But it's still early. That might not occur until later."

On the contrary, I told her. Early in the day during a large voter turnout is precisely when I'd expect to see knees doing the twist and grind.

You gulp down three or four cups of coffee and then stand in line for 45 minutes, sister, and your knees are gonna be slappin' each other silly.

New uses for campaign signs

August 11, 1994

C ongratulations are in order for all the candidates in the last election. Not for running for public office, of course. Why anyone would put up with the expenses, the handshakes, the speechmaking, the mud-slinging and the paybacks is beyond me, especially when they must do it all over in a few years.

Instead, they need a well-deserved pat on the back for cleaning up after themselves. From my perspective, the sign removal of 1994 was the fastest and most thorough in recent history.

Road rights-of-way that were waist-deep in campaign posters just a few days ago have been scoured clean—leaving only waste paper, beer cans and bottles, hub caps, coffee cups, plastic bags and

other all-American litter to mar the landscape. Utility poles once ringed with politicians' faces have been replaced with pictures of lost dogs. Front yards and empty lots previously dotted with Vote-For-Me pleas now only sport an occasional "For Sale."

True, some candidates have been more diligent than others. Based on my tours, the majority of signs still standing belong to the losers. Mayhaps they need one more session with the crying towel.

Collecting all this campaign trash is tough, but finding a good use for it is even tougher. The last thing our packed-to-the-max landfills need is another ton of manure.

Fortunately, there are alternatives for this mountain of garbage. Among them:

■ Book covers—You can kill two birds with one stone with this approach. The kids get a cheap, effective jacket to protect their new school books, plus an intimate view of government in action. When these same politicians get indicted by a federal grand jury for the games they love to play, students will have a complete set of up-to-date pictures.

■ Halloween masks—Gather a variety of head shots and dole 'em out to the kids in October, along with scissors and string, and let them create their own false faces. Some of the children in your neighborhood might even want to band together by political party and make their raids as a group. Whether we're talking Tootsie

Rolls or taxes, the shakedown principle is the same.

■ Wrapping paper—Looking for an unusual wrap for your holiday presents? Why not nestle them inside the smiling face of your favorite politician? There is one drawback for the recipient, however. Returning the gift to the store is one heckuva lot easier than recalling the winner from office.

■ Energy sources—Bring all those billboards, posters, speeches, signs, business cards, wooden stakes, 2-by-4s and other campaign rubbish to your nearest steam plant and let TVA sacrifice them as a burnt offering. Surely there is enough of this official offal throughout the Tennessee Valley to make a significant reduction in the use of coal.

And just think. If we could bottle the hot air emitted during this campaign, TVA wouldn't need to generate any juice till the year 2010.

Don't look now

August 22, 1995

It's a good thing I don't work for Carl Markus. Otherwise, I'd be fired faster than you can say, "Go clean out your desk."

Markus is a city official in Minneapolis, Minn. He made news all around the country a few days ago by issuing a "no-ogling" order for the street paving crews he supervises.

Seems a woman called Markus' office to complain that some of the pavers had stared at her when she walked by. Instead of saying something sensible like, "Yes, ma'am; these things tend to happen," Markus picked up his Bureaucracy 111 textbook and studied it intently. Then he issued a decree stating people on the sidewalk can only be looked at for nine seconds. After that, Markus ruled, it's ogling—an offense punishable by a verbal warning and, if repeated, termination.

Which is why I'm so happy Carl Markus isn't my boss. I'm staring at people a lot more these days, and I'd surely get caught in his dragnet.

My staring has nothing whatsoever to do with women, though. I am an equal opportunity starer.

I stare at men too. And dogs. And buildings. And trees. And cars. And signs. Quite simply, I stare at anything and everything that comes in front of my eyes.

I don't have a choice in the matter. I have just been fitted with my first set of bifocals.

I have suffered poor vision, of the faraway variety, all my life and worn contact lenses for years. They still work fine most of the time.

But, as any Baby Boomer-Geezer In Training will tell you, the people who publish newspapers, books, magazines, catalogs and telephone directories have switched to smaller, fuzzier type in the last couple of years. So when we BB-GITs are not wearing our contact lenses, the only way we can see close up and far off at the same time is with bifocals.

Not the split-image bifocals our parents wore, of course.

We BB-GITs are too cool for that. We buy fancy new "no-line" (translation: more dough) bifocals that look like any other type of spectacles.

Until we put them on, of course. Then we stand and stare, just like our parents did when they tried their first set of the hateful things, desperately attempting to bring the world into focus.

We do more than just stare. We also bob our heads, trying to locate the visionary sweet spot.

It is a maddening experience. No matter what we are attempting to see—a sports story in the morning newspaper or a wren chirping from the oak tree 25 feet away—our eyes are focused on the wrong part of the lens. So we sit there like a bunch of head-bobbing dogs in the rear window of a '57 Chevy, running our noggins up and down, staring and swearing.

But that's not the worst part. Just watch some poor BB-BIT wearing bifocals attempt to negotiate stairsteps, and you'll know what I mean. The way he staggers and misplaces his feet, you'll swear he's drunk.

Have a heart, America. Don't stare at us.

At least not for more than nine seconds at a time.

Tightening someone else's belt

February 18, 1993

T he chair recognizes the honorable Senator Bigbucks from the distinguished state of Utopia.

"Thank you, Mr. Speaker. Since we're about to vote on some very important budgetary items, I'll keep my remarks as brief as possible.

"As President Clinton told the American people so eloquently the other night, it is time to sacrifice if we hope to regain control of this nation's economy. Truly, the challenge he issued is nothing less than a call to arms. We must defeat this enemy if our republic is to survive. Also, we must purge Washington of the greedy special interests that put such an awful drain on our resources.

"Fortunately, I have every reason to believe the people of the United States have the determination to follow through on this mandate.

"I don't relish the thought of revenue enhancement any more than the rest of you, my fellow members of the Senate. It is a bitter pill, particularly during this era of domestic economic chaos. Still, it must be done.

"At the same time, I have a few minor adjustments to make on the president's sweeping economic reform package. I'm confident I can count on the support of my colleagues, just as I have always supported your adjustments.

"First, I noticed that my request for $25.8 million in beef tongue research at Utopia State University has been stricken. This is intolerable. As you honorable senators know, Utopia State University has long been a leader in beef tongue research and technology. To eliminate this valuable mission would be ruinous to the important beef tongue industry.

"Second, I must demand that my request for $32.7 million for the Utopia Air Base be put back into the budget. Even one penny less for Utopia Air Base will have a drastic ripple effect on the military strength of our nation. For 40 years, the wingnut instructional program at Utopia Air Base has taught legions of mechanics how to apply Wingnut A to Bolt B. This training is indispensable if we expect the United States to maintain its position of military superiority.

"Third, there is this matter of $52.6 million for sidewalk crack repairs in Utopiaville. Only last week, Dr. I.R. Nutz, chief of staff at the internationally renowned Utopia Chiropractic Hospital, reported that sidewalk cracks are a leading cause of the spinal alignment misery suffered by many of the residents of Utopia. As a result, these people must call in sick. Not only does this eliminate their ability to pay income taxes, it creates higher health-care costs throughout the country. Clearly, this is a national tragedy, and I beg your assistance in helping to alleviate it.

"Finally, I must also insist that $78.5 million for a preliminary study of the Utopia Valley Chain of Lakes project be implemented. Engineers and economists estimate that harnessing Utopia Creek and creating a series of ponds throughout Utopia Valley will, in turn, produce billions of dollars in benefits sometime between now and the year 2750.

"The people of Utopia are happy to sacrifice, Mr. Speaker. All they ask in return is their fair share of the pork. I mean, pie."

It's a gas

July 2, 1995

G overnment scientists are afraid the Earth is going to melt, and it's all the fault of a bunch of rude cows.

If you keep up with world events, you are familiar with this situation. It's been in the news for years. Has to do with methane gas and its effects on global warming. Researchers believe grazing cattle—and to a lesser extent, sheep and goats—are responsible for as much as one-sixth of the methane produced on this planet. Now, they're out to prove it.

The U.S. Department of Agriculture has begun tests with a fancy new sensing device that monitors the methane emissions from every cow in a particular field. This high-tech thingamajig is hooked to an ultra-sensitive machine called a laser spectometer.

All of which is a fancy way of saying that every time Bossy burps or toots, the blast is duly noted.

I don't know how much money the feds are spending on this project, but they could save a lot by simply hiring some school kids to hold their noses, point to the guilty party and shout, "SHEW!"

Then again, maybe not. The animal rights crowd would blow a fuse because of the embarrassing emotional distress this will cause to the offending cow. So forget I mentioned it.

Perhaps a better way would be to teach cattle not to burp and toot in the first place.

Of course! What a perfect government program! It would be costly, exceedingly technical, require hundreds of thousands of employees and be burdened by miles of logistical red tape. I'm surprised someone in Washington hasn't thought of it already.

Farmers would be required to notify their county agent upon the birth of each calf. At a given age—three or four months, perhaps—calves would be shipped to a central location within the county. There, they would undergo social training.

Under the guidance of government experts, calves would learn to not gulp air as they eat and chew their cuds. This one step alone should cut the belching rate in half.

Accidents will always happen, of course, so the curriculum

must include lessons in discretion. Thus, when a calf feels an uncontrollable explosion coming on, the very least he or she can do is walk to an unoccupied corner of the field. Or, if taken by surprise, moo something on the order of, "Pardon me. Must be the wild onions."

Once calves pass the course, they may return to the farm—hopefully to pass on their valuable lessons to pigs, chickens and horses.

I see this as a win-win situation. For one thing, the methane gas problem will cease to exist, thus guaranteeing the future of planet Earth. Two, the nation's farms will become a picture of hygiene and social decorum. And best of all, this will give Congress and the president something new to argue about.

The way things have been going lately in Washington, about all I can do is hold my nose, point my finger, and shout, "SHEW!"

Let's get 'em scrubbed!

July 5, 1994

Thanks to those hygienic men and women of the Tennessee General Assembly, we all know to wash our hands! after using the bathroom.

Not a quick rinse, either. We are not talking about a gentle hint to run your pinkies through the tap water after pottying—whether you wee-weed on them or not. Instead, you must wash your hands!

The "!" is of utmost importance. By law, it must be included. If not, there's a $50 fine.

But don't take my word for it. Check out the walls of any public restroom. A new state law requires a sign, at least 6 inches tall and 14 inches wide, that reads, "For good health, please wash your hands!"

One of the sponsors of this gem was Sen. John Ford (D-Memphis). Yes, the same John Ford who recently tried to make it rough on a state trooper who clocked him at 94 mph on the interstate.

The senator raised a stink with the officer because lawmakers have "legislative immunity" to and from Nashville. For all I know, they may also have immunity from washing their hands! after performing No. 1 or No. 2. They might as well. At 94 mph, there's no time to zip up their trousers, let alone flush or turn on the faucet. But I digress.

I suppose there is merit to this law. Anyone with half a lick of common sense knows that scrubbing after The Business is the polite, sanitary thing to do. It gets rids of germs. Helps stop the spread of disease. Cuts down on illness.

But must lawmakers waste their time and our money enacting such inane legislation? If so, why don't they put their sanitized heads together and draft laws requiring us to use a hanky!? Or brush after each meal!?

You know the answer, of course. Legislators engage in silly exercises like this because they're afraid to tackle the real health issues. Smoking, for instance.

The germ-conscious lawmakers who passed the wash your hands! rule also enacted a piece of legislation called The Prevention of Youth Access to Tobacco Act of 1994. Sounds honorable enough. What better way to advance the cause of public health than by keeping cigarettes out of the hands of children?

Ah, but way down there in the itty-bitty print, guess what? With the assistance of the tobacco lobby, these same hygienists included wording that prohibits Tennessee cities from enacting restrictions against smoking. Meaning non-smokers must continue to breathe the fumes of those who wish to pollute their own lungs.

These same lawmakers also leaped fearlessly into the issue of drunken driving. They dressed the windows of public safety by passing the Open Container Law, which stipulates drivers may not hold an open bottle or can of hooch.

As for passengers in the vehicle? Heh-heh. The law doesn't apply to them, thanks to our public health guardians and their liquor lobby friends.

What a bunch of jellyfish. If we had any sense, we'd wash our hands! of them next election day.

Thou shalt not park illegally

May 5, 1992

T racey Farr is a senior at the University of Tennessee. She graduates in a couple of weeks. Her majors are political science and economics. She hopes for a career in human resources or public administration.

In four years at UT, Farr has received a broad education— English, math, business, natural sciences, the works. But recently, she learned the most important lesson the university teaches, inside the classroom or out: Don't ever mess with the system.

A couple of months ago, Farr signed up for job interviews offered by UT's office of career planning and placement. She turned in resumes and talked with representatives of several companies in her chosen field.

One of them asked for a copy of her grades, and Farr filled out the necessary paperwork. Then she waited for a reply from the company, possibly for a follow-up interview or maybe even a job offer. The reply never came.

What did come was a form letter from UT's career planning office. It said her transcript had not been sent. What's more, the letter said the company had been notified that Farr owed a fine.

Turns out Farr had two outstanding parking tickets. She immediately wrote a check for $52.50, but it appears to have been too little, too late. Because the next day, she received a Dear John from the company.

"It could have been they didn't want me in the first place," said

Farr. "But it also could have been that they got UT's letter about the fine and dropped me. If so, that seems like very harsh punishment for a couple of parking tickets."

True. The what-ifs from this situation, extrapolated over the next 30 years, could wind up costing Farr thousands and thousands of dollars. A lucrative career could have been deep-sixed before it began. But, as anyone who ever set foot upon The Hallowed Hill can testify, thou shalt not park illegally.

"It's not only parking fines; it's any money owed to the institution," said Bert Sams, associate vice chancellor for administration and student affairs. "It could be a damage fee from chemistry lab, a food services fee, a housing fee, anything. The rules clearly spell out that students must pay all outstanding debts."

In addition, Mary Boyd, assistant director of the career planning and placement office, said students are reminded via newsletter to pay what they owe, no matter how small.

"It goes out weekly during the job interview periods," she says. "There's always a notice at least once about the importance of paying all fines. Still, it is very common for transcript requests to be turned down because of this. I'd say it happens at least 10 percent of the time."

That's life, Tracey. Tough luck, kiddo. What a hard way to learn a lesson. But rules are rules.

Besides, if you'd had sense enough to have been born a boy and knew how to catch a football, you wouldn't have to worry. You could have dropped out of school, gotten drafted by the pros, told 'em to take their fine and shove it—and still be welcome to park your Jaguar wherever you want anytime you visit the ol' alma mater.

Tempest in a, uh, teapot

May 9, 1993

Dear Bubba:
  Hit's me, Cuzzin Clem from Tennessee. I know I ain't
  wrote you in quite a spell, but thangs has been powerful
busy down here on the farm. The late freeze 'bout tore us a new
one. Knocked everything off kilter. We're jest now gettin the last of
the crops set out.

Anyhow, I wanted to tell you another reason why Tennessee is
sech a crazy state.

You know what we're about to get? A new law to protect us
farmers and hunters and fishermen, that's what. Hit's been
bounced around in committees over in Nashville fer the last few
days, and I 'spect they'll get around to votin on it fer shore sometime next week.

This is a law that says hit's OK to pee outside, as long as
nobody is lookin.

I ain't making this up, Bubba. I know what you always say
about them legislator people. You say they ain't got enough sense to
pee without 25 other people tellin them how to do it. But this
proves you wrong. As fer as I know, they is less than 25 people on
them committees.

Here's how this thang came to be: Two Republicans, Randy
Stamps of Hendersonville and Carol Rice of Clarksville, was tryin
to figger a way to keep people from shuckin off their clothes in
them juke joints. So they wrote up a law against "public indecency"
and figgered it'd slide through slicker'n bear grease on a bedpost.

Boy, was they ever wrong!

You see, them smarty-pants legislator people never figgered
what happens when fellers like you and me is out in the fields and
hit's been a good hour since we drunk all that iced tea at lunch. Or
else what happens when we sit on a deer stand all mornin atter a
breakfast of fried aigs, catheads and gravy and coffee. Or when
we're in the bass boat, soakin up a few suds, and hit's a long way to
run back to the dock.

They never figgered on a whole lot of other thangs, either—like wimmin that's wet-nursin their babies or sports people takin showers in a locker room or patients at the doctor office or any other time you gotta peel off yore britches.

Whee doggies! Them crazy legislator people stirred up a bigger hornets' nest than the one you and me flung a rock through when we was kids!

Nacherly, anybody with half a lick of common sense would have throwed the whole thang out and been shed of it. But not the Tennessee legislator people. Since their brains is rotted worse than a barrel full o'catfish bait, they started writin exemptions for 'bout nearly everybody in the whole state.

That's why we're about to get us an o-fficial, guaranteed, put-it-in-writin law that sez anytime we need to pee and they ain't a privy handy, all we gotta do is run behind a bush and let 'er rip.

I jest wish Paw was around to see this foolishness. I shore know what he'd have to say. He'd say hit looks like the Tennessee legislator people have done peed away another bucket full of money wastin time on crazy laws.

And then he'd probably pick up the paper this new law is wrote on and tote it with him on his next trip to the privy. That'd be puttin it to the best possible use.

What this country needs

March 14, 1995

Precisely 141 years ago today, Thomas Riley Marshall was born in North Manchester, Ind. I know this scintillating news makes your week complete. But instead of baking a cake in honor of the occasion and breaking into a rousing chorus of "Happy Birthday, Old Geezer," let us ponder how the course of American history would have been altered if Marshall had been born, say, 100 years later.

Surely he . . . huh? What's that? Who in blue blazes was Thomas Riley Marshall? I thought you'd never ask.

He was the governor of Indiana, that's who. And from 1913

until 1921, he was vice president of the United States under Woodrow Wilson. Technically, he could have served as prez in 1919 when Wilson became ill. But, being a good lieutenant, Marshall would hear nothing of the idea and dutifully continued to play second fiddle.

Everything in the preceding paragraph is 100 percent true. But don't look for it on the final exam because it is totally unrelated to Marshall's place in history. You see, despite his years of dedicated

public service and despite any legislation he helped enact, Thomas Riley Marshall is best remembered for one sentence he uttered:

"What this country needs is a good 5-cent cigar!"

Marshall made the remark in front of the U.S. Senate, sometime in the 'Teens. At the time, and for decade-upon-decade thereafter, it was considered a pearl of Yankee wisdom—a to-the-point statement with direct applicability to virtually any aspect of American commerce and manufacturing. It was the ultimate sound byte before sound bytes were cool. But it sure wouldn't play today.

In the first place, Marshall would need to update his finances. Economists differ about these things, but given the ravages of inflation and skyrocketing costs of agricultural production, that 5-cent cigar would cost in the neighborhood of, oh, $4.78 today.

As any political spin doctor can tell you, "What this country needs is a good $4.78 cigar!" fails miserably in the charisma department, along with "Give me liberty or give me a caning!" They just don't have the same punch as the original.

Economics notwithstanding, any politician today who praised the widespread consumption of cheap tobacco products would be attacked by the American Medical Association, the American Lung

Association, the American Heart Association and the American Cancer Society within 10 minutes after his remark was faxed coast-to-coast. Unless, of course, he was from a tobacco-producing state, in which case he would be nominated for Grand Poobah of the Universe.

Still, everything that goes around comes around. Particularly in politics. There is plenty of room in Washington today for Thomas Riley Marshall's kind of thinking, and I'm just waiting on some genius to rediscover it. Something along the lines of:

"What this country needs is a good 50-cent bowl of cornflakes!"

Yeah, it's a little rough. But I'm working on it.

Credits where they're due

May 17, 1992

G ood ol' TVA. Always showing up at the right time with an absolutely ingenious plan to bring peace, prosperity and pollution to our valley.

The agency announced the other day that it will spend a bit of pocket change—somewhere between $2.5 million and $4 million, but who pays attention to details?—to buy "emission credits" from a Wisconsin power company.

An emission credit is what power producers earn for complying with environmental regulations. The more they fall in line with the Clean Air Act, the more credits they receive.

It's sorta like what happens in prison. If Inmate XR1385-B is in for 10 years and behaves like an angel, he might get two years knocked off. Conversely, if Inmate TP5829-C is a meanie, he might have extra time applied to his sentence.

But there is a significant difference between convicts and utility companies—in some ways. Convicts can't swap their time with anyone else. Utility companies can. And that's what TVA is doing.

Wisconsin Power and Light has extra pollution credits, and TVA is forking over wads of cash for them. This gives TVA permission to spew an extra 10,000 tons of sulfur dioxide into the air around here.

See? Didn't I tell you—*cough, cough*—it was ingenious?

I just can't wait until this marvelous plan trickles down to the rest of society.

Let's say you're clicking along the interstate at 76 mph and get nabbed by a radar unit. Ouch. This could be bad. You've already got three tickets on your record. The judge is likely to be steamed. Your insurance rates could soar. You might even lose your license.

Are you worried? Not in the least. You reach for your cellular phone and dial a friend.

"Hey, Freddie. It's me—Luke. I'm calling to see if you can help me out of a little jam."

"All you gotta do is ask, pal. What's up?"

"A state trooper is standing outside my car right now. He's just popped me with another speeding ticket. How are you fixed for credits?"

"No problem. I haven't been busted in a good 10 years. I must have at least 200 mph worth."

"Great! Looks like I need 11 mph. Name your price."

"It's the standard rate—$50 an mph. But since you're a friend, I'll let you have 'em for $40. I'll drop 'em in the mail tomorrow and you can send me a check."

"Freddie, you're the best. What a pal. If there's ever anything I can do, just call me."

"Well, now that you mention it, Luke, the IRS is breathin' down my neck, big time. What's your tax credit situation?"

"Not great. I can probably spare $7,000 worth. But my cousin, Louie, is loaded. Last time we talked, he had over $150,000 in credits just waiting to be used. I'll call him first thing tomorrow morning and set it up."

"Excellent!"

"Gotta run. Give a kiss to Beth and the kids."

I love it. The crime rate bottoms out and the economy rebounds like a rubber ball on concrete. It just doesn't get any better than this.

What's in a name?

May 21, 1996

N ow that Bob Dole has officially resigned from the Senate so he can officially accept the Republican presidential nomination, there is one itty-bitty matter of foreign diplomacy that the man from Kansas must officially worry about.

His name.

On American soil, "Bob Dole" sounds great. It's short, simple, snappy, easy to remember and rolls off the tongue much smoother than "Rutherford B. Hayes" and "Warren G. Harding," two Republicans who ran for office when a middle initial was officially required.

(Indeed, "Bob Dole" has such a nice ring to it, Dole often uses it as a third-person reference when speaking of himself. "Bob Dole has always been tough on crime," he'll say in one campaign speech. "Bob Dole has always been against higher taxes," he'll say in another. Frankly, Sam Venable is growing rather weary of this oratorical quirk and fears it may spread to the masses. But Sam Venable digresses.)

In certain foreign countries, however, Dole's name is not so perky. It's downright offensive. This has nothing to do with Yanqui imperialism, capitalist pigism or any other insults foreigners sometimes hurl at American politicians.

Instead, it's the word "dole" itself.

In Iran, that's exactly the way the term for "male reproductive organ" is spelled.

I hold in my hands a Reuters news dispatch from Tehran that discusses the thorny (ouch, poor choice of words) issue. The story quotes Majid Fanni, a prepress specialist at a Tehran service bureau: "At first it might seem funny to some people, but it's creating a serious issue for us. How can we write headlines using that word?"

(Once again, Sam Venable is tempted to digress and point out to Majid Fanni that his last name, in English, means "butt." Then again, mayhaps Sam Venable should keep his imperialist thoughts to himself. So forget Sam Venable mentioned it.)

In all fairness to Bob Dole, there's not much he can do to remedy the problem, aside for saying, "Hey, just call me Bob," when traveling in regions where his last name creates such embarrassing confusion. It's not like he went out and shopped for a name that causes people in some cultures to squirm.

And it's not like we capitalist pigs haven't suffered the same nervous moments with foreign names. In 1979, when Chinese leader Deng Xiaoping visited the United States, American TV and radio broadcasters had to remain straight-faced every time they correctly pronounced his surname. I'll guarantee you more than a few heads turned when news that "President and Mrs. Carter joined Dung at a White House dinner today . . ." came across the tube.

Quite frankly, Sam Venable got over this juvenile name-game nonsense a long time ago. So did anyone who attended Young High School in the early 1960s. One of our classmates—Sam Venable swears he is not making this up—was named Richard Long.

He didn't go by "Richard."

A new wrinkle in campaigns

May 22, 1994

The filing deadline for state elections passed last week, so now we know who is officially in for the grand campaign. Great. This is the perfect time to introduce all candidates to the Caligiuri principle of politicking. Tennessee office-seekers will have several months to go on diets and improve their tans— maybe even have a surgical cosmetic tuck here and there—so they can hit the campaign trail with full disclosure.

I have named this principle after Richard Caligiuri of Wilkinsburg, Pa., a candidate for his state's 18th District seat in the U.S. House of Representatives.

Caligiuri, a former Libertarian Party official who is running as a Democrat, recently purchased a full-page advertisement in a weekly Pittsburgh newspaper.

In it, he posed nude.

No joke. The advertisement came complete with a headline exclaiming, "I'll kick your ass philosophically!"

Caligiuri, who described himself as a "philosophical outlaw," told reporters that taking off his clothes was the only way he could generate media coverage.

"This is what attracts people and media attention, and that's a shame," he said. "It's also a comment on our society."

Sadly, he is correct. Americans are far more interested in TV reruns than who's running for public office.

They've also grown numb of tired old debates in which Candidate Jones and Candidate Smith trade blows over taxes, inflation, trade deficits, crime, health care, blah-blah-blah, and their indifference is reflected at the polls.

But under the Caligiuri principle, I expect an immediate and dramatic reversal of this trend. Just think of the advantages:

Political speeches will be shorter. It won't even be possible to speak off the cuff, mainly because candidates won't have a cuff.

It will be exceedingly simple to separate the heavyweights from the also-rans.

Every candidate can proudly and truthfully proclaim, "I have nothing to hide!"

Male candidates will be relieved of the loosened-necktie-and-coat-slung-over-the-shoulder pose they feel obliged to strike whenever they visit a factory, warehouse or other blue-collar setting.

Terms like "pressing the flesh" and "getting caught with your pants down" will take on entirely new meanings.

I can even imagine a time when the Caligiuri principle spreads across the general population and people truly begin to see each other as equals.

Well, more or less.

Indeed, this bold notion reaffirms my faith in the power of the people to work for the common good by simply sitting down together.

As long it's not on vinyl seatcovers.

Playing the percentages

November 4, 1993

In some respects, the 12.2 percent voter participation in the city elections was a rousing success. It was twice the 6 percent who voted in the September 28 primary. And considering there wasn't a boiling-hot, city-wide issue at stake, it wasn't that bad of a showing.

"It's hard to get people to the polls when there isn't a lot of controversy," Election Commission Chairman Dennis Francis told

reporters after the ballots had been counted. "There just wasn't a lot of 'throw the rascals in, throw the rascals out' mentality."

Irene Lovely, registrar at large, echoed Francis' comments. She said the volatile 1992 presidential election brought voters out in hordes. The 76 percent participation last November was the largest she's seen in 27 years at the commission.

Perhaps these veteran election watchers are correct. Perhaps we should be content with 12.2 percent for this ho-hum campaign.

But anytime 87.8 percent of the voters take absolutely no part in deciding who wins and who loses a race, something is out of kilter. It's like trying to build a car with only an ignition switch, a battery, two tires and a muffler, and then expecting the thing to roar to life.

Yes, yes; I know. Editorial writers have harped on this issue for eons. Anytime there's an election, you can expect someone to blow the dust off an old get-out-the-vote essay and play it one more time. This is journalism's version of the Christmas carol. We sing it on cue, season after season.

Not that it makes one whit of difference, unfortunately. Voters continue to find 10,001 excuses for not casting their ballots and 10,001 reasons to gripe after the winners are sworn in. So since only 12.2 percent of the eligible voters in Knoxville took part in this one, I say everybody in city government should adjust their schedules likewise:

Only 12.2 percent of all employees—the mayor and staff, members of council, police officers, firefighters, anyone and everyone who draws a check from the city—should be kept on the payroll. Send the other 87.8 percent packing.

Those 12.2 percent who are left can only work 12.2 percent of the time they're officially on the clock. The other 87.8 percent is considered free time. They'll be paid, however, at a 100 percent rate.

During the 12.2 percent of the time these people are actually working, they only have to give a 12.2 percent effort.

Only 12.2 percent of calls to the police and fire departments will be answered. Only 12.2 percent of streets will be maintained. Only 12.2 percent of the city's recreation areas will be open and, of course, for only 12.2 percent of the time.

What's that, you say? The citizens of Knoxville will blow a fuse? They'll turn out by the tens of thousands at the next City Council meeting, carrying pitchforks and torches and demanding to know what-for?

Big deal. Only 12.2 percent of them will be given a chance to speak.

Sensitive to sensitivity

October 24, 1991

I t's 6 a.m., Oct. 25, 2050. All across Anytown, U.S.A., clock radios are sounding off:

"Good morning, Americans—and that includes all you Native Americans, African-Americans, Italian-Americans, German-Americans, French-Americans, Mexican-Americans, Polish-Americans, Russian-Americans, Turkish-Americans, Asian-Americans, Arab-Americans and anyone and everyone else within the sound of my voice. I'm Phil Goode, your sensitive newscaster from your sensitive station, KARE.

"How's does my voice sound today? Too loud for those of you who didn't get enough sleep? Too soft for the hearing-impaired? I'm so sorry. Let us know what you think. Because at KARE, we care about you. Now, for the news:

"Several people were killed in various parts of our city yesterday. Some died in automobile accidents, some in hold-up attempts, and some committed suicide. Several people also were arrested for a variety of crimes. On the other hand, the vast majority of people in Anytown did not die and were not arrested. Of course, in keeping with KARE's commitment to avoid offending anyone, no details about any of these events will be made public.

"In holiday news, the Anytown Police Department is warning drivers to be extra careful next weekend when youngsters will be trick or treating. In addition, the department also called attention to the Halloween sensitivity law, which specifies that children may wear only plain paper bags, with eye and nose holes, for masks. Children dressed as nurses, bandits, witches, actresses, lawyers, athletes, soldiers, politicians—or any uniform that could be construed as insensitive to the feelings of people in these and other walks of life—will be sent home and given a gentle talking-to.

"On the sports front, here's the rundown from last night's high school football action: Teams Y-17, W-5, J-92 and R-12 won.

"For you couch potatoes—and, please, don't think we're being insensitive; we know there are many people who enjoy sitting on the sofa for hours at a time, eating non-nutritious food and watching athletics, and we're happy for them—there's a full menu on tap this weekend. Several football teams will play key games, including the nationally televised clash between Team H-12 and Team D-4, followed by the match-up between Team K-2 and Team P-4 from the West Coast.

"Also, all eyes will be on the final game of the World Series, featuring Team A vs. Team G, formerly known as the Braves and the Indians—Oh! How it pains me to say those words! After that, stay tuned for live coverage of psychological consultations with the players: 'Coping Sensitively With Success' for the winners and 'You're Still a Good Person' for the non-winners.

"On the weather front, it looks like rain for Anytown. This is bad news for area farmers who are trying to harvest their crops, and we apologize. We realize the financial stability and general well-being of our farm families are tied directly to the harvest, and we sincerely hope they can cope with the possibility of showers.

"That's all the news for now. I'm Phil Goode for KARE, the station that cares. Thanks so much for listening, and have a nice day.

"I mean, have a nice day if that's what you have in mind. If having a nice day is the very last item on your agenda, far be it from me to be so insensitive as to force my feelings on you. Have whatever kind of day you want to have. Please."

CHAPTER FIVE

Food for thought on thoughts of food

Some scientists argue that the urge to reproduce is the strongest force in all of humanity.

Don't believe them. I say it's the urge to fill our bellies.

Figure it out for yourself:

How many times a day do you eat? And how many times a day do you engage in, uh, "reproductive pursuits," even at the top of your game?

Case closed.

All this talk about research has made me hungry. You gonna finish that doughnut?

Ever a burger

May 19, 1996

I ate one of McDonald's new Arch Deluxe hamburgers the other day, and I'm excited to report that this revolutionary combination of bread, ground beef, bacon, cheese, spicy sauce, onion, lettuce and tomato tastes exactly like (a drum roll, please)—a hamburger.

What else would you expect a hamburger to taste like? A wool sock?

If I bit into a hamburger and it tasted like smoked turkey and Swiss cheese on rye bread with deli mustard, I'd say, "Wow! This is like no hamburger I ever ate before!"

Of course, I'd probably never eat another one, since I'm in the quaint habit of ordering smoked turkey and Swiss cheese on rye bread with deli mustard, not a hamburger, when I'm in the mood for smoked turkey and Swiss cheese on rye bread with deli mustard.

Nonetheless, I've got to hand it to the geniuses at McDonald's who cooked up this gem. Regardless of whether they invented a new hamburger, they've definitely scored points in the marketing category. These new Arch Deluxes are destined to break sales records.

Why?

Because they're not being targeted to kids. Repeat: Not being targeted to kids.

If you've seen any of McDonald's commercials for the Arch Deluxe, you know what I'm talking about.

This is an "adult" sandwich. McDonald's goes out of its way to turn kids off. The company all but says to everyone under 30, "Gag! If you order an Arch Deluxe, your face will break out in zits, you'll grow up to be an accountant and you'll start dressing dorky like your parents."

So how will teenagers and other hungry youngsters react?

They'll buy Arch Deluxes as fast as they come off the grill, that's how.

Not because they're afraid of zits and careers in accounting, but because someone has told them not to buy a hamburger. And, by golly, nobody's going to tell them what to do!

If I was one of the big dogs at McDonald's, I'd go a step farther. I'd establish a minimum age for purchasing an Arch Deluxe—just like for beer and likker—and card everybody who comes through the door.

The age can be 18, 21, whatever. Doesn't matter. Just make sure that anyone under the minimum knows he/she absolutely, positively cannot purchase one of the new burgers.

Talk about mega-sales. Every McDonald's from Seattle to Miami would be overrun with frantic teens demanding to be served.

True, a few of these young folks would file a lawsuit, costing the parent company several million dollars. So what? The resulting publicity would be worth billions.

All the other kids wouldn't mess with legalistic mumbo-jumbo. They'd simply get hold of a fake ID and gorge themselves silly on forbidden Arch Deluxe fruit.

Either way, McDonald's would need a new fleet of tractor-trailer trucks to haul its money to the bank.

Goodbye to plain ol' coffee

April 9, 1996

I knew the world had fallen completely off its axis when I walked into my favorite truck stop the other morning and discovered a cappuccino machine.

Yes. Cappuccino. That foamy, sweet, Beautiful People coffee wannabe, right there in amongst the girlie magazines, CBs and

10W-40. This stuff even came in two flavors: mocha and French vanilla. I was certain that somewhere, all the pieces of Jimmy Hoffa were turning in the grave.

It's bad enough that cappuccino machines have invaded service stations, delis and lunch counters all over town. But a truck stop? Heaven help us.

I don't have anything against cappuccino, per se; if you want to spend good money on a beverage that tastes like coffee-flavored meringue, have at it. It's just that cappuccino is the latest volley in a never-ending assault on plain ol' coffee.

If you are over the age of 40, you may well remember when it was possible to sit down in a restaurant and order a cup of eye-opener without being quizzed beyond, "You want sugar and cream with that?"

Not today. Ask for a simple cup of coffee in the 1990s and you might as well submit to an audit from the IRS.

You want regular or decaf?

One-hundred percent Colombian or a blend?

Amaretto?

Irish cream?

Swiss mocha?

Hazelnut?

Espresso?

With mint or a cinnamon stick?

No, ma'am. I want non-fancified, old-fashioned, clear-your-throat coffee! Black.

Don't think you can escape this madness by asking for tea, either. That merely compounds the problem.

First, you've gotta choose between hot or cold. Then, will it be: Herbal or regular?

Sugar or artificial sweetener?

And what about flavors—orange, raspberry, peach, cherry, tropical, cinnamon, apple or cranberry?

Huh? Cherry? Ma'am, I want tea, not fruit punch!

It gets worse. They've even found a way to screw up all-American lemonade.

I made this discovery several weeks ago when I walked into a general store in Hancock County and spied a cooler full of lemonade in such exotic flavors as peach and tangerine. Finding this harsh truth in the outback of Hancock County was just as shocking as seeing the cappuccino machine in a truck stop. When did the world run off and leave me?

"Don't you have any regular lemonade?" I wanted to know.

"Guess not," the woman replied.

"Well then, just give me water, please."

She didn't blink an eye: "You want it from the tap or out of a bottle?"

You know, when you steel yourself to it, dying of thirst ain't all that bad.

The real truth about labels

October 6, 1995

The more I learn about truth-in-food-labeling laws, the more I long for the good ol' days when "wholesome" and "nutritious" were used to promote everything from candy bars to cigarettes.

Sure, it was sneaky to mislead the public Back Then. But what has changed? Despite all the new regulations about labels, the sneakiness continues.

I picked up a Moon Pie the other day and flipped it over to look at the label. I figured anything that tastes as good as a Moon Pie, is stuffed with goo like a Moon Pie, and is coated with chocolate like a Moon Pie must have a fat content measured in gallons.

Wrong. According to the label, there are but 5 teeny-tiny grams of belly-swelling, artery-clogging fat in one of these delicious delights.

And then I noticed the fine print: The "serving size" is half a Moon Pie. In other words, the total fat content is 10 grams.

OK, so the label is technically accurate. But who eats half of a Moon Pie? Eating half of a Moon Pie breaks every law of human nature and is a direct violation of the U.S. Constitution, the Bill of Rights, the Taft-Hartley Act and the Paris Peace Accords. Go look it up.

But sneakiness is nothing compared to confusion. I recently went to Wendy's and ordered a grilled chicken sandwich. While it was cooking, I moseyed over to a side counter and picked up a copy of a pamphlet called "Good Nutrition News From Wendy's."

According to this chart, a grilled chicken sandwich contains: "Chicken breast fillets (with rib meat), caramel color added; containing up to 17 percent of a solution of water, seasoning (salt, dextrose, grill flavor from vegetable oil), modified food starch, corn syrup solids), sodium tripolyphosphate, garlic powder, grill flavor from vegetable oil, onion powder, maltodextrin, beef flavor (beef stock, maltodextrin, salt, flavor, caramel color, disodium inosinate, disodium guanlylate, lactic acid), polysorbate 80, caramel color, BHA, BHT), partially hydrogenated soybean and/or cottonseed oil."

That ain't all. The bun is made up of "Enriched flour, water, high fructose corn syrup, soybean oil, yeast, vital wheat gluten, salt, calcium sulfate, sodium stearoyl lactylate, calcium stearoyl-2 lactylate, tumeric, paprika, whey solids, sodium caseinate, monocalcium phosphate, potassium bromate, and azodicarbonamide."

Can't forget the reduced-calorie honey mustard, either. It comes packed with "Honey, soybean oil, corn sweetner, Dijon mustard, water, distilled vinegar, modified food starch, egg whites, egg yolks, salt, xanthan gum, spice, sodium benzoate and potassium sorbate (preservatives), dehydrated onion and garlic, natural flavor, lemon juice concentrate, calcium disodium and EDTA (to protect flavor)."

Frankly, I don't care whether my wheat gluten is vital or merely optional. But I wasn't hungry any more and canceled the order.

Oddly enough, though, I did have an unbelievable craving for a wholesome candy bar and a nutritious cigarette.

The future looks great

November 2, 1995

I am delighted to report that the youth of America are well-adjusted, rational little urchins who are perfectly suited for the rigors of the 21st century.

Because they are making better grades than ever?

Because they have mastered high-tech computer skills?

Because they have rediscovered that ol' can-do, never-say-die mental and emotional toughness made famous by the founders of this sovereign republic?

Heavens, no. It's because they have sense enough to know Halloween treats are supposed to be sugary, sticky, chocolaty globules of fat.

I was worried at first. Parents, as usual, had attempted to draw a pall of gloom over this year's celebration by offering "healthy" options for trick-or-treaters. Indeed, a national news report earlier in the week attempted to give credibility to this holiday heresy by suggesting homeowners dole out "single-serving packages of instant oatmeal or Cream of Wheat, bagels, raisins and sunflower seeds" when the kiddies came calling in their costumes.

I like oatmeal as much as anyone. Always have. But not in my trick-or-treat bag!

To make sure my hunch was correct, I conducted an informal

survey with some of the monsters and ghouls that called upon
Venob Manor on Halloween night. To the person, they gave a rousing thumbs-down to anything but candy.

I asked them, "What would happen if someone gave you Cream
of Wheat?"

"I'd throw it away," replied Jeffrey Williams.

"I'd give it back," said Sue Masterman. Samantha Smith opted
for a more charitable route: "I'd give it to my grandmother, and she
could give it to Fish."

But perhaps Jessica Huskey offered the most realistic response: "I'd give it to my
Dad. He'll eat anything,
even licorice jelly beans."

Of the 20 or more
goodie bags I inspected,
the only treat remotely
associated with nutri-
tion was an apple in
Jeremy Holliday's pos-
session. He said it
ranked well below
Snickers.

I did get a shock when Uvette White showed me her wares. I
asked about her favorite treat, and she held up what I thought was
a red toothbrush. On closer inspection, it proved to be a strawberry
Twizzler. Thank goodness.

Sam Thompson, who is surely destined for a career in accounting, dumped the contents of his plastic pumpkin on my floor and
proudly displayed his plunder, one piece at a time. The inventory:
two suckers (orange), four packs of Sweet Tarts, one pack of
Skittles, four Milky Ways, two Reese's Cups, two sour balls (lime),
one Tootsie Roll, one Wacky Wafer, one roll of Gummi Savers, one
piece of bubble gum, one Jolly Rancher (lemon), and one fruit strip
(strawberry).

But Raleigh McNamee gave me the greatest hope for the
upcoming leaders of our country. Amid what surely was two pounds
of assorted sweets in his bag, I saw two huge candy bars.

"You mean somebody's giving out the big stuff this year?" I

wanted to know.

"Nope," he replied. "I bought those at the store before I started trick-or-treating."

Atta boy, Raleigh. Loosen your belt, pay your dental bills, and grow up to be a good American.

All you gotta do is ask

November 22, 1994

S hould you and your family enjoy a delicious turkey dinner this season, there's a chance Jean Schnelle and her 47 assistants had something to do with it.

In a typical Thanksgiving-Christmas season, they help put more than 200,000 turkeys on the tables of America. Sometimes, right at the last minute.

"Oh, yes, we occasionally hear from folks just as they are ready to eat," said Schnelle, director of the Butterball Turkey Talk Line in Chicago. "They get the turkey cooked but don't know how to carve it. I've coached some of these people along and heard their electric knife in the background, hitting a breastbone."

This is T-Week for Schnelle and her staff of home economists. As they have done for the last 14 years, they'll sit by their toll-free telephones and field a variety of calls from frantic cooks.

"People are not stupid," she told me. "The last thing we'd ever do is laugh at them. It's just that many have never cooked a turkey before, or else they are unfamiliar with their kitchen equipment and they simply need some help."

It's really not that difficult. The trouble comes when wannabe chefs get it in their heads that a holiday meal must be prepared with sauces, herbs, spices and other culinary secrets handed down, generation to generation, since the Indians and Pilgrims dined together.

Ah, but problems do occur.

"Often it's because they don't understand terminology," she explained. "I have recommended cooking the turkey breast-down and had people ask me, 'Where is the breast?' Other times, when I say 'baste,' they think it means sewing the turkey up."

There are even those who don't understand some basic grocery nomenclature. Such as the caller from Virginia who wanted to know how to thaw a fresh turkey.

"Also, I learned a long time ago that when I recommend putting the turkey on a rack, I need to explain that means a rack inside a pan. Otherwise, people might plop it down on the oven rack itself."

Wow. Talk about overworking the ol' smoke alarm. Not to mention the Herculean cleanup job. Even a self-cleaning oven would strain under such a load, eh?

Not really. It seems that Schnelle and associates have heard from Thanksgiving chefs who've deposited their bird into the oven and then mistakenly set it on self-clean.

"That's when they should call the fire department instead of us. The door of the oven gets locked shut during self-cleaning—even though I've had men who called and said they took it apart. After self-cleaning is over, there's nothing left but a lot of ash."

At least these folks did manage to turn on the heat. Schnelle and her crew occasionally are summoned by perplexed homeowners who complain their microwave ovens won't perform.

"Usually, the power has gone off," she said. "We have to gently explain if there's no electricity, the microwave won't work."

And to think the Pilgrims and Indians managed quite well with fire.

Sgt. Fatso and his tubby troops

September 17, 1992

Today's news tip is so exciting, I may have to dash out for a cheeseburger before I can begin organizing my thoughts.

Oh, what the heck; I'll make it a double. A tidal wave of glowing health has suddenly washed across my chubby little body. I may even add a slice of coconut cream pie.

This joy comes courtesy of the Institute of Medicine, which is an affiliate of the National Academy of Sciences. On request of the U.S. Army, IOM experts have been studying height and weight guidelines for Uncle Sam's fighting troops. The other day in Washington, they released their startling findings.

The bottom line: Fat is where it's at.

Permit me to quote directly from the news report. "The Army system fails to recognize that a slightly overweight person may outperform a lean person," the study said in part.

What's more, the Army "fails to take into account the ratio of fat to muscle. As a result, a person who is extremely muscular, including many professional football players, could actually not meet the current military restrictions."

According to the IOM, the Army's physical training program stresses running, push-ups and sit-ups. Fine, if you happen to be in retreat. But, says the IOM, in combat there's a lot of lifting, carrying and moving heavy equipment. Thus, it is essential to have a bunch of Sgt. Fastos on hand to do the job properly.

I could have given the experts this information all along. It's what I've been telling my doctor for years. Those height-weight charts are completely out of kilter, and those of us who cast wide shadows actually perform better than the bean poles.

Oh, sure. I can hear the naysayers now.

First, they will argue that 99 percent of us are not in the military and don't engage in combat.

So? That means we should just drop our guard completely? You never can tell when Saddam Hussein might try to sneak some of his crazies into East Tennessee. If that happens, the Pudge Patrol will be at the peak of conditioning to counterattack.

The disbelievers will also argue that the key word in the IOM's report is "slightly" overweight. They will whip out more charts (no doubt with the same erroneous figures as before) showing that "slightly" overweight means three or four pounds.

Details. Mere details. It's all a matter of relativity.

What's 10 pounds—or 15 or 40—in comparison to, say, an F-16? It's insignificant, that's what. Or "slight," if you choose. And since the IOM has concluded that chubs can outperform the willow sticks, I say, "Pass the butter," and quit worrying.

I say quit worrying about that fat-to-muscle ratio business too. My body contains prime examples of fat and muscle; but, gosh-darn the luck, everything's hidden by a layer of skin, and I can't tell one from the other.

Other people have the same predicament. William "The Refrigerator" Perry, for example. He plays football for the Chicago Bears. According to what the IOM said about certain professional athletes, I doubt he would qualify for military service.

All of which speaks well for the IOM study but poorly of America's fighting machine. If you were an enemy of the United States and it was show time, whom would you fear more: some wiry G.I. Joe built along the lines of Michael Jackson, or The Fridge? I rest my case.

Now that I'm in training, I might order some onion rings too.

June hath 30 days—for eating

June 9, 1995

Loosen your belt, folks. We have descended upon the eatingest region of the calendar.

June is home to National Dairy Month, National Turkey Lovers Month, National Fresh Fruit and Vegetable Month, National Frozen Yogurt Month and National Surimi Month—all washed down with National Iced Tea Month.

Buuuuurp! Thank you. I feel much better.

Dairy Month, of course, is the granddaddy of these events.

According to Chase's Calendar of Events, the Bible of festive occasions, Dairy Month dates back to 1937. Specifically, Chase's says this is "a time to salute American dairy producers who provide quality dairy products all year long."

So don't just stand there. Run to the refrigerator and pour yourself a cold, refreshing glass of cholesterol in honor of the gala occasion.

And while you're at it, carve off a slice of turkey breast so you can "promote awareness and increase turkey consumption at a non-holiday time."

Also, munch some celery and a handful of grapes to recognize "the abundance, variety, good taste, good value and importance to good health of fresh fruits and vegetables."

By then, a big bowl of pecan praline will be perfect to "inform the public of the benefits and colorful history of frozen yogurt," although you might not want to mix the yogurt with surimi salad, despite the "convenience, taste and versatility of imitation crabmeat, lobster and shrimp."

But don't fret. Once you have slammed down a quart of iced tea, your tastebuds will have ceased to register any complaints because they will be enjoying "one of the most widely consumed beverages in the world and one of nature's most perfect, all-natural, low-calorie, refreshing thirst-quenchers."

I think I know why all these food festivals are crammed into June—besides celebrating, promoting awareness and informing the public. It's because our defenses are at the absolute lowest.

June is when everybody's hearts, not to mention their stomachs, turn to thoughts of grub. It's been six long months since the excesses of Christmas and New Year's. Valentine's Day chocolates and gooey candy Easter eggs are but a memory. Now's when we want to load the platter with some real tooth-sinkers.

Nobody starts a diet in June. If embarrassing thoughts of stretched-to-the-max swimming suits came into your mind back in March, that's when you attacked the problem. Or should have, anyway. By now it's too late. So you just let the cellulite hang out and be done with it.

It doesn't get any better next month.

July is when we're supposed to celebrate National Baked Bean Month ("to pay tribute to one of America's favorite and most healthful and nutritious foods"); National Hot Dog Month (celebrating "one of America's favorite hand-held foods with fun facts and new topping ideas"); National Blueberries Month ("to make the public aware that this is the peak month for fresh blueberries"); and National Ice Cream Month—not to be confused with National Dairy Month from June—("to promote America's favorite dessert.")

If you're starting to detect a pattern here, go to the head of the class.

According to the promoters of these special events, each of their respective food products is America's "favorite" or "best-loved" or "most nutritious." For example, way back in February, there was National Pie Month ("to emphasize home preparation of America's favorite dessert"). Now the ice cream crowd says the same thing.

How can this be? Is there no truth in advertising? Perhaps nobody connected with these events is the least bit concerned about conflicting claims. But I am.

And I say that we host National Food Fight Month to see who comes out the winner.

Fry my sushi, please

April 28, 1994

Maintain your guard, brothers and sisters. There could very well be infidels amongst us.

I bring you this admonition after reading the "Southern Focus Poll." And I came away with the distinct impression some of our own kind may have betrayed us.

The "Southern Focus Poll" is a detailed survey conducted by personnel from the Center for the Study of the American South at the Institute for Research in Social Science at the University of North Carolina at Chapel Hill.

Yes, I know. A fancy title like that is enough to choke a hog and should immediately arouse suspicion in all circles. But the best I can tell, these folks are on the level.

What they did was gather 800 people from 13 Southern states and ask them 148 questions about likes, dislikes, attitudes and opinions Down Here. Then they asked 400 non-Southerners the same questions.

After poring over their findings, I have concluded that either (1) the New South is not as Southern as it used to be, or (2) sinister infiltrators from Up There have warped our psyches. For example:

■ People claiming Southern heritage said they would rather eat a hamburger than barbecue. They also chose grilled chicken over fried.

■ By rather substantial margins, more non-Southerners expressed an interest in stock car racing, golf, hunting, camping and boating than Southerners did. By a mere four-tenths of 1 percent, we did beat them in the fishing category.

■ A full 6.8 percent of respondents from Down Here said they did not like corn bread.

■ Finally—and this pains me to no end—12.3 percent not only confessed to eating sushi, but actually admitted they liked it.

Where have we failed, sons and daughters of the South? Is nothing sacred any more? Is this the bitter harvest we have reaped for allowing immigrants from Up There to move freely in our midst?

Fortunately, there were some comforting findings. Among them:

■ By wide margins, people from throughout the United States said Southerners were more courteous, more religious, less pushy, more patriotic, less violent and more contented with our lives than anyone else.

■ We had more full-time workers.

■ A whopping 95.1 percent of us said we were definitely proud of our Southernness.

But this business about food still bothers me. Particularly the part about sushi. If my math is correct and the researchers' findings were accurately reported, that means 98 of those 800 Southerners enjoy eating raw fish.

If I had been in charge of this study, I would have asked these people a few more questions about their initial nibble. Such as:

Was this part of a fraternity initiation?

How many beers did you consume first?

Had your mother-in-law come for an extended visit and you were encouraging her to leave?

Or did the motor on your bass boat conk out, and it was either eat bait or starve?

Health food

April 16, 1991

For those of us who think a six-pack of light beer and two Slim Jims constitute a healthy meal, it's getting tougher to select a balanced diet.

The other day in Washington, a group of doctors asked the Department of Agriculture to throw out the four recognized food groups—meat, fish and poultry; grains; dairy products; fruits and vegetables—and adopt a radical new plan.

The group, which calls itself Physicians' Committee for Responsible Medicine, believes the new food groups should be fruits, legumes, grains and veggies. Under the proposed listing, meat and dairy products would be reduced to "minor options" in the daily diet.

"The typical Western diet, high in animal fat and protein and lacking in fiber, is associated with increased risk of cancer, heart disease, obesity, diabetes and osteoporosis," the doctors' report said.

"Meat and dairy products should have a much smaller place on the menu," added committee member Dr. Oliver Alabaster, a disease prevention specialist from George Washington University Medical Center.

Maybe. Maybe not. The way nutritional researchers wax and wane on the benefits and risks of certain foods, it wouldn't surprise me to see them recommending four pounds of marbled beef daily before the year is out. Do the words "oat bran" ring a bell?

The case for or against meat and dairy products notwithstanding, I am concerned about narrowing our choices simply to "fruits, legumes, grains and vegetables."

I don't have anything against those foods. I try to eat them regularly. Why, only today, I consumed something from each one.

For fruit, I had a four-pack of raspberry Zingers. They went nicely with coffee, my choice for the most nutritious bean in the legume division. Grains? Surely you jest. Barley is still a grain, isn't it? I downed a full 12 ounces. And a huge platter of okra, deep-fried in bacon grease, filled not only the vegetable requirement but also took care of my "minor option" for meat.

See? Who said eating healthy is a chore?

Nonetheless, there are many delicious, body-building foods that don't fall into one of the four new categories, and I hope the physicians' group will come to its senses and make allowances for them.

Chili cheese dogs, for instance.

Oh, sure. I know what you're saying. You're saying, "Is this guy insane? Chili cheese dogs are loaded with meat and dairy products!"

Hah. A lot you know. Thanks to preservatives, artificial flavors, fillers, MSG, hydrogenated soybean oil, enrichers, enhancing agents, emulsifiers and salt, it is possible to pull the handle on virtually any vending machine in this great nation and be rewarded with a week-old, semifrozen chili cheese dog that contains NOT ONE MILLIGRAM of meat or dairy product!

These babies are so healthy, I recommend eating at least three.

The 10 C's of survival

March 21, 1993

Y ou probably won't find this listed in any official survival guide, but if you want to be prepared for the next Worst Snowstorm of The Century, always remember the 10 C's: Cookies, cake, chips, chocolate, chili, cheese, corn bread, crackers, cereal and coffee.

I reached this monumental dietary conclusion after polling several hundred East Tennesseans who have finally shaken the sludge off their boots, restocked groceries and dined on food—real food, you understand, that hasn't been "cooked" (insert laugh here) on the hearth.

After viewing the results, I am convinced it is possible to endure not only blizzards, but also pestilence, boils and locusts, as long as you continually ingest selections from the C-food group. With electrical power or without, East Tennesseans tamped down these goodies in vast quantities during the Blizzard of '93.

Cookies were, by far, the leading C-food member, with Nutter Butter a decisive first, followed by Girl Scout cookies (all flavors) and Famous Amos.

Sure, there were other popular foods—soup, hot dogs, burgers, raw veggies (bleech!), peanut butter, pinto beans, pork and beans (air raid! air raid!), tuna, steak, popcorn, 'taters, aigs and bacon, and snow cream by the gallon. But the 10 C's worked overtime to keep the arteries of local refugees amply clogged.

Then again, many folks had to settle for what was on hand, like it or not. Herewith some more or less, uh, "original" selections from the menus of East Tennessee's snowbound cafes:

"Snowcones from snow and melted fruit juice concentrate," Richard Henighan, Seymour.

Pudding and yogurt "because I had my wisdom teeth pulled out the day before the blizzard and couldn't eat anything else," Becky Hughes, Kingston.

"All the bread crumbs and chips under the cushions of my couch," Rod Richards, Spring City.

"Everything in the freezer, because it was thawing," Amy

Stewart, Oakdale.

"Everything good because the doctor wasn't looking," Doris Teague, Newport.

"Everything in sight," Paige Presley, Lenoir City.

"I was stranded in Lexington, Ky.—do the numbers UK 101, UT 40 ring a bell?—and ate crow for three days," Jim Chisholm, Seymour.

"Junk food from vending machines; I was snowed-in in Gatlinburg," Kim DeBusk, Knoxville.

At least five families who filled out my questionnaire dined elegantly throughout the ordeal, thanks to wood-burning stoves, ample supplies of dry fuel and well-stocked larders.

Three others four-wheeled or walked to fast-food joints. "I waited two hours in line at McDonald's," said Kimberly Pack of Knoxville.

Many others fed the hungry. Mark Smith, a German teacher at Jellico High School, helped prepare hot dogs and kraut for 700 folks seeking shelter at the school. And Roger and Kathy Douglas of Newcomb scraped Interstate 75 with heavy equipment and ferried food to stranded motorists.

But my all-time favorite food story—a story of grit, determination, can-win spirit and let's-talk-about-some-swamp-property sales appeal—came from Betty and Bertha Douglas, who live in the Stinking Creek section of Campbell County:

"We ate bread and water until we heard the trap snap and, to the mouse's misfortune, we had meat that night."

As the stomach churns

March 17, 1994

W hen did antacid tablets became an important source of calcium instead of a relief for heartburn?

Perhaps you've seen the latest advertisements and noticed this evolution for yourself. Instead of stressing the acid-fighting qualities of, say, Tums over Rolaids, commercials attempt to impress us with the fact that one brand delivers a full day's dose of calcium.

No offense, but if my guts were on fire from atomic burritos, I wouldn't give a royal rat's rump if the tablets contained vitamin B-12, or if they freshened my breath and relieved constipation. I'd want something to extinguish the flames.

Conversely, if I was in the market for calcium, you'd find me in the dairy aisle or the medicine section, and—surprise!—I wouldn't care one whit if the product helped prevent bunions.

This is not an isolated example. Lately, automobile shoppers have been subjected to advertisements that praise not the long life of the transmission, nor the safety of construction, nor the power of the engine, nor the reliability of the brakes, not even the choice of exterior paint.

Instead, the big pitch is for the radio.

Huh? I'm about to drop 20 G's on a vehicle that I hope will give me 150,000 safe, carefree miles, and the most important factor to consider is the quality of Clint Black's voice on a country music station? I don't think so.

Oh, well. Perhaps such convolution is the way of the future. Stands to reason that I'd be the last to know. Whatever the latest fad, I'm always bringing up the rear. I can just imagine what'll happen some day when I sit down at a lunch counter and order a tuna salad sandwich.

"You want stain block on that?" the waitress will say.

"Beg your pardon?"

"For an extra dollar, tuna comes with stain block. If you dribble on your tie, all you gotta do is wipe it away, clean as a whistle."

"No stain block," I'll say. "Just tuna salad on toasted wheat bread."

"I recommend rye," she'll reply. "It goes better with your socks."

"My socks? What does bread have to do with socks?"

"If you had on brown socks, wheat would be OK. But you're wearing blue. You should definitely have rye."

"Look, I'm hungry. All I want is a plain tuna salad sandwich on plain, toasted wheat bread with a plain piece of lettuce."

"Will the lettuce be with color or without?"

"Isn't all lettuce green?"

"Not the color of the lettuce, mister. I'm talking about hair. You want lettuce that gently restores your youthful color or lettuce that highlights the gray?"

"Forget the lettuce, forget the rye bread, forget everything! All this foolishness has cranked up my heartburn something fierce. You got any antacids?"

"Antacids? Never heard of 'em. But if you've got an upset stomach, I've got just the thing."

"What?"

"Calcium tablets. Personally, I'd get the Tums. They give you a full day's dose of riboflavin."

A true turkey tale

April 7, 1994

What I should have done is stopped everything and gone to the store to buy butter and lard.

But that was impossible. Even in this era of 'round-the-clock supermarket shopping, I was positive no food stores would be open at 8 a.m. on Easter Sunday. At least not in my immediate neighborhood. Perhaps if I had driven all over town I might have located butter and lard, but I never would have gotten back in time to commit The Great Transgression, let alone made it to church before the benediction.

I do not often yield to The Great Transgression. The Knoxville Academy of Medicine has seen to that by scaring the bejabbers out of me with sermons on cholesterol, blood pressure, fatty foods and other pleasures of life. Thus, when the chance to transgress arose, my inventory of sinful ingredients was woefully low. Here's how it happened:

Mary Ann had gotten up before the sun and gone to sing at the early Easter service. I had finished the newspaper and was starting to think about eating a bowl of oatmeal when I remembered a chore left over from the day before: There was a dead bird in the refrigerator.

Permit me to explain.

Last Saturday, in addition to being Mary Ann and my 25th wedding anniversary, was also the opening day of the wild turkey season. Hopeless romantic that I am, I only hunted half the day. By the time I got home and performed preliminary preparation of my gobbler, it was time for anniversary celebrations. So I made the very logical decision to cram what was left of the beast into the refrigerator.

Mary Ann understands these things. After a quarter of a century with me, she never reaches for the milk without looking very carefully.

Anyhow, just as I fetched the turkey, I spied a paper bag. It was full of morel mushrooms Carson Brewer had given me a couple of days earlier. Immediately, the devil appeared on my left shoulder and said, "To hell with oatmeal, Venob. On this fine spring morning, you deserve a hearty, old-time breakfast. We're talkin' East Tennessee soul food, brother."

Sometimes the devil makes a lot of sense.

I carved three slices of turkey breast, dusted them with flour, salt and pepper, and flopped them into a skillet. That's when I yearned for lard. If a sin is worth committing, it's worth doing whole-hog. Alas, I had to limp by with dietarily correct canola oil.

As the meat sizzled, I washed and sliced the morels. Butter, I thought; I need butter. The only civilized way to saute morel mushrooms is with pure, yellow, clog-'em-shut creamery butter. We had no butter, of course, so again I had to make do with canola oil margarine. It was a poor second choice.

By the time the meat had fried to a crispy brown, The Great Transgression hit high gear. I cracked two large eggs into the sea of grease and let them bubble into over-medium bliss. I sliced a wedge of Mary Ann's homemade bread and toasted it, wishing again for real butter.

And then, like Little Henny Penny, I ate it all by my very own self.

If you must sin on Easter Sunday, this—*buurrrrp!*—is the heavenly way to do it.

A problem with raisins

February 25, 1994

Here it is almost March, and I still haven't broken any of my New Year's resolutions for 1994. Then again, I didn't make any New Year's resolutions for 1994, but why fret over minor details?

I am, however, going to get the jump on 1995. Even though it's a full 10 months before we welcome the next new year, I hereby resolve to finish my box of raisins before the expiration date comes due.

I've got plenty of time to work on the matter. A label on the top of the box says my raisins must be used by October 13, 1995. It's a big box, but even if I eat only one or two raisins daily, I'll surely have them all consumed by then.

I happened to notice the expiration date a few days ago when I dug the raisins out of the refrigerator and sprinkled some on my oatmeal.

"Huh?" I thought. "Do raisins go bad? I always figured they were more or less ageless, like peppermints in the bottom of the candy dish at Aunt Prunella's house."

Assuming raisins do have a finite existence, though, why such a precise date for their demise?

An expiration label that says, "It's better to have these things eaten by late summer or early fall of next year," would make a lot more sense, although it would take up a lot of space on the top of the box.

Talk about confusion! Does this mean on October 12, 1995, I can eat these raisins with reckless abandon and suffer no ill effects, but if I wait two more days before nibbling I will keel over deader than Kelsey's mule?

Will my raisins sit in the box, all plump and sweet, until midnight on October 13, 1995, and then—*zap!*—turn into mouse poop? And if I do eat them sometime after October 13, 1995, and croak, will it be ruled suicide or accidental death?

The whole business of expiration dates on food products baffles me. I never know how much faith to put in them.

Let's say I decide to eat a bowl of cereal before going to bed. I reach into the cupboard, pull out a box of Sugar-Coated Zippy Flakes and start to pour them into a bowl. Then I happen to notice that the expiration date passed two weeks ago.

Are my Sugar-Coated Zippy Flakes too stale to eat now? Is it just my imagination, or have they gotten mushy? Or are they just as crisp as the day I brought them home?

And what about the milk I just started to pour? According to the expiration date, it went sour 24 hours ago. Even if it passes the sniff test, does this mean it still might be infected with jillions of newly hatched bacteria and other cooties that will make me spit up at 3 o'clock in the morning? Inquiring minds want to know.

Yikes! I just flipped over to my 1995 calendar and looked up October 13. It's a Friday. Any Friday the 13th is a bad omen in and of itself. But when you consider this same date is oh-so-close to Halloween, it surely has sinister overtones.

Maybe I'll start eating 10 raisins a day, just to make double-dog certain they're gone in plenty of time.

CHAPTER SIX

Seriously speaking

I've never been accused of being a pulpit-pounding crusader. Don't ever expect to be, either.

When I feel a serious thought coming on, my first reaction is to take a cold shower and hope the mood passes.

But not always.

As the title suggests, the entries in this chapter are presented without any hint of tongue in cheek.

Even though humor is the medium I use most often to treat the ills of society, there are times when laughter is not the best medicine.

Eddie's grave

June 4, 1992

More than six years have passed since Eddie Brown was buried in a donated grave at Lynnhurst Cemetery. Despite the traffic clattering along North Broadway, it's a peaceful site where Eddie rests. The red clay above his casket has compacted nicely; there is no hint of undue settling. At varying intervals on hot summer days, Eddie's grave can catch shade from a white oak to the southeast and a hemlock to the northwest. A carpet of neatly clipped grass covers the plot, and if you kneel, you will see sprigs of clover woven among the stems.

I fingered through the thatch on Eddie's grave a few mornings ago, hoping to find a four-leafed clover. There was none, which really didn't surprise me. Eddie Eugene Brown didn't have an ounce of good luck when he was alive. Why should things be any different for him in death?

Eddie died April 10, 1986. He was 4 years old. According to a detective who investigated the case, Eddie had been beaten almost continuously for nine hours.

I quote from court transcripts: "Various examinations indicated that the child had suffered two, possibly three, skull fractures. The CT scan revealed a hairline fracture in the front right temporal portion of his skull, as well as a blood clot and swelling in that area of the head. . . . Blood coming from Eddie's ear indicated that he had a fracture at the base of his skull which had caused an injury to the middle ear."

There's more: "The pathologist who performed the autopsy noted the presence of vomit in Eddie's lungs. . . . According to the expert, this pressure in the skull resulted in Eddie's aspiration of his own vomit and his ultimate death."

Please continue reading, as painful as the words may be: "Eddie had bruises of varying ages on his face, scalp, ears, neck, chest, hips, legs, arms, buttocks and scrotum. . . . X-rays revealed a broken arm which had not been treated and which had occurred three to five weeks before his death. The injury to his arm was confirmed by a witness who had noticed his arm hanging limply . . ."

Eddie's father, Mack Edward Brown, admitted beating his son. He and his wife, Evajean Brown, were charged with first-degree murder. But a strange thing happened on the road to reprisal. Technicalities got in the way.

During Evajean Brown's trial in 1987, Criminal Court Judge Ray L. Jenkins and defense attorney Herb Moncier bickered frequently, resulting in the judge's abrupt declaration of a mistrial.

Later, an appeals court issued a lot of fancy words—"acted precipitantly rather than as the result of that scrupulous exercise of judicial discretion"—to say Judge Jenkins blew it. But because of her constitutional protection against double jeopardy, Evajean Brown was freed.

Mack Brown's trial came up in 1989. He was convicted and sentenced to die in the electric chair.

News-Sentinel staff writer Jim Balloch was in court that day. Prophetically, he reported, "The lengthy appeals process, however, makes it highly unlikely that the (execution) date will be met."

Ain't it the truth. Earlier this week, the state Supreme Court reduced Mack Brown's first-degree murder conviction to second-degree. Brown was ordered off death row. He could be eligible for parole within two years.

Another technicality.

You see, even though Eddie Brown was pounded into lifeless pulp, Justice Martha Craig Daugherty ruled the state failed to prove (1) Eddie's death was premeditated and (2) Mack Brown deliberated before killing his son.

I have read Justice Daugherty's decision. I understand the fine points of law she makes. In no way does she condone this heinous act. Rather, she is attempting to clarify the technicalities of a first-degree murder conviction.

But as I knelt over Eddie's grave, trying to imagine the terrifying four years this child lived and attempting to square that with fine points in the law, none of the pieces fits.

There are times when a bunch of technicalities can all go straight to hell.

Profits from false prophets

March 25, 1993

T his must be a terribly frustrating time to be God.
Wherever the poor guy turns, people are stamping his seal
of approval on everything they do. I don't know how he
keeps from suffering an identity crisis.

Spin the globe and plunk down your finger on any spot and I
guarantee you'll find agents of God working in direct opposition to
each other.

If it's not in Ireland, with Protestants and Catholics exchanging bullets and car bombs, it's in Bosnia-Herzegovina, where Serbs
are praising the Almighty, passing the ammunition and cleansing
themselves of unrighteous Muslims.

Or else it's in New York City and Calcutta, where buildings are
being blasted for the greater glory.

Or in Waco, Texas, where a cultist and his band are shooting it
out with cops.

Or in Pensacola, Fla., where a doctor who performs legal abor-
tions is gunned down by a religious zealot.

Or in Maryville and Knoxville, where crowds of cheering, jeer-
ing churchgoers badger county commissioners into passing laugh-
ingly toothless resolutions telling homosexuals their kind isn't
wanted.

What's so puzzling is that this killing, bombing and oppression
is being carried out under the umbrella of God, the ultimate symbol of love.

A classic case of trademark infringement, if you ask me. That's
why I wouldn't be surprised to see the Big Guy crack down one of
these days.

Not by hurling bolts of lightning. Or causing floods, plague,
locusts and boils, either. Environmental messages don't get near
the respect they did 4,000 years ago. Too many flood-control projects, insecticides and high-tech medicines these days.

Instead, what he might do is start licensing his name. Set up
franchises. You know, just like they do at the University of
Tennessee.

Let's say you're a dedicated Tennessee football fan, 100 percent orange to the core of your being. You want others to join this great cause too. So in the name of academic loyalty and athletic zeal, you design a T-shirt with the UT symbol, add a sketch of Neyland Stadium, dye it that eye-piercing shade of orange and offer it for sale three hours before kickoff.

Will an agent from the university drop by your souvenir stand and thank you for your continuing support?

Not hardly.

He'll stop by, all right—with a cease and desist order and a cadre of cops to confiscate the goods. And when your day in court arrives, you will discover these things are licensed by UT, administered by UT, subject to UT approval; and until you go through proper channels—a surtax here, a percentage there, here a charge, there a levy, everywhere a buck-buck—the Hallowed Hill is a dark and foreboding place.

Perhaps God will get frustrated enough to try a similar approach. All he's gotta do is appoint one of the archangels as chief agent, select a licensing board, and he's in business.

You want to firebomb a high-rise office building in God's name? Pay the fee, brother, and light the fuse.

Starve political prisoners? Oppress the meek? Silence the opposition? Deprive basic human rights? No problem, sister. Just sign on the dotted line, show your cash, and have at it.

Of course, this concept does beg a formidable question: What's God going to do with the mountains of money—we're talking billions upon megabillions—he's going to raise?

Since the streets inside the Pearly Gates are paved with gold, I doubt there's much demand for cash. Besides, you gotta wonder who winds up there in the first place.

Based on the testimony and actions of some of God's agents down through the years, the Muslims don't qualify. Nor the Jews. Nor the Catholics. Nor the Protestants. Nor anyone else who doesn't fall into one particular lockstep or another.

Wow. Heaven must be a lonely place.

Grandma's Hoe

May 12, 1996

I f you saw the old hoe leaning against a barn or lumped with an assortment of other hand-me-down garden tools, you probably wouldn't buy it for a dollar.

Smart economic thinking on your part. This hoe is slap worn out and ready for the dump.

But take another look before you cast it aside. Some things have value that transcends economic measure, and here is one of them. In our family, "Grandma's Hoe" represents a link to the land that has been handed down, mother to daughter to granddaughter, across the length and breadth of the 20th century.

I cannot tell you when, or for what amount, the hoe was originally purchased. That nugget of information was lost when my wife's grandmother, Clara Waggoner, died in 1991 at the age of 94. Doesn't matter. The hoe has been in our tribe for so long, Grandma might as well have forged the metal blade and carved the hickory handle herself.

A major portion of Grandma Waggoner's life was spent coaxing plants from the ground. In her generation and station in life, this was not a form of recreation. It was what made the difference between eating and going hungry, and her hoe was part and parcel of the process.

She and that hoe scratched their way through the soil of a Union County farm while her lawyer husband tried to earn a living in Depression-era Maynardville. She always grew a patch of tobacco—"bakker" in the rural parlance of this region—for cash in the fall, plus bountiful gardens of corn, beans, tomatoes, okra and strawberries.

Hard work? You betcha. But when it is the kind of work you enjoy, the energy is expended freely. Grandma Waggoner loved nothing better than going up and down those rows under the hot summer sun, bent over her hoe and bringing life from the good earth.

It was her calling. It was her passion.

Grandpa Waggoner died in 1972, but Grandma continued to

live alone and raise her garden. Failing health finally sent her to a nursing home in 1979.

The hoe earned no rest, however. It was passed along to Grandma's daughter, Opal Steinhoff—"Gran" to our children—who used it in the garden and flower beds of her home in Seymour. Just before Gran moved to a condo in South Knoxville, the hoe came to live with us.

Not to retire, that's for sure. Despite an elaborate inventory of newer tools lining one wall in our garage, Grandma's Hoe is the implement of choice every time Mary Ann takes to the garden or flower bed.

Nor do I see a respite in the future. Our daughter Megan, who graduated from college only a few days ago, will likely have the hoe in her hands some day, for she has inherited a love of growing things from the women who came before her.

Lord only knows the tens of thousands of hours this hoe has scritched and scratched its way through the dirt. Its handle is worn smooth from years of use. Indeed, it is actually thinner a foot or so above the gooseneck, just where three generations of left hands have grasped it.

But it is the blade itself that I find most fascinating, and I can't think of a better time than Mother's Day to tell you about it.

The blade on a new-issue hoe measures 6 inches in length; on Grandma's, it has been worn down to 5½. Fresh from the shelf, a hoe blade stands 4¼ inches tall; Grandma's is one full inch shorter. All told, then, we're talking the erosion of 1½ inches of hardened steel, filed away, micron-by-micron, one stroke at a time.

Look even closer. The blade of Grandma's Hoe is no longer straight across the bottom like it came from the factory. It is rounded on either side, sloping upward toward the hump of its shoulders to form the rough outline of a heart.

What else would you expect?

When Grandma Waggoner worked in her garden and sang her old-time gospel hymns, she was sowing love right along with those beans.

Leaving home

April 12, 1992

Befi she walked out of the old house for good, she said goodbye one room at a time.

Her fingers ran along the wainscoting in the dining room. Ricky's handprints are beneath here, she was saying. I cried when I found them. He couldn't have been more than 2. He'd poured orange juice on the floor and was sitting right here, dipping his hands in the puddle, then sticking them on my brand new wallpaper, like he was some kind of printing press. He'd worked all the way around one wall before I realized what was going on.

She touched the wooden panels tenderly and spoke again.

Funny, isn't it? I thought I'd never get over having my new wallpaper ruined. But later on, when we put up these boards and I knew I'd never get to see those cute little handprints again, it hurt me even worse.

She moved into the living room and looked at the fireplace. Must have been the winter of '52, she spoke. The one with the big snow. The power was off for days, and the children were sick. We kept a fire going to stay warm and to cook. It seemed so awful then. But looking back, it was like a big, long picnic.

Her gaze turned to the light fixture in the middle of the ceiling. Used to be a crystal one in its place, she said. But you know how boys are. They were horseplaying one day, and things got out of hand. That's been, what?—at least 35 years, I suppose—but the boys still laugh about trying to vacuum up all those little slivers of glass before I got home.

Slowly, she made her way up the front stairs. Their familiar creak was comforting to her ears. Some stairs are just meant to creak, she spoke, even if they're padded. Gives 'em personality.

I won't miss not having stairs at my new place, she said. Everything's on one floor, and that's going to be nice. But you know, I sure will miss hearing these old creaks.

She stood in the room on the second floor and pointed to the spot where her husband was working the day Pearl Harbor was attacked. He was putting down hardwood floors and listening to the radio, she said. He always listened to the radio when he worked. Sometimes two radios at the same time, if two ball games were being broadcast. He came running downstairs and got me and we stayed in this room all afternoon, glued to that little radio.

She descended the creaky staircase and peered into the living room once again. Over there, she said. Over in that corner.

That's where my favorite chair used to sit. After his unit got called up, I'd sit in that chair late in the afternoon and look out the window across the hills. A big oak tree grew out back in those days. During the war, I'd sit here and stare at its limbs stretching toward the house and wonder how much it would grow before the fighting was over. I never quit worrying and hoping and praying he'd make it home safe.

On she walked and talked: To the kids' bedrooms and memories of just-one-more-story. To the basement that flooded after heavy rains. To the kitchen, home of a million happy meals. To the front hall linen closet where she chuckled aloud once more—did I ever tell you about the time Suzy got into the talcum powder right here? She had it all over herself, all over the floor, what a mess. Gosh, that's been 45 years. But I swear whenever I open this door I still smell that powder.

It was time to go. A spanking new home, with new memories of its own to be built, was waiting closer to town. There were no more boxes to pack. Hours earlier, the movers had loaded the last of the furniture and appliances and driven away.

She stood near the back door, coat and purse in hand. Tears welled in her eyes.

It's hard to leave, she said. Fifty-two years in one place is a long time. It's been a good house. A very good house with a very good family. I watched them both grow up, and I wouldn't take anything for the memories.

That's what my mother ws saying to me.

Then she stepped outside, turned the key in the lock and walked away.

McNamara's confession

April 14, 1995

J ohn Lippincott vividly remembers the day in 1983 when he became oh-so-painfully aware of one of the ugliest truths about America's involvement in Vietnam.

"I wasn't sleeping well," Lippincott says. "I awoke about 4 that morning and began to read Stanley Karnow's 'Vietnam: A History' and learned about the memo (then-Secretary of Defense) Robert McNamara sent to President Johnson in May 1967. It was an assessment drawn up by all the principal policy makers of that time. Their conclusion was that Vietnam did not affect the national interests of the United States and that there was no strategic justification for our being there.

"Everybody at the top levels of government knew it. Unfortunately, no one had the moral fortitude to act. Even Johnson was unwilling to accept responsibility.

"It was at that moment that I realized, deeply and completely for the first time, that because the leaders of this country were unwilling to sacrifice their careers for the good of the country, the burden would fall upon its young men."

This flagrant sell-out—only recently admitted by McNamara— ripped Lippincott to the pit of his soul.

"I started weeping around 4:30 that morning," he said slowly and softly, a deep, rich, Southern drawl reflecting Mississippi roots. "By 3 that afternoon, I was so weak from grief, I could not stand up."

After three decades of official silence, McNamara made international headlines a few days ago by admitting the escalation of the war had been a colossal mistake. In his just-published memoir, "In Retrospect: The Tragedy and Lessons of Vietnam," the former defense chief blames himself and other government leaders (including Johnson) for miscalculations, misunderstandings and other blunders that led to the deaths of more than 58,000 Americans half a world away. Acknowledging that his "sense of grief and failure is strong," McNamara himself broke into tears while being interviewed by Diane Sawyer of ABC News.

Hot news, for sure. But it's no revelation to Lippincott and hundreds of thousands of other soldiers who served in Southeast Asia.

"It's only new to the public," said Lippincott, who teaches history and English at Webb School, "not to anyone who was there or who has studied the history of this event.

"I know McNamara is sincere. I credit him for being in the minority of public officials who have confessed their guilt, remorse, grief and cowardice. Even at this late date, I credit him for standing up and saying, 'God knows, I was wrong'. There's not a veteran of that war who doesn't know what the man has been through.

"But the difference is, McNamara was a leader, a policy maker. The soldier can't make his own policy."

Lippincott, an Army lieutenant in combat military intelligence, served in Vietnam from June 1967 to June 1968. His experiences are forever branded into his psyche.

"I never drive to work a single morning without being consciously aware of, and grateful for, the fact that the highway has been secured," he said. "I never walk into a building without noticing the overhead cover and where all the entrances and exits are."

Once a week, he and other combat veterans meet at the Vet Center on Magnolia Avenue. "I go there for fellowship, for sanity, to help listen," he noted. "I've spent a lot of time with people whose lives are still broken by that war."

Lippincott, who earned his Ph.D. from Oxford in England, intends to chronicle his own perspective of Vietnam. Some day. As he muses, "Some of the better books about the Civil War have just come out in the last 20 years."

Will there be a lasting benefit to society from more public soul-searching like McNamara's?

"About the only thing we ever learn is that we never learn," the educator replied. "There is no substitute for good leadership, for courage. And we've been running short on courage for a long time."

The vicious, endless cycle

December 7, 1993

S ince I wasn't born until half a decade after the attack on Pearl Harbor, I never experienced the gut-wrenching hatred mainstream America felt toward Japan during World War II.

I do, however, understand it.

This is the nature of war. Any war. No matter the issues, the venue or the participants, war has an incredible habit of bringing out the evil in everyone it touches.

Fifty-two years ago this morning, Japanese aircraft unleashed a fiery surprise offensive on the U.S. Pacific fleet. More than 2,400 Americans were killed, including 1,177 crewmen who went down with the U.S.S. Arizona. Twenty-one U.S. ships were damaged or destroyed, along with 323 airplanes.

No country can inflict that devastating degree of mayhem on another and expect immediate forgiveness. Which is why, on an August afternoon 3½ years later, crowds of jubilant Americans danced in the streets and waved newspapers with headlines blaring "Japs Face Atomic Doom" in black type six inches tall.

However understandable and predictable it may be, this cycle is surreal when viewed from half a century away: Hundreds of thousands are dead on both sides, billions of dollars worth of property lies in ruins, history is forever altered. Then Johnny comes marching home again, hurrah, hurrah, and foes become friends.

Part of me wants to think this will never happen again. So do others. When I visited the Arizona Memorial in Hawaii last year, I spent some time leafing through the guest register and jotting down comments. Among them:

■ "The Japanese and the Americans will always have different points of view regarding the air strike at Pearl Harbor and the atom bombing of Hiroshima and Nagasaki. And, sadly, there will always remain an element of hate between the two parties because of these differences. This type of thinking is not good. Both sides experienced difficulties because of the war and thus we should concentrate upon not having any more wars. This should be passed on to the children of both sides."

- "All of the names (on the memorial) were human beings who were killed because people could not settle their differences peacefully. How can we allow ourselves to make rockets and many things involved in the waging of war? This is foolishness. Each person, every race, every country—we all have value."

- "I want to tell every human being, every survivor, to pass the good life to the next generation. (The war) was a bad, terrible thing. We should not have it happen again."

- "I went to Hiroshima before I came here. I think that both were tragedies. My proposal is to show the video of Pearl Harbor at Hiroshima and the video of Hiroshima at Pearl Harbor."

- "The occurrence of war is the responsibility of all nations, whether they won the war or lost. There is no difference in that death and destruction are wrought on both sides."

Warm, wise words, these. But—again, tragically and predictably—they are ignored by each succeeding generation when tensions mount and tempers rise. That's why the other part of me is convinced war will forever plague the human condition.

God forbid this planet will ever be revisited by engagements on the same magnitude as World Wars I and II, but rest assured hostilities will be with us until the end of time. Whether with clubs, knives, arrows or missiles, humans have been creating innovative ways to eliminate each other since the dawn of creation.

And that is the most damnably predictable notion about war: The knowledge it will happen again. Not if; but where and when.

It's odd, actually. In spite of this season of goodwill and peace, I almost cringe to think which old enemies will next embrace, and where the next war memorial will be built, and how eloquently orators of the future will decry the taking up of arms against one another.

Because I know none of it can occur until there is yet more smoke to clear and more bodies to be buried.

Abandoned by Uncle Sam

December 19, 1995

Mary Gabbard isn't a student of the political process. Nor does she understand, or suffer kindly, the practitioners of bureaucratikspeak.

She does, however, recognize a broken promise when she sees it. And as far as she's concerned, the United States of America has backed out of a solemn vow it made with the men and women who answered their call to duty.

One man in particular. Garvey Cheek. Her father.

"Is this the America my Daddy fought for?" she asks. "Is this the America my Daddy worked for and believed in? No. This is the America that forgets its promises and steals from those who have little to give. If a 'Contract With America' really exists, then what it has done to my Daddy is neither honest nor fair."

While President Clinton and Congress continue to argue and blame one another for the nation's fiscal woes, more and more people like Gabbard's father wind up in the crossfire. For them, the battle is as real as it was 50 years ago when German troops were shooting bullets.

Mary Gabbard lives in Lenoir City. But her heart belongs in North Wilkesboro, N.C., where her 78-year-old father slowly wastes away in a nursing home. The pain is made worse by the fact that both the Veteran's Administration and the state of North Carolina, with whom Cheek spent his working career, have written him off.

"From the time I was a little girl, I can remember Daddy saying that if something ever happened, Mother wouldn't have to worry because the government would take care of him. He had paid his dues."

Then he tried to collect.

Garvey Cheek fought through bloody months of combat with the 69th Infantry Division in France and Germany, helping free dozens of towns and villages from Hitler's forces. Dead soldiers, German and Allied, lay along the way. The traumatic experience haunted him for life.

"He was never able to talk much about it," says his daughter.

"For years after his return from Europe, loud noises of any kind caused him to react in fright. Little by little, I learned Daddy was pinned down in a foxhole for several days and that most of his friends were killed. Their bodies kept him alive in the freezing cold."

Cheek returned from the war and pieced his life back together. He worked 30 years for the North Carolina Department of Transportation, doing everything from weighing stone at the state quarry to driving a tractor and a snowplow.

In later years, his health declined rapidly. He had bypass surgery in 1987, followed by a stroke in 1991. He has been hospitalized with Alzheimer's and Parkinson's diseases. And old demons have begun making return visits.

"One night in the hospital he became confused and started fighting the Nazis again," said Gabbard. "He ripped off a piece of water fountain and used it as a weapon. His language was terrible. This was a man from whom I had never heard profanity before.

"Most of the time, Daddy doesn't recognize anyone, his wife or his children. He requires medication and skilled medical attention. He is now in diapers. He has to be fed, bathed and dressed."

Despite the tragic state of Cheek's health, however, the Veterans Administration and the state of North Carolina have ceased his medical coverage. The family got the word on—of all days—December 7.

"Odd, isn't it?" said Gabbard. "The V.A. chose the day Pearl Harbor was bombed, the day that changed Daddy's life forever, to kick him out."

Since then, Gabbard's 73-year-old mother has paid nearly $4,000 to continue coverage. The family is seeking relief through legal and political circles. And they continually ask, "Why?"

"They say Daddy isn't sick enough to get coverage," Gabbard noted. "Pray tell, how sick does the man have to be?

"When the government called, he did not hesitate to do his duty. Now, when he calls out of need, America refuses to honor its duty."

Santa Sam

December 25, 1994

W hen you are 17 years old and wise in the ways of the world, you have no reason to believe in the magic of Santa Claus.

Even if he is your father.

I speak from vast experience in this matter for my dad was the real McCoy. Eleven months out of the year, he assumed an alias—Sam A. Venable Sr. He also had a variety of disguises—college professor, coach, referee, school board member, Sunday school teacher and volunteer worker among them. But between Thanksgiving and Christmas, he went by his real name and practiced the profession he was born to pursue.

Here was no actor for hire. This was a man on a mission, a living, breathing Knoxville Kris Kringle whose joy in life was spreading the wonder of Santa Claus to all who would believe.

Don't take my word for it. Just ask the thousands of youngsters who sat on his lap and whispered their wishes or watched in awe as his float passed by them in Christmas parades.

Even now, nearly a quarter of a century after my father's death, I hear stories from these tykes-turned-thirtysomething with young ones of their own.

They still tell me about how their parents would bring them to Santa Sam's front yard, a winter wonderland of colored lights, Christmas trees, music, candy canes and laughter.

They remember climbing into the giant wooden sleigh, the feel of his red corduroy suit, the belly that needed no artificial padding, the sparkle in his eyes, the gentle hands that held them against the cold, the warm smile on his lips and, most of all, the thunderous "oooh-ho-ho-ho-ho!" that roared from beneath his white beard. Keep your amateur sound effects, thank you. When Santa Sam uncorked a ho-ho, it was recorded by seismologists.

All of which was well and good for the wee ones, I reasoned back then. The magic of Santa Claus was strictly for kids. Certainly not for sophisticated 17-year-olds wise in the ways of the world.

Then one December night I learned the truth about Santa Claus, and it sent waves of goosebumps racing down my neck, just as it did right now as I typed the words.

I was in my bedroom, preparing to leave for the evening. I don't know if I was headed for a date, a ball game or a few hours of running around town with my buddies. Doesn't matter.

But I do remember that it was nearly Christmas, and dozens of anxious youngsters were waiting for St. Nick's arrival out front. Just as I turned off the lights, I glanced out the window and saw something I can recall in infinite detail to this day.

If children were already in line, Santa Sam camouflaged his entry. Always the planner, he knew that kids know Santa comes from the North Pole, not the front door of somebody's house. So he'd sneak out the back, duck into the woodlot that ran alongside our yard, weave through the pines and emerge among his flock. "Feeding the reindeer" is what he told them.

My father was a big man. Thanks to old sports injuries and a ravenous appetite, he had terrible knees. This tended to give him a limping, rolling gait, particularly when he was tired.

The person I watched as he made his way through the shadows at the edge of the woods, out of sight of the children, was Sam A. Venable Sr., college professor, coach, referee, school board member, Sunday school teacher and volunteer worker. A middle-aged, going-on-worn-out old man with an unhealthy heart whose remaining Christmases, unknown to any of us at the time, numbered only in single digits.

But the elf who stepped into the wonderland of colored lights and music seconds later was Santa Claus. The real one. A red-suited, ho-hoing, kid-hugging Father Christmas who walked without a limp and could have, I am certain, hitched reindeer to that wooden sleigh and vanished into the sky.

When you are 47 years old and not nearly so wise in the ways of the world, memories like that can make you cry.

Twisted sympathies

February 23, 1995

I f an Old West bounty hunter came back to life today, he'd forget about tracking down murderers, bank robbers and other undesirables with a price on their heads. Instead, he'd concentrate on a bigger source of bucks: rewards for the people who harm animals.

I have reached this conclusion after watching developments in the wake of crimes against humans and beasts alike.

Up in Greene County, for instance, there's a $2,500 state reward for information leading to the arrest and conviction of the person(s) who killed Edwin Frazier Jones. The Baileyton shopkeeper was found dead in his store on January 4. He had been shot in the head.

Here in Knox County, a $3,500 reward has been set for the killers of Lester and Carol Dotts, who were shot February 3 in their Village Green home. Sheriff's deputies say the reward is funded by $2,500 from the Dotts family and $1,000 from an anonymous donor.

Fine. I hope these incentives do help solve the crimes. No amount of money can compensate for human life, but someone out there knows who the culprits are, and if $2,500-$3,500 is required to bring them to justice, so be it.

However, the payoffs are more lucrative in crimes that weren't committed against humans.

Last Christmas Eve, a 542-pound black bear was killed and left hanging in a tree in the Great Smoky Mountains National Park. This cowardly act enraged people throughout the community, and a reward campaign began.

A spokesman for the Tennessee Wildlife Resources Agency told me his department will pay up to $3,000 for information leading to successful prosecution of the poacher(s).

But that's merely the state's money. TWRA says many anonymous donors have also come forward with pledges, pushing the total above what's being offered in the Dottses' slayings.

Still, we're talking peanuts. Bounty hunters on the trail of some serious money might want to poke around the Ames Plantation in West Tennessee.

Last December 4, during the running of the National Amateur Invitational bird dog trials, someone poisoned a champion entrant named Miller's Silver Bullett. Fortunately, the dog survived. No one has been arrested. In the meantime, dog fanciers have posted a $10,000 reward, including $5,000 from Terrel Miller, owner of the 6-year-old male pointer.

This phenomenon is not new. In April 1994, a California jogger named Barbara Schoener was killed and partially eaten by a mountain lion. Schoener left two small children. A trust fund was established to help pay for their education.

About a week after Schoener's death, wildlife authorities tracked down and killed the mountain lion, which turned out to be a female with one cub. Well-wishers started a drive to raise funds for its upkeep. And, as anyone who follows national news events can tell you, the cub fund soon outdistanced the children's fund by more than $12,000.

The more I try to understand society's reaction to tragedy, the more confused I become.

Brotherly love

February 11, 1992

One of my favorite memories of Alex Haley occurred a couple of Octobers ago during the Fall Homecoming at the Museum of Appalachia.

It was quite early in the morning. A thick fog hung over the valley. Dozens of craftspeople were clustered around campfires, coffee cups in hand, exchanging opinions on subjects as far-ranging as white oak baskets to Tennessee's prospects for victory in a football game two days hence.

On a typical festival day, there wouldn't be many visitors at this hour. But this wasn't a typical day. Spencer Christian, the weather forecaster for ABC's "Good Morning, America," was broadcasting from tiny Norris, and a throng of locals had turned out for the spectacle.

Perhaps people from New York or Hollywood wouldn't understand, but something like this is about as close as East Tennesseans ever brush—live and in the flesh—with bright lights, big city. Makeshift studios had been erected in a cabin and on the grass. There was a national weather map so Christian could warn Los Angeles commuters about smog and remind Miami sun worshippers to carry an umbrella. A crew of lieutenant directors showed everyone where to stand.

This sort of broadcast never lasts long. Christian did a couple of quick interviews with Haley, gave the weather, and that was that. Except for the fact that fog made it impossible to see farther than 15 feet, everything came off without a hitch.

Afterward, Christian climbed into his limousine and rode off to the airport for another assignment in another location. Haley, on the other hand, picked up his sausage biscuit and continued roaming the grounds as nonchalantly as a tourist from Indiana.

I don't mean to be harsh on Spencer Christian. For all I know, he disdains his celebrity status and the glittery trappings that come with it. What's more, Haley held a distinct location advantage. An adopted East Tennessean, he had been homefolks around here for years.

Still, I couldn't help but see irony in the fact that a network meteorologist would be whisked away in a stretch limo while a Pulitzer Prize-winning author with one of the most recognized names and faces in the world calmly ate a biscuit and talked to his neighbors about the merits of homegrown tomatoes.

But that was Alex Haley. He was unassuming, unpretentious, the antithesis of 20th century fame and fortune. The millionaire who rubbed shoulders with presidents, princes and potentates was just as comfortable—perhaps even more so—shooting the breeze with everyday folks.

Alex Haley never met strangers. To him, everyone was "brother" or "sister."

This was not a mere catch-phrase, either, not some homespun persona he adopted to be country chic. It came straight from the heart. His rich, gentle, deep, "How'ya doin', Brother Venable?" was as sincere the first time we met in 1983 as it was the last time we shook hands at his home in August.

Alex always signed his autograph, "With brotherly love," and I am convinced he meant every word of it to the men, women and children he encountered throughout his travels.

Now he is gone from us, felled by a heart attack at the age of 70.

I just looked at the various wire-service directories in my word processor, and they are full of stories about this man and his life.

Typical news stories, these. They speak of his literary accomplishments, of his immense impact upon human history, of the works he had in progress. There are quotes of mourning from admirers all over the country. Plus a list of survivors. But if Alex Haley's obituary was written like a typical death notice, the survivors' list would require hundreds of thousands of additional pages.

He left a family of brothers and sisters all over the world. And we shall miss him very much.

Tending to the flock

February 23, 1993

Not all the Good Samaritans rendering aid in tornado-ravaged Lenoir City drive ambulances, police cars, fire trucks and military vehicles. One of them arrived in a 1986 red Chevy pickup with four bald tires, an aging muffler, 137,000 miles on the odometer and a bumper sticker proclaiming, "God Is a Good God."

Based on what I saw last Monday morning, God's messenger is pretty good, too. Also very persistent.

"Oh, it's not much," said Alvin Ellis, a short, slender man with silver hair, piercing hazel eyes and a soft smile. "It just shows what you can do with a little faith and a little prayer."

Alvin Ellis lives in Englewood. Through the week, he works as a sandblaster and painter; you can tell the moment you shake his weathered hand that here is a man familiar with manual labor. On Sunday mornings, though, you'll find him in the pulpit of Mount Cumberland Community Church, an independent house of worship in Etowah.

Ellis didn't report for work Monday morning. Instead, he climbed into the cab of his red pickup and pointed it toward Lenoir City—for the third time in as many days.

You see, Brother Ellis calls on two elderly shut-ins who live on Cherry Street in Lenoir City. He's known Ola Beeler and her mentally handicapped daughter, Edna, for four years. Ellis and his wife, Hazel, visit every Saturday, bringing bread, cake, biscuits and other baked goods. While Hazel sits with bedridden Ola Beeler, Alvin drives Edna Beeler to the drugstore and supermarket and helps her buy supplies.

Ellis and his wife made their customary visit last Saturday afternoon, then headed home to McMinn County. When he heard about the killer tornado that struck Lenoir City on Sunday, he returned to Lenoir City to check on the Beelers.

"I didn't know nothing about 'em," said Ellis. "I couldn't find out if they was hurt or dead or if their house had been hit. I just knew they'd be callin' for me, and I had to help."

He wasn't successful at first. Law enforcement officers turned him away from the disaster zone. He argued, to no avail. There was nothing to do but wait.

Ellis drove home. At first light Monday he was back. He was among dozens gathered at a command post in the Wal-Mart parking lot, each seeking permission slips to enter the damaged area.

Sorry, he was told. Nobody gets in. The town is sealed.

Still, Ellis would not leave. He saw me interviewing business people, insurance agents and office workers who also had been rebuffed and pulled me to the side.

"Maybe you can help me," he said, spilling his story as I jotted notes. "I know those women don't have nobody to look after them. Mrs. Beeler is bad sick. I'll take 'em home with me if I have to. I just can't leave this town till I find out if they're OK."

"Follow me to the high school (where evacuees were being

taken)," I said. "Maybe you can find them there."

Foiled again. The gymnasium was filling with elderly, infirm Lenoir Citians. But Mrs. Beeler and her daughter were not among them.

No problem. Ellis told his story to Sgt. 1st Class Jennifer Martin and Pfc. Clayton Welda of the Tennessee Defense Force. They located an ambulance. Everyone headed for Cherry Street.

Just in time, too. The electricity had long been off, and the Beelers were cold and scared. Ellis hugged both women repeatedly, assuring them everything would be fine. Arrangements were made for the Beelers to be taken to a hospital in Loudon and cared for until power was restored.

"I'll follow you to the hospital," Ellis told the women as the ambulance door closed. "Then my wife and I will come back and visit tonight."

Interesting, isn't it? Whether preachers wear sandals and carry a shepherd's crook or drive a red pickup truck with four bald tires, when it comes to caring for the flock, they never give up.

Tobacco warnings

January 22, 1993

A friend of mine who has tried to quit smoking repeatedly and unsuccessfully is now considering the new "patch" therapy.

Surely you've seen this thing advertised on TV and in newspapers and magazines. It's an adhesive bandage containing a nicotine solution. The patch goes on a smoker's arm, and small amounts of nicotine are absorbed through the skin. Theoretically, this helps wean the body of nicotine's physical addiction, letting the smoker concentrate on breaking the mental habit of reaching for a cigarette, lighting up, tapping the ashes and crushing the butt.

But my friend is worried about using the patch. With some very good reasons.

You can't get it without a doctor's prescription, for one. If this stuff is too powerful to buy over the counter, like dandruff shampoo or toothache ointment or hemorrhoid cream, what sort of high-powered mischief does it pack?

"I've heard all kinds of horror tales," my friend was telling me. "One guy had screaming nightmares the whole time he was using a patch. It's made some other people awfully sick, especially if they smoked a cigarette while they were wearing a patch."

I've heard the same war stories. A woman I work with tried the patch for a while, and it gave her a dose of the Barney Fife shakes.

But people who are contemplating patch therapy don't have to rely on office hearsay to get the bejabbers scared out of them. All they have to do is read the fine print on advertisements for the thing.

Don't take my word for it. Pick up any publication and see for yourself. There was a patch ad in last Sunday's Parade magazine, for instance. It covered almost all of two pages.

The first page showed the perky face of a woman who is proud to be a quitter. Below her picture was your basic advertising gibberish, the brand name of the product, a 1-800 number, blah-blah. Plus a small line that read, "See next page for additional important information."

I turned the page and—*ba-boom!*—was smitten square in the jaw by a 10-by-7-inch block of extremely small print overflowing with complex warnings and precautions. Some random samples:

"In a six-week, open-label dermal irritation and sensitization study . . . 22 of 220 patients exhibited definite erythema at 24 hours after application. Upon rechallenge, three patients exhibited mild-to-moderate contact allergy. . ."

"Caution should be exercised when (patch) therapy is administered to nursing mothers. The safety of (patch) treatment in nursing infants has not been examined. Nicotine passes freely into breast milk . . . An infant has the ability to clear nicotine by heptic first-class clearance; however, the efficiency of removal is probably lowest at birth . . ."

"Signs and symptoms of an overdose . . . would be expected to be the same as those of acute nicotine poisoning including pallor, cold sweat, nausea, salivation, vomiting, abdominal pain, diarrhea, headache, dizziness, disturbed hearing and vision, tremor, mental confusion . . ."

And on and on and on.

Is all this warning necessary? I suppose. Given the litigious nature of today's society, it's a wonder we can pop two aspirin without signing notarized statements absolving our doctor, the supermarket and the drug manufacturer of all responsibility should we cough two days later.

Still, the irony of this patch precaution panic is incredible.

The only warning on a pack of cigarettes is a simple sentence from the surgeon general's office. You plunk down your money and strike a match and suck great globs of tar, nicotine and carbon monoxide straight into your body. But if you want to quit, you've gotta go to the doctor, get a prescription, wade through 300 lines of legal/medical gobbledygook and run the very real risk of making yourself sick as a dog.

Only in America.

The livin' ain't always easy

July 15, 1993

Except for two precious little ladies—an official niece named Jessica who loves Milky Way candy bars and has all but outgrown her childhood, and an unofficial niece named Brigitte who is 4 and always greets me with a cheerful, "Uncle Sammy!"—there are no more youngsters in my life.

As the father of two college students, I'm in that in-between stage: Too old to have toddlers around the house, too young (I hope) for grandchildren.

I miss the little people. I miss their spontaneous laughter, their bright eyes, their gentle touch, their off-the-wall questions. I miss kissing a hurt knee and making it better. I miss walking into the bedroom after a bad dream and chasing monsters from the closet. So perhaps you will understand why I drove to Nanny's Nursery, 100 Fort Sanders West Blvd., yesterday and asked Miss Pat, the director, if I could visit with her 2- and 3-year-olds for a while.

I chose 2- and 3-year-olds for a very good reason. In a set of circumstances almost too tragic and too bizarre to be believed, Knoxville lost two children from that age group in less than 24 hours. A third is hospitalized, as is a fourth child, age 6.

Three-year-old Kaile Lynn Lee was abducted from her West Knoxville home, allegedly by a friend of the family. Her raped, sodomized, strangled body was found a day later near Tellico Lake.

Then there was 2-year-old John R. Hughes of Columbus, Ga., whose death was every parents' absolute worst nightmare. John and his mother and father, Mary Baker and Matthew Hughes, were visiting relatives here in Knoxville. John got into some of his mother's prescription medicine and was poisoned. He died at University of Tennessee Medical Center.

On the heels of those tragedies, West Knoxvillians Kirby Lewis, 2, and Emily Prince, 6, were bitten by copperhead snakes.

Kirby's injuries occurred on the Abrams Falls trail in the Great Smoky Mountains National Park, Emily's at the Big South Fork National River and Recreation Area. Both girls were listed in stable condition at UT Medical Center.

Four young, dear, innocent children. It makes you wonder why.

It also makes you want to be near some wee ones, and I'm grateful to Miss Pat, Miss Margaret, Miss Martha, Miss Anna Marie and all the others who allowed me to sit down with their kiddies during lunch. I had a wonderful time.

Miles was making a mustache with the lettuce from his salad. Kelley told me how the cake fell over at her birthday party. Taylor finished his food quickly and ran to play with blocks. Katy spilled her milk, and Miss Margaret showed her how to clean it up.

Matthew told me he'd spent the summer playing on swings and going down the slide. Which reminded Bijan to tell me Daniel had thrown up on the slide. Jordan burped and politely said, "Excuse me." I told Daniel and Jordan not to worry; things like that happen to all of us.

Corey and Michael have been playing basketball all summer. Cody has been swimming. Ellen, who has the biggest eyes and the curliest hair this side of Shirley Temple, has been to Atlanta to visit her two grandmothers.

When lunch was finished, Miss Anna Marie led the angels back to their classroom. It was time for a nap. But first, she let them sing "America" for me. Sing it twice, actually, because Eric couldn't remember the words the first time. Then we all gave each other a big hug and a big kiss.

If I were a magician, I'd make every day like that for children all over the world. There would be love and fun and laughter and games and pizza. And a big piece of cake for dessert. It would always be summertime, and the living would always be easy.

So hush, Uncle Sammy. Don't you cry.

The speaker learns a lesson

July 26, 1994

D uring some commencement exercises the other day, the guest speaker got royally upstaged by a member of the student body. I know this for a fact because I was the guest speaker. And on a scale of 1 to 10, I got outscored by an even 10 points.

This occurred at Morgan County Regional Correctional Facility near Wartburg. I had been asked to address the summer graduation program, during which 25 inmates were to be honored.

Seventeen of these men had earned their high school GED. Seven others had successfully completed vocational classes. One other, Andrew Whitnel III, was presented a bachelor of science in psychology from the University of Tennessee.

Whitnel stands 6 feet tall. He is trim, muscular, blue-eyed and Hollywood handsome. Eleven of his 47 years have been spent behind bars. Currently serving time for armed robbery and attempted second-degree murder, he is due for release in 2004.

"I hope to get a state position counseling young people when I get out," he told me after the program. "I want to talk to them about drugs, alcohol and having sex too early."

"Would that type of counseling have helped you?" I asked.

Whitnel looked off into space for a moment and sighed. "I don't know," he replied. "I came from a good family; I don't have the excuse a lot of these fellows do. I was just too rebellious."

It had been 29 years since Whitnel, of Mt. Juliet, enrolled at Tennessee Tech on a partial football scholarship. As time went on, though, his education became sidetracked by drugs and a quick temper.

He eventually earned his college degree via correspondence courses from UT-Martin and UT-Knoxville, along with in-prison instruction by teachers from the Knoxville campus.

Whitnel has already used his educational skills to help others; he is an aide for Janice Sparkman, an English teacher at the prison school. But when he stood up before his fellow graduates and another 250 student inmates, he gave them a lesson from the heart as well as the head.

"Why waste this time in bitterness and despair?" said Whitnel, wearing a black graduation gown over his prison-issue blues. "Study so that you will approve of yourself. You are the one who has to live with yourself. You are stuck with you for the rest of your life. You are the one who benefits most from education. Not your teachers. Not your family. Not the prison system—YOU.

"Choosing education has many advantages. Most of these can be summed up in one word: Choice.

"There are more and better jobs to choose from when you have an education. If you are working for the Saturn car company instead of pumping gas into a Saturn, you are going to have a higher standard of living.

"Maybe some of you are in here because you didn't think you had any other choice. Maybe you felt that you could only survive by committing crime. One thing is certain. When you came in here, your choices decreased.

"I don't know what choice you will make next. You must choose according to your own ability. My only advice is: Don't quit! Go as far as you can to further educate yourself. I don't mean that you must go to college or a vocational school, although for many of you that would be your best choice. I mean never stop learning!

"Read things that are educational. Learn from your job. Learn from your life. Pay attention to those with new ideas, especially those who have proven themselves by their own choices for success.

"Don't lie down and let the world run over you. Educate yourself. Give yourself choices.

"Most of all, the choice of education can give you the choice that all of us in here would most like to have: The choice of freedom."

The guest speaker from Knoxville was then introduced. He fumbled with his notes, said little of consequence, and sat down.

Worry

May 8, 1994

I was at my mother's condominium a few nights ago. It was chilly outside. She had a fire in the fireplace.

Not a real, honest-to-gosh fire with real, honest-to-gosh wood. That was a luxury she gave up when she moved out of her old house. In the condo, she has gas logs that dance with yellow and blue flames at the flip of a switch. Cleaner and more convenient, certainly, but not nearly as soothing to the ear and the soul as seasoned hardwood.

We visited for a while and Mother decided to extinguish the fire. She walked to the hearth and turned the switch to "off." The flames disappeared.

"Where's the pilot light?" I asked. "I can't see it."

"It's way down at the bottom," she answered. "It's on. Don't worry about it."

"But how do you know it's on?" I pressed.

"I just know it is."

That did not suit me. I worry about pilot lights. Especially at my mother's place. So I got down on my hands and knees and looked under the gas logs.

"I don't see a flame anywhere."

"You're not looking in the right place," she replied.

I scrunched down even lower and turned my head sideways.

My cheek brushed the carpet. Still no flame. I crawled to the right three or four inches and turned my head sideways again.

Finally, there it was—a small blue arc, burning faithfully.

"Satisfied?" Mother asked as I rose to my feet.

"I am now."

She started to shut the doors on the fireplace.

"Wait a minute!" I said. "You shouldn't close those doors all the way. That'll cut off the oxygen and put out the flame. Then gas will seep into the room."

She gave me one of those looks.

"Everybody in this complex who has a fireplace keeps their doors closed, and their pilot light doesn't go out," she said. "I talked to the man at KUB about it. He said it would be just fine to let it burn all summer. It won't cost much at all, and it keeps them from having to send someone out here in the fall to light it. Quit worrying about it."

What? Me, worry?

Of *course* I worry. That's what families are for.

People on the parent side of the equation are supposed to worry about their children. As the children grow older, the formula changes. It is then time for them to worry about the parent.

When I was a teenager, I could not leave the house—to go fishing, run my newspaper route, drive to the store, whatever—without my mother saying, "Be careful."

She said this because she was worried something bad might happen to me. Every parent worries, if he or she is worth so much as a pile of pocket lint.

No, not hand-wringing, oh-my-God-there's-going-to-be-a-horrible-wreck-and-you'll-be-killed kind of worry. Instead, just an awareness of the jillion things that can go wrong Out There, so please, child, take care of yourself.

I say the same thing to my kids, even though they are virtually adults themselves. It is a trait handed down, generation to generation. I trust they will pass it on in due time.

Mother and I talked a little while longer. I needed to go. We walked to the door together. She asked what I was doing the next day. Going turkey hunting early in the morning, I told her, then coming back to town and working late.

"You going to the mountains alone?" she asked.

"Yes'sum."

"Well, for goodness sakes be careful. You might fall or get snakebit in those woods."

I said I would be careful. I kissed her on the cheek and walked to the car. She waved goodbye from the door. I tooted the horn and waved back.

Mothers. God love 'em. I hope today's celebration of Mother's Day is the happiest they've ever known.

As for my own mother, I wish she'd go check that pilot light again, just to make sure. I worry about these things.

Ten kisses on V-E Day

May 11, 1995

H itler was dead. The war in Europe was over. Happy days would be here again. Someday.

As was his nightly habit, an Army infantry captain stationed in France penned a letter to his wife and infant daughter in Knoxville. Like GIs scattered all over Europe, he simply wanted to be done with the business of making war. He wanted to come home. Yet he sensed many months would pass before his young family could be reunited.

The letters he mailed faithfully are now yellow with age. But his messages of love and loneliness ring as true today as they did on that first V-E Day, 50 years ago:

"Dearest Sweethearts. 'Fini le guerre.' The war is over. Those are the words on everybody's lips tonight.

"It seems that everybody is immensely relieved, but I haven't seen very much loud or boisterous celebrating.

"People seem to feel it's just a job well done or partly done— and now let's finish it all the way. Then too I think this has come more or less as an anti-climax. Things have been progressing towards it for so long that people just weren't excited when the time came, although I understand from radio reports that England and America have practically gone wild with demonstrations and rejoicing.

"We first received official news at the 3 p.m. radio broadcast, but I had gotten word early this morning that it was all over. One of my drivers had just gotten in from Paris, and he had been up all night driving a general on various business. The general told him that the pact had been signed at 0241 and that hostilities were to cease as of 0500.

"The thought that's uppermost in everybody's mind now is when are we going home? What to do now? Where do we go from here?

"The Stars & Stripes devoted a full page today with info about troop movement, redeployment, demobilization and discharges. I've read the whole thing over, and I can't find anything in there that gives me much encouragement.

"I'm afraid it's going to be at least a year and maybe longer. Maybe the Pacific first. I sure hope not. However, we don't know anything yet, and I think the best plan is to just wait and see what happens and hope for the best.

"I do so wish I were coming home now because I love you both more than anything else in the world. Just like you said once, V-Day won't be here until we're all three together again for good. Then we can really celebrate. That's going to be wonderful.

"This has been a beautiful day, warm and sunshiny. It was made brighter and nicer by a letter from you. This one was dated April 28th and was the first one I'd gotten in a week. I don't have ones from the 26th and 27th yet, but maybe they'll be here tomorrow. Your letters are so sweet, and I just love the things you say about our Blue Eyes. I'd love to see her.

"Tonight I can't think of too much to write except that I love you and miss you so terribly much. You're everything in the world to me.

"Good night, my loves. Sweet dreams. Be good and take care of each other for me. Here's ten big kisses for Mommy and ten little ones for my Scrapper."

Ever-so-slowly, the weeks turned into months. It would be the following April before the homesick captain made it safely back to Tennessee and picked up civilian life where it had been interrupted.

A son was born to the family. Then another. And another. As time wore on, World War II faded into a memory.

The captain returned to his teaching career. He became a leader in local athletics. He championed the cause of civil rights. He served on the school board. He raised funds for dozens of charities. He died, much too young, in 1972.

But his wife still has the letters he wrote every day from France. From time to time she opens the envelopes and unfolds the onion-skin paper and rereads his tender words.

And she gives each one of us ten kisses from our father.

A prayer of a chance

May 27, 1993

Before I began writing this column, I said a little prayer that the words I type will help make some sense out of the school prayer issue.

Even though there is a window across the front of my office—a relatively clean window, at that—nobody saw me pray. I didn't seek a court order for the right to invoke God's help. Nor did anyone come charging in with a decree, demanding I not contaminate the secular workplace with thoughts divine.

Instead, I simply paused for a few seconds. I looked away from my desk. I thought, "Lord, please help my fingers convey to this keyboard what my mind is trying to say. Many thanks." And that was the end of that.

To the best of my knowledge, I broke neither the laws of this sovereign nation nor the work rules of the publishing house for which I work. All I did was pray. Quietly. To myself.

Surely you have seen people perform a similar act in restaurants and cafeterias. Then again, maybe you haven't.

Perhaps the woman sitting at the table next to you was speaking passionately with God, even though her head was not bowed. Maybe the man across the room was thanking the Lord—or Buddha, Allah, Great Spirit or whomever—for his daily bread and asking that his wife be spared the ravages of breast cancer and singing praises of thanksgiving for a newborn grandchild and beseeching peace in the world when, from all you could tell, he was applying pepper to his mashed potatoes.

That is because prayer—or meditation or whatever name it goes under—is best practiced between the individual and whatever higher power he or she wishes to call upon.

Make no mistake. If any group of people needs praying over, graduates-to-be are high on the list. Right at top, in fact. As I have written before, there are times when all human beings—those with religious convictions and those without—simply need to stop and think about what has taken place in their lives.

Graduation is one of those times.

Graduates should be thankful—oh, so very thankful—for the parents, teachers and friends who guided them through their formative years, who still care deeply about them, who want them to find a lifetime of happiness.

Graduates should ask for continued strength, wisdom, judgment and courage as they begin the next chapter of their journey.

Graduates should remember those who are less fortunate, bearing in mind that cozy thoughts alone are worthless without positive action.

This is precisely what every person attending a graduation ceremony in Knox County has both the right and the power to do. Indeed, this is what every person, everywhere on the face of this planet, can do. Every second of every minute of every hour of every day.

Prayer does not require an official place on the program. It does not require microphones and soft background music. It does not require anything except a desire to pray.

Then, as the commercial says, just do it!

Amen.

The real monsters walk among us

November 6, 1994

I didn't make an official count, but based on casual observation—plus the mountain of candy Mary Ann and I are nibbling away at daily—only a handful of trick or treaters came to our door on Halloween night.

Seven or eight, I'd guess. Surely no more than a dozen.

If we lived in a remote area, perhaps at the end of a long, winding road, I could understand; a miniature Mars bar would hardly be worth the effort. But we're in the heart of Subdivision, U.S.A. Drive along any of our streets during school bus hours and you'll see children galore.

There are many reasons for scant participation in this annual shakedown for sugar.

It was a school night.

The weather was questionable.

A good friend was hosting a party.

All legitimate excuses, for sure. But if the truth were known, I bet a lot of parents simply refused to let their kiddies out of the house because they, Mom and Pop, were afraid of the bogeyman.

It's easy to find bogeymen. They're everywhere.

They are convicted murderers out on parole. They are dope peddlers willing to destroy lives for a few dollars. They are pedophiles lusting for the opportunity to take advantage of trust. They are child abusers freed on a technicality. They are paramilitary crazies armed with grenade launchers and machine guns.

You've read about these bogeymen in the newspaper or seen their stories on TV, haven't you? By the tens of millions they lurk in the shadows outside our doors. They will get us sooner or later. No family will be spared.

So we lash back at them before they can touch us. Whipped into a frenzy of paranoia, we buy pistols for our bedstands and double bolts for our doors. We put bars on our windows and install burglar alarms. We have our kids fingerprinted and insist they never, ever, not-under-any-circumstances speak to strangers.

That's what's so tragic. In our fervor to lock out the bogeyman, we often let the real monster walk among us.

I hold in my hands a U.S. Department of Justice report called "Murder in Families." It was issued last July and charts more than 8,000 homicide cases that occurred in 1988. Statistically, it gives chilling credence to the notion "you always hurt the ones you love."

According to this report, 80 percent of murder victims were killed by a family member (16 percent) or acquaintance (64 percent). Only 20 percent were slain by a complete stranger.

Consider this quote: "A third of family murders involved a female as the killer."

Or this: "In murders of their offspring, women predominated, accounting for 55 percent of killers."

Another: "When a mother killed her own child, the offspring she killed was more likely to be a son than a daughter: 64 percent sons versus 36 percent daughters."

The local pattern pretty much matches those national statistics, says Mike Hyde, a homicide investigator for the Knoxville Police Department. In the majority of murder cases he has worked over the last six years, a relative or friend of the victim turned out to be the killer.

According to prosecutors on opposite sides of the United States, that is precisely what occurred in two of the most publicized murder cases in a decade. How bitterly ironic it was that news of Susan Smith's arrest in the killing of her two young sons in South Carolina came the same day that a jury in Los Angeles was seated for the double murder trial of O.J. Simpson.

Yes, there will always be ghouls who strike out of the blue, picking victims randomly on which to unleash acts of unspeakable horror. We have every reason to stay vigilant.

But panic not. As crime statistics show all too well, bogeymen usually leave murder to the experts. More often than not, the person who wields the knife or pulls the trigger is the very last one you'd expect.

Unless you're a cop.

Charley's war

November 11, 1993

There are so many things Marianne Wells would love to do with her daddy on Veterans Day. She'd like to introduce him to the grandsons and granddaughter he never knew. Maybe go fishing again and tell him, over and over and over, how much she misses him.

But more than anything else, she'd like to talk to her daddy about World War II and the demons that filled his head and haunted his dreams until the day he drew his last ragged breath.

"He blotted it out," says Wells. "That's the way he handled things. If he were alive today, I'd do my best to get him to a veterans center and let them help him work it out. But . . ." Her eyes fill with tears and she looks away.

First Lt. Charles J. Garvey Jr. was a P-47 fighter pilot. In the spring of 1944, he was shot down over Belgium, landing safely, if ingloriously, in a potato field. Friendly civilians gave the handsome young American a change of clothes and got him into the underground. His route to freedom was blocked by Nazi infiltrators, however, and Garvey spent the rest of the war in prison camps.

"I remember being told that he nearly starved to death, lost his hair from a scalp disease and almost lost his feet to fungus," said Wells. "Other than that, it was never mentioned."

Not until years later, when she was reading Alexander Solzhenitsyn's "The Gulag Archipelago," did Wells broach the subject of German prison camp with her father.

"He said, 'They slapped me around a little bit,' and then he stopped," Wells related. "The only thing he'd say after that was, 'I don't want to talk about it.' "

On March 19, 1980, Garvey died of emphysema. He was a very old man at the very young age of 59. When the personal effects were distributed, Charles Garvey III acquired his father's prison diary and the scrapbook he had made from cardboard and pieces of tin cans. Through these items, he and Marianne have discovered a chapter in a life neither of them had known.

In the space of this short column, I cannot begin to reveal all of

Garvey's fear, loneliness, hope, despair, and incredible wit and insight under such trying circumstances. Nor can I show you the cartoons and intricate drawings he created. But trust me when I tell you it was like looking into a man's brain and watching the thoughts form, hour by hour, as the days behind barbed wire turned into weeks and then months.

This has been a personal journey for me as well as Marianne Wells, for her daddy was a friend of mine. I knew him as a quiet, friendly man, a skilled outdoorsman with a warm smile and a strong handshake, yet with a haggard face and a voice hoarsened by too many cigarettes and too much beer. A man who, just as his daughter observed, often seemed burdened by something he could never quite escape.

Perhaps part of the answer lies in this diary entry from Oct. 22, 1944: "I suppose most people think of war as an unending, angry conflict between two armies—one made up of soldiers fighting nobly, for the right, the other of brutal venal wretches, deliberately battling for something they know to be wrong.

"In reality, war is mostly waste, idleness, dirt, fright, discomfort and uncertainty; and damn near everyone in his waking hours wishes with all his heart he had never let himself be drawn into it. He comes to know that the war which has him by the heels can accomplish nothing that could not be accomplished by honest discussion between a few reasonable men—accomplished without loss of life, loss of property, loss of freedom; loss of all things which men fight for.

"He forgets, if he ever knew, the principles for which he is fighting, and they seldom enter his mind except when he hears them mouthed by politicians who have never, under any circumstances, faced enemy bullets and would never endure the hardships and discomforts which make up a soldier's life."

God rest you, Charley Garvey. You and all the others whose wars never ended. I can only hope you are finally at peace.

Garth's big sacrifice

September 1, 1992

Garth Brooks, the country music superstar, has made a startling discovery: Fatherhood is a full-time job. Which is why he announced over the weekend that he is considering retiring from the business this December.

According to Brooks, "retire" means flat-out, 100-percent, burn-your-bridges quit. No more records, no more tapes, no more CDs, no more concerts. Nothing except staying around the house and helping the missus take care of their new baby girl.

If that's truly the case—please understand my "if" is roughly the same size and shape as the state of North Dakota—I say more power to him. Kick off your boots, pardner. Pull up a chair and enjoy the good life.

Early retirement for Garth Brooks makes a lot of financial sense. He is a kajillionaire many times over. Since 1989, he has released three albums that have sold a combined total of 20 million copies. That doesn't touch what comes in from stage appearances, endorsements and other lucrative trappings of the trade.

Assuming he has one-hundredth of an ounce of business sense—or, more realistically, knows someone who does—he'll never have to worry about food, clothes, shelter, dental bills, car payments, summer vacation and an education for the kid. For Pete's sake, he can pay someone to worry for him. Or a whole crew of worriers, if he takes a notion.

It makes a lot of sense from the entertainment point of view, as well. Brooks is surely smart enough to know that fame is fleeting, even for megastars.

When Brooks hit the national scene, some industry observers immediately branded him the next Elvis. Of course, they said the same thing about two or three dozen hot singers ahead of him, and they're saying it right now about Billy Ray "Achy Breaky Heart" Cyrus. Apparently there are more Next Elvises in the music industry than there are Elvis sightings in doughnut shops and hamburger joints across the face of this land.

Another thought: As far as Brooks' detractors are concerned, nothing could be better than for him to retire immediately. Is he too busy to sign the papers today? Just think how more beautiful the musical world would have sounded if, say, Slim Whitman had retired at an early age and never "sang" again. Or Prince. Or Ice-T.

Still, Brooks lists none of the above as the official reason he wants to quit. He says he wants to be a full-time dad to 2-month-old Taylor Mayne Pearl Brooks. He's plumb wrung out from all those days and nights on the road, and he wants to play patty-cake and go to tea parties.

"I'm having an inner battle about fatherhood and entertainment," he said in a published interview. "If I don't have the strength or find out I'm not going to do them both, the choice hands down has got to be fatherhood."

Sounds great. But forgive me if I laugh.

Not that I doubt Garth Brooks' intentions. On the contrary, I'm sure he is sincere. Based on magazine articles and newspaper profiles I've read about this guy, he appears to be a very sensitive, very caring person. A man of "family values," as politicians would put it.

But I also realize he's a man who has made an extraordinary mountain of money in an extraordinarily short period of time by writing and singing songs about, and to, the people of middle America.

These are the people who get up before sunrise and hit the road to a boring factory job 65 miles away. The single parents who juggle free time and stretch paychecks. The dads who lead Boy Scout hikes and teach Sunday school classes. The moms who drive car pools and coach softball teams. The parents who pinch budgets so there's a package to unwrap on birthdays and at Christmas.

Take my advice, Garth. Don't mock these folks with gallant talk about quitting your job. They've managed to work and raise their families without the safety net of platinum records on the wall and $50 million in the bank.

A trip to the attic

September 11, 1992

I n the corner of my garage is a cardboard box I have been bumping into and tripping over for the better part of the summer. Next time I go up to the attic, I'll take the thing with me and get it out of the way.

Then again, maybe not. I've been "next timing" that hateful box for months, and it is no closer to ascension than it was the day I carried it in.

Purebred procrastinators surely understand this logic. They know it is more sensible, not to mention far more emotionally satisfying, to rub your shin and curse a box that gets in the way— maybe even kick it—instead of spending the two minutes required to pull down the attic ladder and lug the offending object out of harm's reach. This is one of life's Great Mysteries we procrastinators figured out long ago.

Our brand of logic is exceedingly systematic. We know, for example, that if the box was a huge obstruction, one that caused us to consistently step out of our way, we would have toted it up to the attic from the very beginning.

But this particular box is not all that big. It's just small enough to fit into the next-time-I-go category. If that means an occasional bump and subsequent oath in the dark, so be it.

In any event, I was in the garage the other morning, preparing to launch myself wholeheartedly into yard work. Well, quarter-heartedly, at the very least. My first chore was ferrying the garbage can and several bags of trash to the curb.

I am talking lots of trash. Indeed, a small mountain of trash, most of it left in the wake of my college-sophomore son's departure. He is studying at a university in Wales this semester. Just before leaving, he had given his room a farewell cleaning, the likes of which it hasn't seen in a good 12 years.

Like his old man, Clay tends to be a pack rat. But for some reason, he had purged his room, big time. His trash pile contained several large, brown grocery bags, each filled to capacity with old tests, reports, essays, drawings, maps, brochures, magazines, you-name-it.

One of them, though, was particularly heavy. When I set it down, a sharp, metallic clack resounded. I peeked inside, and a stinging lump immediately ballooned in my throat. With a daughter living in a college dorm and a son living outside the country, I am empty of nest summa cum laude, and my throat-lump threshold has sunk to an all-time low. This nearly took me over the edge.

There, in a pile, lay all of Clay's trophies from high school, middle school and beyond—two from math competition, a couple from his old soccer team, a small statuette he'd won at a kids' fishing tournament.

Nothing fancy, mind you. Just cheap, plastic-and-brass mementos that had been gathering dust on his shelves. I'm sure Clay had long-since grown tired of them.

Parents, of course, never grow tired of these things. We have a much different perspective about them than our children, and you know before I can type the words what I did: I marched back inside the house and got me a new grocery bag and rescued the trophies from landfill oblivion.

Get rid of them? You gotta be kidding. You don't just throw things like this away, I told myself. Some day, these trophies will mean a lot to Clay. Years from now, he'll be happy I saved them for him.

Then gently, almost reverently, I rolled up the top of the new bag and carried it back into the garage and carefully tucked it into that hateful cardboard box I have been bumping into and tripping over all summer.

That's the same box my mother gave me months ago when she moved out of her house. The same box that is packed full of junk: yellowed clippings, cracked photos, scrapbooks, vacation souvenirs—plus two very tarnished high school football trophies that she rescued from my own purge more than 25 years ago.

Next time I go up to the attic, I'll take the box with me and get it out of the way.

CHAPTER SEVEN

The sporting life

Anybody who lives in the South and doesn't follow sports leads a lonely existence.

Between football, basketball, baseball, softball, hunting, fishing, hiking, golf, tennis, skiing, racing and horseshoes, Southerners can find enough wholesome activities to keep themselves occupied 22 hours a day—leaving just enough time for trivialities like working and sleeping. Not necessarily in that order.

Critics say we Southerners put too much emphasis on sports. They say it's scandalous that a college football coach can earn half-a-million bucks a year when a fully tenured professor tops out at $50,000.

Could be. When they start packing 98,000 screaming fans into History 111, we'll talk about it.

The evil lure of fishing

June 7, 1996

I f you read the comics page—and who doesn't?—you know Garfield the cat and his goofy-geek owner, Jon Arbuckle, have been on a fishing trip for the past few days.

There is a very good reason why: This is National Fishing Week, and cartoonist Jim Davis, creator of the fat cat with an insatiable appetite for lasagna, is the honorary chairman.

"Fishing, like Garfield, is truly for everyone, young and old," Davis said in a prepared statement. "There are no cultural, financial, gender, physical or mental barriers. Just drop your line in the water and enjoy. There are more than 50 million anglers in the United States. With your help we can interest many others in a sport that is truly universal and truly fun."

Fine. I truly agree with everything Jim Davis truly says—with three exceptions.

As an anglerperson myownself, I'm here to tell you there definitely are financial, physical and mental barriers to fishing. I speak with a lifetime of experience in this regard.

The first myth we must dispense with is this nonsense about "no financial barriers."

Clearly, Jim Davis has spent too much time in the cane pole section. He does not realize that today's angler is a fine-tuned machine who must stay on the cutting edge of technology in order to master the sport.

Translation: Dough, and I ain't talking carp bait.

Before you make the first cast, you must go to a banker and establish a $400,000 line of credit to cover boat, motor, trailer, plus a four-wheel-drive vehicle to tow everything with; not to mention (we're talking bare minimum from here on out) a dozen graphite spinning and casting rods; three fly rods of finest Tonkin cane in various weights; 15 suitcase-sized tackle boxes filled with crankbaits, spinnerbaits, buzzbaits, jerkbaits, jigs, plastic worms and grubs; 25 assorted bottles of pork rind; spoons, spinners (not to be confused with spinnerbaits); depth finders, pH meters, thermometers; dry flies, wet flies, nymphs, streamers; 155 miles of

monofilament, braided line, Spiderwire, fly line, leader material
and backing; fly-tying vise, feathers, dubbing, thread, hooks;
waders, hip boots and dip nets (one for boat, one for fly-fishing vest,
which I forgot to mention); two fillet knives (one electric, one manual); polarized eyeglasses; subscriptions to Field & Stream,
Outdoor Life, Sports Afield; and memberships in Trout Unlimited
and Bass Anglers Sportsman Society.

Now, for the "no physical barriers" malarkey. Try hiking to, and
wading silently along, some secluded mountain stream with even
one-tenth of the aforementioned equipment. I rest my case.

Finally, let us broach the matter of "no mental barriers." This
one covers a multitude of sins.

Anyone—and there are at least 50 million of us, as Jim Davis
points out—who spends that kind of money and energy in the
name of recreation has dubious mental capacity. Even worse, we
use it attempting to outwit a cold-blooded animal whose brain is
the size of a pea.

It's too late for addicts like me. But I implore the impression-
able youth of America: Save yourselves! Just say "no" to fishing!

Scratch the scratching

March 28, 1993

Nearly everyone associated with major league baseball—
from the owners to the managers to the players—agrees
the game is too slow.

The average game last season took just under three hours to
complete. This sluggishness has been increasing yearly since the
early 1980s. Fifteen years ago, baseball games lasted 24 minutes
less than they do today. Then again, 15 years ago you didn't need
an inheritance and a $300,000 line of credit to buy tickets, either.
So maybe the goal is to give fans more for their money.

In any event, baseball officials recently announced several
changes for the upcoming season, changes they say will speed up
the process by as much as 20 minutes per game.

Hitters will be encouraged to stay in the batter's box between pitches, for example. Catchers and infielders will take fewer trips to the pitcher's mound. Public address announcers will call the next hitter quicker.

Ho-hum. This is a nickel-and-dime approach, as far as I'm concerned. Why settle for a piddly 20 minutes? Why not make two or three sweeping changes that will pump life back into the ol' contest and keep it there, inning after inning, game after game?

Once my recommendations are implemented, baseball will launch into orbital speed. Games will no longer drone on endlessly. Who knows? Mayhaps we'll finish the World Series before the All-Star break of a traditional season.

To achieve this lofty goal, I propose that baseball officials:

■ Make players refrain from spraying tobacco juice anytime they are on the field.

Please understand: It's OK for them to chew; they just can't spit.

I daresay each player averages 10-30 minutes per game fiddling with the wad of tobacco in his jaw. If he's not forming a fresh chew, he's spewing streams of ambeer, wiping his lips on his sleeve, clearing his throat, or extracting stray stems, crossties, 2-by-4s, fence posts, barbed wire and other materials cleverly concealed amongst the tobacco leaves. (If you've ever chewed, and I did for years, you know what I'm talking about.)

This step alone will carve a serious dent in the time it takes to play the game. Hey, who's going to delay, even for 10 seconds, when he's up to his eyeballs in liquefied Red Man?

■ Permit each player only one crotch scratch per game.

Again, we're talking about a drastic step that will slice deeply into baseball's dawdle time. And it's as much a matter of fairness as anything else.

I ask you: What other high-dollar profession allows its players the luxury of indiscriminate crotch-scratching?

Surely there are times when lawyers, doctors, dentists and Fortune 500 CEOs are smitten with The Itch. But do they have the privilege of clawing and groping in public?

No. So why should baseball players be treated any differently?

■ Eliminate the ridiculous system of "secret" signals from the third base coach.

Talk about a time waster! We're dealing with the blinding speed of a sundial here, folks.

Watch a third base coach next time, say, there's a runner on first.

Depending on the count at home plate, he'll probably tug at the bill of his cap, touch his left elbow, lick the fingers on his right hand, pat his right knee, rub his belt buckle, touch his nose and nod three times.

All of which tells the runner, "Try to steal second base if you think you can make it."

Of course, it can also mean, "Yeeii! There's a bee in my britches!" In which case the runner, confused as heck by this time, thinks he's being told to make a sprint for home on a simple dribbler to left field. All in all, third base signals are a costly waste of time and manpower.

Besides, if the guy on first is slick enough to negotiate a $7 million contract, don't you think he's got sense enough to know when to run?

Never try to explain

May 7, 1991

I flicked on the television one night last week and happened to catch the final inning of the Texas-Toronto baseball game, the one where Nolan Ryan pitched his seventh career no-hitter.

"Wow!" I yelled to Mary Ann. "Seven no-hitters! Incredible! This guy is 44 years old! He was playing professional baseball before some of his teammates were even born!"

"So?" Mary Ann replied. "You'll be 44 in a few days. I suppose on your birthday people are going to jump up and down and say, 'Wow! Venob is 44 and he showed up for work today! Incredible!' "

"That's not the same thing."

"You're right," she said. "ANY day you show up at the office is incredible."

I ignored her feeble attempt at humor.

"You don't understand," I said. "Seven times in his career, Nolan Ryan has pitched a no-hitter. Nobody has even come close. Ever. I just saw history in the mak . . ."

"What's a no-hitter?" Mary Ann broke in.

"Exactly what the name implies. Nobody on the other team got a hit."

"You mean throughout the entire game, not one soul hit the ball?"

"No. A lot of people hit the ball."

"So how can there be a no-hitter?"

"They either grounded out or flied out."

"You mean 'flew out,' " said Mary Ann. " 'Flew' is the past tense of 'fly'. Not 'flied'."

"It's different in baseball terminology," I answered. " 'Flied out' means they hit the ball into the air and someone caught it. 'Grounded out' means the ball bounced along the ground, but some-one picked it up and threw them out before they reached first base. Either way, nobody got a hit, and Ryan's no-hitter was preserved."

"That makes no sense whatsoever," she responded. "If it's OK to say 'flied out' when the ball goes into the air, it ought to be 'grinded out' when it's on the ground."

"It just doesn't work like that!" I shouted. "I don't know why! I didn't make up the language! It's just a term! People eat hot dogs at baseball games, but nobody thinks it's really dog meat, do they?"

(I should be used to it by now. For more than two decades I have lived with a mathematician, and I know that everything in a mathematician's life is precise. There is no nonsense, no imagina-tion. Mathematicians would have you believe their lifestyle is logi-cal and orderly. They like the metric system too, so you figure out who's right.)

"In any event, I don't see why it's such a big deal," Mary Ann said. "This guy has been playing baseball for years, and he's only had seven good games? Doesn't sound like a very productive employee to me."

It was no use. I left the room and went into the kitchen for a snack. Rummaging in the back of the refrigerator, I found a pack of hot dogs and ate one. Cold. It was awful.

And in reflecting back on the experience, I wondered if ballparks did start selling parts of Rover and Fido, would they be advertised as "grinded-up" dog?

When you're not shackled by logic, these things cross your mind.

A gift from Jerry

November 11, 1992

I'd love to be standing in the corner of a certain Iowa hardware store the next few days and watch what happens when a farm kid strolls in. A left-handed farm kid, that is. A left-handed farm kid who enjoys the game of baseball and maybe is a little short on cash.

He—or she, if that's the case—is in for a wonderful surprise.

I know this is going to happen because I was in that store one week ago last Friday and saw the surprise take shape.

I travel to Iowa with a group of friends every fall. We come from all over the South—Virginia, Tennessee, Georgia, South Carolina, Louisiana and various points between—and gather at an abandoned farmhouse 10 miles west of a town called Allerton, which is roughly the size of a grape.

Officially, we go to hunt pheasants and quail. If you checked our freezers right now, you would see evidence of successful teamwork between men and dogs.

But, more importantly, this is Our Time.

Our Time to renew old acquaintances. Our Time to cook ghastly suppers of greasy meat and wash them down with more beer than we drink at home. Our Time to tell lewd stories, argue politics, loll around unshaven and unbathed, scratch whenever and wherever it itches, and unleash visceral noises, north and south, deemed inappropriate elsewhere. My wife calls it one of those Ychromosome things.

But back to the hardware store.

The reason I'm at the store in the first place is because we're driving a rental van from the airport in Des Moines, and one of my buddies has just purchased a big box of toys for his children. He wants to ship it home instead of lugging it back onto the plane. So we stop in your basic, plain-brown-wrapper, microscopic Iowa farm town and ask about a UPS office.

It's over at the hardware store, someone tells us. Just across the street.

Indeed it is, and it's right off the cover of Saturday Evening Post. There's seed, feed, fertilizer. Boxes of hog nose rings. A pegboard studded with work gloves. Coils of barbed wire.

At the end of one aisle, there's also a Spartan display of sporting goods: dog-eared boxes of shotgun shells and .22 cartridges, three or four hunting knives, a half-dozen fish stringers, boot laces, a couple of tubes of boot grease. And three left-handed baseball gloves.

While the UPS transaction is taking place, another of my buddies picks up one of the gloves. Jerry slips it over his large right hand and slowly begins pounding the pocket.

"How come they're all left-handed?" he asks.

"Sold the righties a long time ago," the shopkeeper replies. "Don't get much sporting goods business around here anymore. Can't compete with the big discount stores, you know. Hard to make a living in a little town like this."

"Yeah," Jerry replies, still pounding, his gaze fixed on the pocket of the glove. "Any left-handed kids around here?"

"Sure. Every now and then one of 'em comes in and tries a glove on, but they hardly ever buy. You know how it is."

Jerry nods and keeps pounding the glove, steadily working the dusty leather with his fist. He tries another and gives it the same treatment.

The UPS business is finished by now. Time to pile into the van and keep driving south.

But Jerry's business is not finished. He scoops up two gloves, carries them to the counter and peels several layers from his money clip.

"A left-handed kid needs a left-handed glove," he says. "The next two that come in here trying on gloves, you give 'em one of these."

The shopkeeper blinks in surprise. "Why, that's mighty nice of you, mister. Who do I tell 'em they're from?"

My friend smiles and walks toward the door. "Jerry," he says over his shoulder.

That's why I'd like to be standing in the store when a left-handed farm kid comes in and starts pounding a glove. I'd love to see the look on his face when he discovers it's free.

And I'd especially like to tell him it's a gift from Jerry May, the former Pittsburgh Pirates catcher—a Virginia farm kid who's never forgotten the joy of playing America's game.

Duck fever

November 14, 1995

It's November, there's a chill in the air, waterfowl are flying south, and I feel a hunting story coming on. If you are offended by that sort of narrative, kindly exit this column immediately and move to the stock market page, where killing is socially acceptable.

Migrating ducks and geese have been making headlines all over the country the last few days, and not just in the sports section. In three municipalities—Kansas City, Mo.; Des Moines, Iowa; and Omaha, Neb.—passing flocks were so large, they jammed radar screens and caused airport operations to temporarily shut down.

Hogwash, you say? One of those yarns old timers tell as they spit and whittle? Don't bet on it.

Normally, bird migration is an autumn-long process. But occasionally a freak, early cold front compresses the activity. That's apparently what occurred several days ago throughout the Midwest.

I'd love to have watched this exodus—again. Perhaps I wouldn't get so flustered this time. But I doubt it. Indeed, I hope I would shake worse than shingles in a hurricane—again.

It happened one cold, clear November morning in 1981 when Mike and Jack McClelland and I were decoying mallards in the cattail marshes of the Missouri River outside Pierre, S.D. The three of us had enjoyed excellent duck hunting all week. But that day I witnessed a spectacle I've never encountered before or since, and that covers nearly three decades of dedicated waterfowling.

I saw "The Migration."

I'm talking tens of thousands of airborne mallards funneling down the middle of the river in one giant, twisting swarm. The cloud extended for miles, so help me.

Since we were hunting ducks and had three dozen duck decoys bobbing on the water in front of us, it only seemed natural to blow our duck calls at this huge, undulating wave of birds. Not that it would have mattered, you understand. Coaxing so many birds our way would have been as futile as trying to push a Mack truck up a 30-degree slope with our shoulders.

But it worked. So help me.

Not all of them came, of course; surely not one percent of the main flock. Yet suddenly, there were untold hundreds and hundreds of mallards—maybe thousands, who knows?—circling, wheeling, milling all around us. They were stacked like pancakes: some paddling on the water 10 yards away, some landing, some still soaring 100 yards up. Everywhere, ducks. The roar of the wind against their stiffened wing feathers was deafening.

To underscore what happened next, let me state that I have killed some ducks in my life. I worked for 10 seasons at a waterfowl club in southwest Louisiana. I wrote a column for a waterfowl magazine for six years. I have guided duck hunting parties, conducted duck hunting seminars, judged duck calling contests. Trust me; I know what to do when it's time to put shotgun to shoulder. So do Mike and Jack.

This time, though, we were spellbound. Gripped by duck fever, if you please. When the shooting belatedly began, we came further unglued, worse than rookies who'd never pulled on a pair of hip boots.

I fired my first two rounds blindly, for naught, knowing better both times I pulled the trigger. On the final volley, my senses finally returned. I picked out a climbing greenhead no farther than 25 yards away, straight up, and brought him crashing into the cattails.

The echoes of all three shotguns faded across the broad river. The main flock continued to pass overhead. I stared into the heavens, slackjawed.

Finally, I turned to my partners and said, "I'm ashamed to admit this, but I only got ONE out of that entire bunch!"

Mike and Jack were trembling as violently as I. They didn't speak for a second. Then they both burst into laughter.

"H-h-h-hell!" Mike sputtered. "We didn't even cut a feather!"

That's the most ducks I never killed, and I'd give a week's pay to do it all over again.

Terror on the river

October 10, 1993

Please forgive Marcia Houser for sitting this Halloween out. Yes, I know it's still three weeks before haints, ghosts, goblins and witches invade the land, but Marcia's had enough of the scary stuff. If she's lucky—and nobody sneaks up behind her and shouts "BOO!"—her pulse might return to normal by the time everyone else is saying, "Trick or treat."

Houser's Halloween started a few days ago when she went fishing. She drove to Three Rivers Dock at the junction of the Holston and French Broad rivers in East Knox County.

"It was late in the afternoon, and I was by myself," said Houser. "I guess that can be a little scary, but I really never thought much about it. All I wanted to do was sit on the bank and catch a few catfish."

So she cast her line into the French Broad and began soaking up the final rays of warmth on an Indian summer afternoon.

That's when she saw "it" coming down the Holston River.

"I didn't pay much attention at first," Houser said. "I figured it was driftwood or just a piece of junk. Maybe a plastic bag."

She turned back to the French Broad and continued thinking fishy thoughts.

"I glanced around a few minutes later. It was getting darker, but there was still some light on the water. Whatever was in the river had floated over toward my side."

Marcia squinted in the fading light. And—*yeeee-ikes!*—her heart very nearly exploded from her chest.

"It looked exactly like a naked human butt!" she exclaimed. "You could see these two big cheeks and . . ., well, you know, everything! It started floating closer and closer to me. I was frozen. The only thing I could say was, 'Oh, Lord! Please don't let it be a dead person!' I'm telling you, I really had to psyche myself to keep from screaming."

The object floated yet closer.

"It was pale-colored! I prayed again, 'Oh, please, Lord! Don't let it be a body!' "

By now the light was virtually gone, and The Thing was but a few feet away. With trembling hands, Houser extended the tip of her fishing rod and gently tapped one of the "cheeks."

It thumped.

She tapped again. Harder.

It thumped back. Louder.

And that is when Marcia Houser sent her blood pressure soaring into triple digits. With laughter.

"It was a punkin!" she cried. "The biggest ol' punkin I ever saw in my life."

Houser waded into the water and wrestled the beast ashore. It was all she could do to load it into her car. She estimated its weight at between 60 and 70 pounds.

I asked if she was going to carve it into a jack-o'-lantern.

"No," Marcia replied. "I got a friend to take a picture of me with it. I kept it for several days, but it was real bruised from coming down the river. It rotted pretty quickly."

Stands to reason. The big ones always do get away.

The Big Orange squeeze

September 1, 1995

I f you are a newcomer to Knoxville and are contemplating your first visit to Neyland Stadium for a University of Tennessee football game, there are a few things you need to know before sashaying up to the ticket window and ordering "two on the 50-yard line, please."

First, make certain you have thick skin because people will laugh riotously at your ignorance. Buying UT football tickets in a conventional manner, as mentioned in the opening paragraph, last occurred during the Mesozoic Era. Since then, the only way to be assured of admission is to (a) donate vast amounts of money to the university or (b) donate vast amounts of money to a scalper.

Both are effective. Method A has a decided tax advantage, but Method B guarantees better seats.

Either way you enter the stadium, though, here are three key elements to remember as you become part of the legendary Big Orange tradition.

CRAMPED QUARTERS: The average width of a seat at Neyland Stadium is 18 inches. The average human butt is slightly wider.

This is of little significance, however, because the average set of human shoulders is half again as wide as the average butt. In other words, even though your thighs do not trespass into someone else's territory, the rest of your body surely will.

This discrepancy becomes apparent to first-timers approximately .0001-second after the singing of the National Anthem. They attempt to sit back down, only to discover their 18 inches were hijacked by Neyland Stadium veterans who hit the planks the instant George Bitzas hit his high note.

But don't worry. This sardine-can condition has the ability to resolve itself if everyone on the entire row sits at an angle and watches the game over one shoulder, mimicking a mass assemblage of the Andrews Sisters or the Coasters.

LIQUOR LOGIC: UT regulations forbid the possession or consumption of alcoholic beverages anywhere on campus. These regulations are strictly enforced by Sniff Police who roam the student section once every 10 minutes, the north and south end zones once a game, the west section once a season and the luxury skyboxes once every other decade.

Nonetheless, many newcomers may be shocked on game day to encounter Vol fans exhibiting obnoxious behavior, slurred speech, a strong smell of alcohol on their breath and other signs of inebriation.

Be not mistaken. These fans are not in a state of drunkenness. They are in a state of hungoverness, stemming from the NCAA's sanctions against Alabama more than three weeks ago.

WAVE LENGTHS: "The Wave" is a popular, spontaneous form of fan expression at sports facilities throughout the nation. Traditionally, it is performed three or four times a game, usually as an act of celebration.

In Knoxville, however, The Wave can get cranked up six, seven, eight times a quarter. Usually by newcomers, drunk or otherwise, who are trying to regain their 18 inches of comfort.

God's team

November 12, 1991

Before the glow of Tennessee's spectacular, 11th-hour upset of Notre Dame last weekend fades into sports trivia, let me pose a question.

Why would God care one iota who wins or loses a football game?

Divinity is not my strong suit, but I have to think that with a world full of hatred, greed and other human shortcomings, The Big Guy has more to worry about than a sporting event.

In the aftermath of the Vols' miraculous victory, though, several people indicated The Big Guy played a role. I quote directly from the sports page concerning Notre Dame's failed field goal as time ran out:

"I hate to ask the Lord for help in these moments, but on behalf of all Protestants in this country, I think we deserved a little bit of help. I put my head down and said, 'Lord, let somebody miss one of these things just once.' "—Tennessee defensive coordinator Larry Lacewell.

"I've heard God is for Notre Dame, and I thought, 'Lord have mercy, there's got to be a Big Orange God.' I looked up and I didn't see him so I said, 'We're on our own now.' "—Tennessee defensive tackle Shazzon Bradley.

"If they'd been kicking toward Touchdown Jesus (the huge mosaic on a campus building near the football field), they would have made it, but they were kicking the other way."—Vol guard Tom Myslinski.

This is far from an isolated instance, of course. In the post-mortems of virtually any athletic contest, the winner often says, "I asked God for that (fill in the blank: touchdown, field goal, extra point, base hit or other miracle) and he came through."

Thus, one can only conclude that God was doing his heavenly best to deep-six the other team. And if that's true, you'd think he'd do it with more flair than a fizzled kick. Why not something really dramatic, like smiting them with the jawbone of an ass?

Ever the researcher, I consulted the Bible. I checked the concordance of the King James version (red-letter edition, so you KNOW it's the straight scoop from Up There to Down Here) and found no direct references to football.

Oh, there were a few passages that could be twisted into athletic application. As in:

Psalms 38:16: ". . . when my foot slippeth, they magnify themselves against me." (Wet conditions on natural grass?)

Proverbs 3:23: ". . . and thy foot shall not stumble." (Artificial surface?)

II Peter 2:13: ". . . sporting themselves with their own deceivings while they feast with you." (The famous fumblerooskie?)

Matthew 13:38: "The field is the world . . ." (What? No crowded seats like at Neyland Stadium? Saints be praised!)

Other than that, there was no mention about which teams have heavenly sanction. So please, jockmeisters everywhere, no more of this God-gave-us-the-victory nonsense.

The Big Guy is a busy person. He has sins to record and golden stars to bestow. He has to make important decisions regarding floods, droughts, pestilence and boils. There's the woodshed thing with Jimmy Swaggart. And, of course, he has to allot several hours a day for conference calls with officials of the Republican Party.

The very last thing God had to fret about last Saturday was the outcome of some piddly, secular-humanist football game between the universities of Tennessee and Notre Dame.

I'm sure he had a lot more riding on Georgia-Florida.

Trickle-down sports

August 6, 1992

I've spent the last few days scanning preseason football stories from all over the South.

Stories about passers and pass rushers, blockers and tacklers, runners and receivers. Stories about tough schedules and weak schedules. Stories packed full of what-ifs and maybes, probabilities and impossibilities.

But nowhere have I read a story about who will be the designated wee-weeer on any given team, and that makes me wonder if SEC football coaches, players and administrators aren't hopelessly behind the times.

Ever since I read a soccer story from Spain last spring, I was certain that the designated wee-weeer would soon take its rightful place on Southern football rosters. Maybe these things take longer than I realized.

This happened last May at a town called Bilboa. A big soccer tournament was in progress. It was halftime of a match.

I don't know what sort of festivities Spanish sports officials normally plan for halftime of a soccer match. Surely nothing so elaborate as the opening of the Summer Olympics or the Orange Bowl halftime orgy. Whatever they had in mind, however, a 22-year-old player named David Billabona stole the show from them.

He walked up to a goalpost and wee-weed on the upright.

The reaction of tournament officials was surprising. They said Billabona's actions showed a "lack of respect for fans."

That's odd. How do you show lack of respect for fans who typically become hysterical in their enthusiasm and wind up trampling a few dozen of their fellow fans to death?

In any event, I was certain Billabona's act of moisture would start mental gears clicking all over America, particularly here in the South. Surely, I thought, the people in charge of football games would see the advantages of designating a wee-weer at every contest.

It's cheap, for one thing. You don't have to spend jillions of dollars on band uniforms, musical instruments, band directors and flag squads. Ten or 12 dollars worth of Cokes and the designated wee-weer could perform throughout the entire intermission.

In addition, it spreads the opportunities for fame to more people. Not everyone has the physiological makeup and athletic skills necessary to be a linebacker or defensive end. But every student on campus has the potential to become a conference champion wee-weer.

Naturally, this broad-based competition lends itself to wee-wee tournaments with lucrative sponsorships from Gatorade, Coke, Tetley and Budweiser, just to name a few.

But the overriding reason to designate a wee-weer for every game—and this is particularly true at the University of Tennessee—is the enormous savings it will bring to the building and grounds committee.

Who's gonna dare try to tear down the goalpost—indeed, even touch it—at the end of the game?

Hunting coyotes

December 15, 1994

I don't think this is how pioneer women did it. Neither does Linda Stooksbury.

As she says, "They had button-up blouses and shirts back in those days. It would've been real difficult to maneuver."

But you never know. When arrows are zinging through the air or hungry bears are growling and spitting at arm's length, the human body is capable of amazing feats.

The story you are about to read is true. I know because Linda told me. I didn't see it for myself, which is fortunate, because we both would have wound up on the ground in fits of laughter.

Linda and her husband, Wayne, live on a farm. It's just outside Clinton, on the banks of the Clinch River. They raise cattle. Lately, coyotes have become somewhat of a menace.

Yes, coyotes—those yip-yip-yip-yiooooo! varmints you see on cartoon programs and TV Westerns. Coyotes have been steadily migrating across the United States for more than 20 years. I saw my first eastern coyote in Lee County, Va., in 1989, and since have spotted three more. Folks who stay in the outdoors constantly tell me they've become commonplace. Which is fine, unless you're in the cattle business and have a few calves hopping about the lower 40.

"They get in packs and try to chase a calf down," said Stooksbury. "We've had to take the attitude that if we see 'em, we shoot 'em."

That's what occurred not long ago. Linda was inside when she heard the family beagle barking from its kennel. She peeked out and there, standing in the garden, was a coyote.

"I keep a 16-gauge single-barrel shotgun right by the door," she explained. "I grabbed it and four shells and ran out."

(We pause here for a lesson in local firearms nomenclature. It's important. When Linda spoke of a "single-barrel," she was using the hillbilly term for a single-shot. In other words, a shotgun that takes one round of ammunition per feeding. It has to be broken open, a shell inserted into the chamber, then snapped shut; and before it can be discharged, an exposed hammer must be pulled into the firing position. Got that? OK, continue.)

"I was runnin' across the garden, trying to get close before he saw me," she related. "I had to do something with those three extra shells so I could use both hands to shoot. I looked down and realized I was wearin' stirrup pants with no pockets. All I had on top was a stretch T-shirt."

So, at full stride, Linda deposited the three spare cartridges inside an undergarment that women wear across their chests.

"Normally, all I ever keep up there is extra Kleenex," is the way she put it.

In the ensuing seconds, Linda perfected a system: She'd fire, reach into the, uh, ammo holder for another round, load, cock, aim and fire again. All on a dead run.

On her fourth shot, she killed the coyote.

It's a good thing too. Not only was her shell supply completely exhausted, the ammo holder itself was dang nigh twisted wrong-side out.

It'd be a lot easier for farm women, Linda decided, if someone designed a bra with loops for shotgun shells sewed in the lining.

Paying for the park

February 11, 1994

The Clinton administration is proposing that visitors to America's national parks and other public lands pay increased user fees to offset the rising cost of staying in business.

There's nothing official yet. Congress turned down similar legislation last year, and it'll be later this spring before lawmakers consider the matter again. Nonetheless, the president's budget proposal calls for an additional $32 million in fees from parks and recreation areas.

Makes sense. The people who enjoy the trails, streams, woodlands and campgrounds of America ought to foot their share of the bill to keep things maintained.

Lord knows the shoddy state of our parks. Some experts believe it would take a whopping $2.2 billion just to whip these facilities back into good condition. That's a huge chunk of money any way you cut it, and it billows into skyscraper proportions when you consider the proposed budget for the entire National Park Service is only $1.4 billion.

But along with increasing the user fees, the president and his park advisers need to find other forms of revenue.

New fines, for example.

I'm not talking about penalties for littering, catching over the limit of trout, feeding the bears, defacing public property and the other standard Ugly American offenses. I'm talking about getting to the heart of the problem—the Ugly American himself/herself.

Trust me. If the big cheeses would tap into this lucrative market, the money would come flowing in. Such as:

■ Assess bony-legged Tommy and Tammy Tourists 75 bucks every time they hit the trail wearing over-the-calf black socks, sandals, a purple Hawaiian shirt, red-checkered polyester shorts and a straw hat with fishing lures dangling from the brim.

■ Slap a $15 surcharge on tacky souvenirs like moose dropping necklaces, rubber tomahawks and goofy T-shirts that say, "My Parents Visited Yellowstone National Park and All They Bought Me Was This Stupid Shirt."

■ Levy a $25 incineration fee for charred hot dogs, hamburgers and other mystery meats "cooked" over an open fire.

■ Institute a $15 permit before stupid questions can be asked, such as, "What time do they turn on the water in the streams?" Or, "How come this wood won't light? I poured gasoline all over it."

■ Require the purchase of a $7.50 camera site nuisance stamp before family or group photos can be snapped anywhere in the park. The price of this stamp doubles if any member of the group wishes to make a silly face or hold "rabbit ears" behind someone else's head.

■ Charge visitors $50 for bringing new/rented/borrowed gear into the park without ever having tried it out at home. Add another $45 for hikers who attempt a 12-mile overnighter with boots that have not been broken in.

No money to run the national parks? You gotta be kidding. All it takes is some innovative thinking.

Super stats

January 26, 1992

Before this day is over, we will be up to our chin straps in statistics.

We will know who won the Super Bowl, of course. People all over the world will know, for that matter, because this most-famous of sporting events will be broadcast domestically by 200 television stations and 315 radio outlets and beamed to 41 foreign countries.

According to the number-spewing technicians at CBS, today's TV addicts will receive their fix through the services of 18 cameras and 12 videotape machines, including two Super Slo-Mo's, two Chyron graphics generators, one telestrator for analyst John Madden to diagram plays, and one Abekas for on-screen player photos.

The final score, which will be forgotten in a week, is only a minor statistic. Within minutes after the buzzer, we will be veritably deluged by digitized data.

You want to know the rushing yardage gained by each team? It'll be there. The passing yardage? No problem.

All you gotta do is ask, and the speedy sports statistics specialists will deliver—average punt, longest return, points by quarter, quarterback sacks, linescores, fumbles, interceptions, TV ratings, total payout.

You don't even have to wait for the main course. The statisticians are happy to deliver double handfuls of hors d'oeuvres for pre-game munching. Such as longest field goal (48 yards, Jan Stenerud, Kansas City-Minnesota, 1970, and Rich Karlis, Denver-N.Y. Giants, 1987); longest completion (80 yards, Jim Plunkett to Kenny King, L.A. Raiders-Philadelphia, 1981, and Doug Williams to Ricky Sanders, Washington-Denver, 1988); most receptions (11, Dan Ross, Cincinnati-San Francisco, 1982, and Jerry Rice, San Francisco-Cincinnati, 1989).

And on and on and on and on.

Funny when you stop to think about it. Here is a single day—one brief, 24-hour segment—from the 1992 calendar. No different from the day before or the day after. Except for those numbers.

But before you sit down to watch today's game, consider a few statistics that won't appear on your screen.

These aren't exact numbers. They're rough averages. Guesstimations, at best. I extracted annual figures from the most recent charts and compilations in the 1992 World Almanac and divided by 366, the number of days in this year.

Nonetheless, it's worth mentioning that on Sunday, Jan. 26, 1992, while the rest of the United States overdoses on football:

- 11,350 babies will be born;
- 5,830 people will die—including 103 infants, 127 victims of vehicular accidents, 14 drownings, 66 from AIDS, 1,981 from heart disease, two from plane crashes, 84 from suicide, 55 from murder;
- 109,407 people will undergo some type of surgical procedure;
- 6,656 marriages will take place;
- 3,197 marriages will end in divorce;
- 39,563 crimes will be committed;
- 1,981 people will file for bankruptcy;
- 437,158 tons of plastic will be thrown away;
- $8,834,153,000 will be added to the public debt.

I'm waiting for the day when John Madden can reduce numbers like those to a diagram board.

Then, as Big John would say, "Hey! We're about to see some real action here!"

Fun nights at the ol' ballpark

June 6, 1993

I n light of the free-for-all that erupted the other night at a major league baseball game in California, Knoxville sports officials might want to re-examine their agenda of "giveaway" promotional events.

Perhaps you read about what happened, or saw highlights on TV. It took place in the bottom of the sixth inning in a game between the California Angels and the Toronto Blue Jays.

The actual slugfest, I mean. From news accounts I saw of this fun-filled evening, members of both teams had been baiting one another constantly since the umpire cried, "Play ball!"

In any event, California fielder Chad Curtis was rounding third on a home run hit by teammate Tim Salmon. In so doing, he exchanged words with Toronto third baseman Ed Sprague. I don't know what the exact words were, but they apparently were along the line of, "Nanny, nanny, boo-boo! We just scored two runs on you!"

And before you could say, "Buy me some peanuts and Cracker Jacks," Curtis and Sprague were exchanging punches as well as words. The dugouts emptied approximately 2.0376 seconds later, and a good time was had by all.

This volatile reaction occurs quite often in sporting events these days. It is due to the scientific fact—substantiated by any supermarket tabloid psychoanalyst—that members of professional football, baseball and basketball teams all have a latent desire to play hockey. Since only the most skilled fighters are allowed on hockey teams, however, the poor wretches must settle for more passive pursuits. But I digress.

Wait. I'm going to digress again. Trout fishermen, professional or otherwise, also belong in that hockey-wannabe group. I recall an opening day in the Cherokee National Forest some years ago when—I am not making this up; a game warden who helped separate the participants told me about it—four or five anglers converged upon a popular hole at the same time. Before calm was restored, several fisherfolk were dunked, kicking and thrashing, into the embracing waters of Tellico River. Then everyone retrieved their nightcrawlers and canned corn and caught a limit of stocked trout.

Back to basebrawl: Any other time, this would have gone into the record books as just another spat in just another game. But this was Baseball Night at the ol' park. Meaning that many of the 24,360 spectators had been given a hard, round orb, perfectly suited for hurling, when they passed through the gates.

And hurl they did. Hundreds at a time.

Indeed, a veritable shower of baseballs cascaded onto the playing field, donking off players' faces and heads and creating one royal mell of a hess. Several players had to be restrained from climbing into the stands for a touch of retaliation. Before play resumed, five players were ejected. One was injured.

The lesson local sports officials should learn from this fiasco? Plan carefully—oh, so carefully!—for upcoming promotional events.

I realize it's difficult to pack crowds consistently into Bill Meyer Stadium for baseball or the Civic Coliseum for hockey. But in the name of peace, I hope team owners immediately dismiss any plans they may have for gate-filling gimmicks like Baseball Bat Night and Hockey Stick Night—as well as Broom Handle Night, Boat Paddle Night, 2x4 Night, Brick Night, Chain Night, Coke Bottle Night, Buckets Full of Toxic Waste Night, Spear Night, Knife Night. Not to mention the ever-popular Uzi Night.

In their place, may I suggest safer alternatives. Such as Foam Rubber Night, Feather Pillow Night, Sofa Cushion Night and Confetti Night. Or, if they insist on being daring, Water Balloon Night.

No matter what type of promotion the big cheeses decide upon, though, there is one giveaway they oughta include with every ticket sold throughout the season.

A helmet.

CHAPTER EIGHT

High tech is a pain in the neck

No doubt about it. I am road kill on the Information Super Highway.

But the truth of the matter is, life was a lot more simple back in those golden years B.C.— Before Cyberspace.

Yes, I know. That kind of attitude makes me a relic, a toothless has-been, one of those old-time checker players who hung around the depot long after the trains quit running.

Big deal. This world has always needed grumpy geezers, and I'm happy to do my part.

"Computers? Bah! Humbug!"

Man, I love the sound of that!

Do V-chips go with bean dip?

September 8, 1995

N ever let it be said Congress drags its feet. This august body of lawmakers approved V-chip legislation even though the V-chip does not exist.

I'm not joking. Congress and President Clinton have officially endorsed the V-chip plan to control violent programs on television ("V" means violence; get it?), yet this gizmo is at least two years away from reality. But who's worried about trivialities?

Assuming technology does catch up with the law, though, I hope TV manufacturers go the extra mile. I hope they install other chips in their sets so we consumers can exercise our constitutional right to zap programming we don't like.

(True, we already have a chip like that at our disposal. It's called the "off" button. But, again, who's worried about trivialities?)

Some chips I'd like to see:

G-chip: Scrambles incoming geezer re-runs, including "Matlock", "Golden Girls" and "Lawrence Welk." Plus any old Geritol commercials still floating around.

R-chip: Bans Rosanne from all performances—stand-up routines, sit-coms or National Anthem solos.

L-chip: Limbaugh is decent radio entertainment if you're sleepy and a long journey on the interstate beckons. But on TV? No way. Even on one of those super-sized screens, his jowls hang off the set.

TS-chip: As in talk shows—Geraldo, Sally Jessy, Oprah, Jerry, Ricki and others of their ilk. You hear one saga about Husbands Who Cheat On Their Wives With Their Neighbor's First Cousin's

Brother's Boss From The Sioux City Symphony, you've heard 'em all.

PP-chip: Political promises. The instant any politician utters the words "I promise" or "I pledge," the screen goes blank and a test pattern appears. Both tend to be boring, but the test pattern doesn't insult your intelligence.

H-chip: Prevents house-ad hokum. You know what I mean—those cheesy, high-praise, magno-fluff, self-promoting commercials that news programs are wont to run 27 times a day.

And speaking of commercials, why not subject them to a dose of chip-chopping? As per:

HO-chip: Hemorrhoid ointments. At least ban them during the dinner hour.

FH-chip: Feminine hygiene products. See above.

SCS-chip: Shouting car salesmen. Do these jerks talk that loud around their own homes?

RC-chip: Stops repeat commercials after the third showing per hour. How many times has that headache tablet commercial with the stupid-dad-who's-talking-to-his-stupid-daughter-while-he-packs-for-a-stupid-business-trip aired in the last couple of weeks? A thousand? I'd like to give 'em both a headache. With a ball bat.

Chip-chip: Quite frankly, I don't care which potato chip contains the most fat. Neither do my arteries. If I'm going to cuddle up next to a pillow-sized bag of Crunchy Saturated Greasies, what's the difference between 50 grams or 500?

Modern mowing

March 18, 1994

This is a promise: I will not be the first in my neighborhood to own a solar-powered lawn mower.

I am a traditionalist in these matters. I believe in keeping my grass trimmed the old-fashioned way. By hiring a kid to do it.

Just teasing. I do all of my own mowing, thank you, and I do it the way God and the American Petroleum Institute intended—with a bone-rattling, smoke-belching relic whose output, for accuracy's sake, should best be rated in units of hamsterpower instead of horsepower.

I started off this year thinking I would buy a new lawn mower. I looked at some slick advertisements in the newspaper. I walked through the lawn care department of a discount store. I kicked a few tires.

Then I looked at one price tag. Several minutes later, Mary Ann nursed me back to consciousness.

But even if I do break down and purchase a new mower, it won't be one of those Robotic Solar Mowers that the Poulan-Weed Eater Co. has just introduced. Not until it has been greatly simplified, anyway.

You may have heard about this new device. It sells for $2,000 and is being test-marketed in Pennsylvania, Maryland, Florida, Texas and California. As the name implies, it (1) uses solar power and (2) runs by itself.

Since this new mower doesn't require the services of a human operator, it does not have handlebars. Instead, it is guided by a small wire that has been buried around the boundary of your lawn—the same principle incorporated by "invisible fences" for dogs.

So far, so good. But when I read the fine print, I knew the Robotic Solar Mower was not the answer to my lawn-care prayers.

Why? Because this pea-picking thing contains a computer and sensing device that must be programmed.

Such a requirement will eliminate ownership by anyone over the age of 45—unless they are computer nerds, in which case they don't need a lawn mower, solar-powered or otherwise, because they always have their noses glued to a video screen and couldn't care less if the jungle in their front yard is 12 feet tall.

People of my generation have never learned to program our VCRs, digital clocks and microwave ovens. And yet we're supposed to be able to push a few buttons and tell Mister Grass Gulper to hang a left at the end of the brick wall, sidestep the tulips and trim around the base of the oak tree? Yeah, right.

I can just imagine myself attempting to fire up one of these babies. I'll push a button on the control panel and immediately have to leap out of the way of whirling blades. Or else inside the house, my VCR will immediately start recording reruns of "Cheers" while the microwave oven torches itself to ashes on Time Defrost. In any event, there will be nothing I can do to stop the monster except sprint into the garage, find a shovel, and beat the cussed thing until it quits kicking.

A $2,000 lawn mower that blinks "12:00" in bright red numerals. Just what every homeowner needs.

No more Richter scale

May 1, 1994

I wonder if the scientific community has any idea of the turmoil it has created by killing the Richter scale.

As we speak, media personnel and earthquake survivors alike are gnashing their teeth in a rumbling ground swell of protests that would easily register 7.9 on the Richter scale—if there was still a Richter scale to measure it on.

This controversy erupted recently when Thomas Heaton, president of the Seismological Society of America, stunned the world by saying, "There is no such thing as the Richter scale."

That's not 100 percent correct, of course. There most certainly was a Richter scale. It was named after the late Charles Richter, a California seismologist who created a formula for determining the strength of earthquakes.

But Richter's system is three-quarters of a century old, and a number of more accurate devices have since been developed. Through the years, Richter scale calculations evolved into a handy buzzword for the media. They were not being spoken by the skilled men and women who study the shifting nature of Mother Earth. So Richter got the thumb.

What a pity.

Most newspaper reporters and radio/TV broadcasters wouldn't know the Richter scale from an oak stump. But because of last week's ruling, they will no longer be able to generate stories that begin, "An earthquake measuring (fill in blank) on the Richter scale devastated the city of (fill in blank) today, killing (fill in blank) people, injuring (fill in blank) others and causing more than (fill in blank) of dollars in damages."

Neither will ordinary citizens be able to impress their friends with tales about how they rode out The Big One. An earthquake is an earthquake, but an earthquake "that measured (fill in blank) on the Richter scale!" is the sort of statistic of which family legends are made.

Oh well. The experts have spoken. What's done is done. I just worry about what sacred tradition will go on the chopping block next. What if the learned people of science decide to change the way hailstones are measured?

Ever since the game of golf was invented, golf balls have served as the standard for hailstones. Have you ever heard a TV reporter, broadcasting live from some storm-damaged farm community, say that hail the size of walnuts, kiwi fruit or Ping-Pong balls had wiped out the corn crop?

Of course not. It's always hail the size of golf balls. If the storm is particularly fierce and the stones unusually large, they are described as "hail twice the size of golf balls."

And what's going to happen when experts in the medical profession decree that grapefruit are not an accurate standard of measure for tumors? How will we be able to communicate, particularly here in the South?

Keep your technocratic mumbo-jumbo about millimeters and microns. When you hear someone say, "Lord, honey, they opened Helen and took out a tumor the size of a grapefruit; wasn't nothin' they could do but sew her back up," you know it's time to call the florist.

Talking cars

June 24, 1994

A car yelled at me the other day, and I wanted to beat its windshield into slivers.

This happened in the parking lot of a shopping center here in Knoxville. I was walking along a row of vehicles, minding my own business, when a shiny red sports car shouted at me in an obnoxious electronic voice.

"Stand back!" it demanded.

I'm sure I jumped. It's not every day a car orders you to get out of the way, particularly in a nasal voice reminiscent of a 1959 Civil Defense documentary on the perils of commie radiation.

I walked back toward the car. It issued the command once more. The message went on to say this car was being protected by a security system, and if I didn't want to hear one of those ear-piercing "wooop-wooop-wooop" sirens, I'd best make myself scarce.

Amazing. A hunk of metal decides its space has been invaded and tells a human being to scram.

For one of the few times in my life, I was speechless—as if talking back or cursing would have done any good. I truly yearned for a base-ball bat. There are times when spontaneous civil disobedience is not only justified, but highly recom-mended.

"Mr. Venable," the judge would say. "You have been charged with assaulting an automobile. How do you plead?"

"Self-defense, your honor. The smart-aleck car mouthed off to me."

"Oh. It was one of those talking cars?"

"Yes, your honor."

"Case dismissed."

This never should have happened in the first place. Car manufacturers had no business putting voices inside their products. Congress should have enacted legislation to stop the silliness before it got out of hand.

Now, I fear it is too late.

I am proud to say I have never owned a car or truck—or any type of machine—that is capable of speech.

A friend of mine once bought a sports car that said stupid things like, "Turn off lights" or "Gasoline is low." He would laugh and say, "Oops! There goes my intelligent car again!" and make a big joke out of it.

I was always uneasy riding with my friend after that. I was afraid I would slide into the passenger seat some day and a know-it-all voice from within the vehicle's computerized bowels would tell me, "Your clothes don't match" or "Still not using mouthwash, eh?" and I would do something hasty in return that might harm our friendship. Like kick the dashboard to smithereens.

But this is the last straw.

I know car theft is a serious matter. I know people have every right to protect their property. I know electronics companies have every right to sell devices that supposedly deter criminals.

But I have rights too. Among them is the right to walk through a parking lot without a machine bossing me around.

Sometimes I think society would be better off if Henry Ford had kept his inventions to himself.

Technology on the talk line

February 1, 1991

I t has finally dawned on me why some of East Tennessee's larger cities—Knoxville and Oak Ridge, to name a couple—have declined in population over the last 10 years. And why so many of the smaller ones—Sevierville, Kingston and Maynardville among them—have ballooned.

The answer has nothing to do with lower taxes. Or business opportunities, school districts and property values. Quite the contrary. People have moved back to the sticks because telephone party lines are officially extinct.

According to a report from South Central Bell, the last party line in Tennessee—"for many years, the only option for phone service, especially in rural areas"—was recently unplugged.

If you ever shared a party line, you can appreciate the impact of that statement. If not, pretend you're trying to call for a doctor's appointment.

"Zat you, Hazel?" a voice says when you pick up the receiver.

"No. It's Lucille. Who's this—Irene?"

"Lord, no! Irene's at work. They switched her to 7-to-3. This is Jo Ella."

"Sorry, Jo Ella. I didn't recognize your voice. You got a cold?"

"Yeah. That's what I was telling my sister, Annette. Say hi to Lucille, Annette."

"Hi, Lucille."

"Hi, Annette."

And on and on it goes until you take the hint and get off the line so Jo Ella and Annette can finish their conversation.

Ten minutes later, you try again:

"Who just picked up?"

"It's Lucille Lickskillet. Who's this?"

"Hi, Mrs. Lickskillet. It's Jimmy Jones."

"Hi, Jimmy. I bet you're talking to that cute girl I saw you with at church."

Silence.

"Uh, er, well, I'll get off the line and let you two finish chatting."

Later, you give it one more shot:

"Zat you again, Lucille?"

"Yes, Jo Ella. Look, I hate to bother you, but I really need to use the phone. I gotta call the doctor and . . . ."

"The knees again? Lord, honey, my cousin's knees—oh, by the way; say hi to Janice Romines."

"Hi, Janice."

"Hi, Lucille."

"Janice is in my garden club and we're planning next month's program. Hang on a second, Janice, and let me tell Lucille about the trouble my cousin Betty had with her knees. They were so sore that . . ."

And for the next 20 minutes, you get an earful of Betty's ligaments, while poor ol' Janice—who only wants to know whether to bring pansies or petunias to the meeting—stands like a statue with a receiver in her ear.

That, dear hearts, is why people moved to the cities in the first place. They were willing to put up with taxes, traffic, smog, crime and other unpleasantries of urban life in exchange for telephone privacy. Once party lines started to vanish, the trend reversed and home owners returned to the outback in droves.

But remember; everything that goes around comes around. You pick up a phone today to call the doctor's office and what happens?

First, you have to play Punch-The-Number for 10 minutes. Then, when a human finally answers, you are put on hold and forced to listen to Muzak. Then you get bounced between receptionist, appointment secretary, nurses' station and the accounting department. When the doc does come on, he hooks you up with a three-way call to some specialist in Boston.

Weird, isn't it? In the old days, economy-minded home owners endured three-way conversation because it was cheap. These days, you gotta pay extra for the honor. This is called progress.

But if business and civic leaders think the census shift over the last 10 years is bad, just wait till figures from the 2000 count roll in. It won't surprise me if two-thirds of Americans are living in caves and talking to each other with giant puffs of smoke.

Mishaps with the microwave

July 2, 1992

Research scientists in California are trying to perfect a microwave clothes dryer.

You'd think people smart enough to be research scientists would have sense enough not to live in the middle of an earthquake zone. But what do I know? As they say in Los Angeles, "Once you get used to a few cracks in the wall, there's no prob. . .*yeeiiiiii!*"

As I was saying, the microwave clothes dryer is about to become a reality. Officials at the Electric Power Research Institute in Palo Alto have already developed a prototype.

According to Dr. John Kesselring, senior project manager, the microwave clothes dryer works on the same principle as the

microwave oven. It heats water molecules inside the garment. It uses 25 percent less electricity than a conventional dryer and reduces shrinkage.

Kesselring does admit a few bugs need to be worked out. Like how to tumble the clothes so heat is evenly distributed.

Great. When he solves that mystery, perhaps he could tell the people who build microwave ovens. Then when we pop in a slice of leftover frozen pizza, we'll wind up with something besides lava and ice crystals.

But as far as I'm concerned, the biggest problem consumers will have with microwave dryers is the same one they have with microwave ovens: When they're using someone else's dryer, how will they know which @#$%! buttons to push?

Unless you live on Jupiter, you've surely encountered this truism. It happens because no two microwave oven control panels are built alike. They're like snowflakes. They may appear similar at a distance, but once you get up close and try to heat a bowl of chili, they absolutely refuse to cooperate.

You think I'm lying? Then I invite thee to pick up thy coffee cup and walk next door and attempt to operate thy neighbor's microwave oven. Or the one down the street. Or the one in the next office building.

See what I mean? The stupid thing sits there and stares at you while you jab-jab-jab buttons like some IRS auditor with an adding machine.

Oh, occasionally, it rewards you with a beep. Or else the clock starts ticking backward. Or the super-smart screen flashes the final market report from the New York Stock Exchange, projected daily temperatures for Reno, Nev., and the latest Top 10 list from David Letterman.

But warm thy coffee? Never.

That's what concerns me about these fancy microwave clothes dryers. Sure as shootin', we'll be on vacation somewhere and need a quick clothes drying. No way. The dryer will sit there like a hickory stump, silently laughing to itself, while we sweat, curse and pound on the buttons, futilely trying to erase the last command.

Save yourself the hassle, folks. Buy a piece of rope and some clothes pins.

Trouble on the line

February 7, 1992

Ma Bell has just sent me a letter describing the newest services available for my telephone.

Oh, joy. Just what I need. More buttons, numbers and gizmos to complicate my life.

I realize this is a terribly outdated notion, but I still believe a telephone has two functions—to place or receive a call. Anything else is fluff.

At my home, I don't have call-waiting, call-forwarding or any other call-nonsense the phone company promoted in the '80s. After looking over the latest assortment of costly trinkets, it is highly unlikely that I will buy them, either.

Ma Bell does make a good sales pitch. Her letter describes several common problems that can be solved with the new services. But I already know how to solve these problems. And it doesn't cost an extra cent.

Take a look at the company's letter and see what I mean:

■ Problem I: The phone is ringing when you get home, but it stops before you can catch it.

Ma Bell's solution: With Call Return, press star-69 and let your phone dial the last number that called you.

Uncle Venob's solution: If it was important, they'll call you back.

■ Problem II: You're too busy to answer, but there's a special call coming through.

Ma Bell's solution: With Caller ID, the calling number will appear on a special display unit (must be purchased separately).

Uncle Venob's solution: Answer the phone. If it's a call you want, continue the conversation. If not, say goodbye and hang up.

■ Problem III: You call a number and it's busy. You must redial again and again.

Ma Bell's solution: With Repeat Dialing, just hang up and press star-66. Your phone will dial the busy number for you every minute for the next half-hour. When the busy line is free, your phone will alert you with a special ring.

Uncle Venob's solution: If it's an important call, keep trying. If not, forget it.

■ Problem IV: Sometimes there are nuisance calls in the middle of the night.

Ma Bell's solution: With Call Block, you can stop unwanted calls—even if you don't know what the number is.

Uncle Venob's solution: Take the receiver off the hook.

■ Problem V: What about repeat, harassing calls?

Ma Bell's solution: Get Call Tracing. As soon as you hang up, press star-57. The number will be traced and forwarded to the phone company.

Uncle Venob's solution: See answer to IV.

■ Problem VI: You want to talk to some special people, but

you're not going to be home.

Ma Bell's solution: With Preferred Call Forwarding, up to six pre-selected numbers can be sent ahead. Then, with Call Selector, these six numbers will each have a distinctive ring.

Uncle Venob's solutions: Tell the special people when you'll be back home.

So how much for all this foolishness? Four bucks a month for the first service, $3 for each additional one. And if you order now, you can save the $23.50 connection fee.

I've got a better deal for Ma Bell. Quit sending me junk mail about stuff I don't want and knock $23.50 off my bill.

Or as they say in the big city, "Don't call us. We'll call you."

Up and atom

January 7, 1992

I f I had $54,000 to spare, the last thing I would spend it on is an atomic clock.

On second thought, mayhaps an atomic clock isn't the very last thing I would purchase. I wouldn't buy one of those dog-ugly neckties that are the rage today. You know the kind—those gaudy, 1957 Floral-Wallpaper-of-the-Year designs that men with lint for brains are wearing these days. As a service to humanity, I would be tempted to spend my $54,000 on mental rehabilitation for these sick men, but only if they wrote, "I will never buy an ugly, stupid necktie again" 250,000 times.

You know how we look at photographs from the polyesterized 1970s—bell-bottom pants, stack-heel shoes, leisure suits—and cringe in sartorial shame? The same thing's going to happen 20 years from now when kiddies start rummaging around in the attic and discover a shoebox of photos from the 1990s. Bet on it.

But back to the clock. It is manufactured by the Hewlett Packard Co. and is called the "HP5071A." This baby retails for $54,000, making it the world's most expensive mass-produced time-piece. But look what you get for your money: It should only err by one second every 1.6 million years!

Let's say you go to a discount store and pay $16 for a knock-about Timex. Chances are it's going to lose a bit of time, maybe a whole 60 seconds every few months.

Over the course of 1.6 million years, the Timex will make you decades late for important meetings, which is certainly not going to endear you to the people you're supposed to be meeting with. For Pete's sake, a lot of these people will have retired and died before you get to the meeting, and their survivors are going to be highly peeved with your rude tardiness. Especially if they wanted you to be a pallbearer.

Another advantage: If you look at the retail price as an investment, the HP5071A is clearly the winner. Fifty-four G's is a lot to drop on a clock, for sure. But over 1.6 million years, it figures out to less than four cents per year. Even if your el-cheapo Timex lasts 10 years, its annual rate will be 400 times that much!

Nonetheless, I am most certainly not going to buy a $54,000 atomic clock, and I recommend you not buy one either.

For one thing, the HP5071A keeps time by calibrating the vibrations of cesium atoms. Unlike God-fearing clocks and watches, it does not contain springs and pendulums.

Think about this for a minute. Which clock do YOU want crashing to the floor in YOUR bedroom when you're on a 4 a.m. potty visit and accidentally stumble into the dresser? Splash some of that cesium around the place and you'll never worry about potty visits—4 a.m. or otherwise—again.

But by far, the most important reason for nixing the atomic clock is because it ruins any excuse you have for being tardy.

The old "Pardon-Me-For-Being-Late-But-My-Watch-(tap-tap-tap on crystal)-Seems-To-Be-Running-Behind" excuse is hard to beat when you're late for a meeting. It's been around since pharaohs told time by sundials, except sundials didn't have crystals and tardy pharaohs were forced to execute a slave or two in lieu of crystal-tapping, a messy experience at best. In any event, it is an accepted excuse throughout the world.

But use it while wearing an HP5071A and everyone else in the room will eat you alive: "What's the matter, Mister Big? Your fancysmancy $54,000 watch let you down? Too bad all us peons with our $16 Timexes managed to arrive on schedule."

And then, sure as the world, they'll get in one more dig:

"And if your watch cost $54,000, how much did you pay for that incredibly ugly necktie?"

War on beepers

July 7, 1992

A judge in Houston, Texas, has won my lasting admiration by declaring open war on beepers. If other public officials would follow this bold initiative, America would become a more peaceful place in which to live.

State District Judge Jo Kegans launched her attack one day last week. She held 40 people hostage in her courtroom until someone 'fessed up to owning a beeper that blasted out in the midst of official proceedings.

Earlier, she had warned spectators, lawyers and others in attendance that beeper outbreaks would not be tolerated. Apparently, no one took her seriously.

Bad move on their part. The next time a beeper sounded off, so did Judge Kegans.

According to news reports, she shouted, "That was the 500th time somebody's beeper went off! They drive me crazy!"

With that, she retired to chambers. For three hours.

No one confessed, unfortunately, and proceedings picked up after the lengthy delay. Still, I daresay Judge Kegans' message rang loud and clear: "Listen to me, people! Don't NOBODY come into my courtroom 'less they park their beepers outside!"

I understand how the woman feels. I just wish I had the power to enforce a beeper ban myself. A ban on digital watch alarms, too. Also car burglar alarms—especially those that blast a loud, "BEEEOOOOOOOOPPPP!" when the owner walks up and sticks a key in the door.

No matter where you are, these hateful things have a nasty

habit of dinging, ringing, beeping, honking, tooting, clanging, banging and blaring when all else is quiet. At the least, these are extremely annoying sounds. At the worst, they can cause an ordinarily calm person to drop dead from a coronary.

Perhaps this is something members of Congress should address this fall. I propose they write a law to protect those of us—and we know who we are—who would dearly love to get through one day without being bombarded by obnoxious beeps.

Call it the Help Us Sustain Hearing (HUSH) Act. Among some of the highlights legislators might want to consider:

Anyone wishing to purchase a beeper must first submit a 2,500 word essay explaining why he/she needs this device in the first place, since a distinct advantage of leaving home or office is getting away from calls. The fee for this application shall be $10,000. Per beeper.

A mandatory waiting period of 15 years between application and purchase of the device shall be strictly enforced. Plus another 15 years between purchase and use.

Before taking delivery of the device, owners must sign a blood oath to keep the volume on lowest possible setting. Penalty for first violation is $75. Second offense, $500. Third offense, 2-5 years at hard labor. Fourth offense, death.

Not that I'm unreasonable or anything. I just think the beeper boneheads oughta learn a little respect.

Smith Corona's last stand

July 9, 1995

Several more hairs in my ever-thinning head turned gray last week when I learned the Smith Corona Corp., America's last major manufacturer of typewriters, had filed for bankruptcy protection.

Unless you are (1) in the newspaper business and (2) approaching that age when the word "retirement" occasionally creeps into conversation, you probably didn't notice this story. But those of us who experienced the professional transition from typewriters to computers certainly did. And we felt like Pony Express riders watching the last of our horses being led off to the cannery.

This news came as no surprise. In fact, I'm amazed Smith Corona hung on as long as it did. The company lost over $12 million last year, a figure I find astonishing. I wouldn't have guessed the American typewriter market was worth $14.27—proving that in matters of economic reality, Smith Corona officials and I have a lot in common.

But progress cannot be denied. There is no question that computerized word processors have decided advantages over typewriters in the business of wordsmithing.

They are infinitely quieter, for one thing. An old-time newspaper office at deadline—"CLACK-CLACKITY-CLACK-CLACK-DING!"—would blast one of today's OSHA decibel charts into lunar orbit. Now all you hear is a timid chorus of click-clicks.

What's more, computers capture the original keystroke. Meaning you can make changes—to different type sizes, margins, versions, whatever—without pecking everything over. The first book I wrote, completed on both manual and electric typewriters, required three manuscripts. I started with the first page and typed nearly 300 more. Then edited and typed them again. And edited and typed them again. The term "labor intensive" took on new meaning during this experience.

Computers are physically cleaner, too. No messy ribbons to stain your fingers. No erasure marks on the paper. No clogged-up e's and o's that look like c's and u's.

Yet for all their techno-qualities, word processors are nothing but robotic dorks. They have neither hearts nor souls. They do not breathe or have being.

Trust your elderly Uncle Venob on this: When you climb into the saddle of an all-metal, desk-model Royal manual typewriter and dig in the spurs, you can feel it come to life beneath your fingertips. In contrast, a word processor lies there, cold and sterile, and speaks—in monotone, no less—only when spoken to.

I still keep a manual typewriter in my office. It is fueled with real, honest-to-gosh paper. It is my medium of choice for letters and memos.

And when I goof, backtrack or change thoughts, I make atonement the way Gawd Hisself intended—with a quick burst of XXXXX's or //////'s. This absolves the sin and refreshes the spirit far better than any cyberspacing "delete" or "rub out" key.

XXXXX//////XXXXXXXyeehaw!XXXX //////XXXyes!////XXXXXXXX////

Thanks. I needed that.

Venting frustrations

July 15, 1994

I was helping my mother run an errand the other day. We took her car. She drove.

"Why don't you turn on the air-conditioner?" I said, approximately 2.763 seconds after we pulled out of her driveway.

"We're not going very far," she replied.

"But it's roasting in here," I protested.

The woman is much too practical. She said, "We'll be there before the car cools off."

"We can also bake a loaf of French bread in this car before we get there!" I complained.

"Well, for goodness sake, roll down your window."

"That won't do a bit of good," I said, sweat beading on my forehead.

"Why? Don't you like to feel the wind blowing in your face?"

"That's just the point," I answered. "Thanks to @#$%! car designers and @#$%! federal regulators, cars don't have side vent windows anymore. The wind can't blow in your face. The only way you can even feel a breeze is to stick your head completely out the window, and that puts a crick in your neck. Besides, it scares the beejabbers out of the driver in the next lane. You don't want me to do something weird like that and cause a wreck, do you?"

(Point of order. I did not say @#$%! in front of my sainted mother. I didn't even say $#@. In fact, I would not even utter a simple #@ in her company. I took the liberty of inserting those cuss words just now so @#$%! car designers and @#$%! federal regulators would understand what I think about their stupid, @#$!-ing decisions. Thank you. I feel much better.)

Alas, I was feeling none too great by the time we finished my mother's errand. Even with her windows rolled down to the asphalt, I am convinced I lost two gallons of precious body fluids from perspiration. We traveled about a mile. Round-trip.

I freely admit it: I am a slave to vehicular air-conditioning. So picket me. Sue me. Beat me. Call me ugly names. This is one creature comfort I cannot live without.

It didn't use to be this way. Back when cars and trucks came with side vent windows, all you had to do was crank those puppies out to maxi-span, sit back, and let the wind work its soothing wonders.

True, you picked up a bit of road noise. And an occasional June bug slapped you on the cheek. Or a stray hornet might ricochet off the pane and carom into the back seat, stinger lashing in every direction. That was always good for a laugh if your dumb sister was sitting back there.

Yet those were small prices to pay for the sensations and scents of sweet summer air, particularly in the early evening after a sudden shower. Then modern technology robbed us of side vent windows and forced us to use AC.

This evolution has been one of those chicken-or-the-egg situations, a bureaucrat's dream: Side vent windows were eliminated to make the vehicle more aerodynamic, which helped save gasoline to power the air-conditioner which was necessary because the side vent windows had been eliminated.

It's enough to make a fellow say @#$%!

If his sainted mother isn't listening.

Tampering with numbers

July 29, 1994

There's a big stink going on in Washington these days because the government wants to make everyone carry a tamper-proof Social Security card.

The feds are in favor of this plan because it will supposedly fight fraud. Government officials say a tamper-proof card will help

prevent illegal aliens from getting jobs and public assistance.

On the other hand, civil libertarians see it as excessive government intrusion. They liken it to a mandatory national identification system and fear an increased threat to privacy.

Both arguments have merit. But they miss the real, frightening issue: Does this country want something else that's "tamper-proof"?

After the experiences we've had with containers, you'd think anybody in Washington who even mentioned the term "tamper-proof" would be tried, convicted and sentenced to hard labor inside of 30 minutes.

The first tamper-proof aspirin bottle I ever encountered nearly gave me a stroke. When I reached into the medicine cabinet that day, I only thought I had a headache. Before the episode ended, I had tapped the stupid bottle on the sink, smashed it against the wall and gnawed the cap with my teeth. I was on the verge of attacking it with a hacksaw when my daughter, then about 4, walked into the bathroom and very calmly cracked the code.

Nothing has changed in the ensuing years. I have accepted the fact that I am tamper-proof-impaired. Meaning that whenever I attempt to open a container of medicine, ointment, food or drink, I either (1) spill most of the contents or (2) say pshaw-pshucks-gosh-dang and abandon the effort.

My two latest encounters have been with yogurt and mouth-wash.

There is a particular brand and flavor of yogurt I enjoy, but an engineering degree, preferably from an Ivy League institution, is required to remove the lid without slinging yogurt halfway between here and Bulls Gap. There is one advantage, now that I think about it: I don't consume as much yogurt as I would if it were as accessible as, say, a six-pack of suds.

Alas, the mouthwash and I have yet to sign a truce. To success-fully open this bottle, one must hold tab A, press tab B and twist cap C. It requires the dexterity of a guitarist and the timing of a comedian.

I don't even know why mouthwash needs to be tamper-proof in the first place. Lye or rat poison, perhaps; mouthwash, no. I assume government regulators would rather we go around exhaling dog breath.

And now they want us to have a tamper-proof Social Security card.

You and I both know this cockeyed scheme will absolutely, positively, never, ever work. Why? Because kids will be the only people smart enough to use the card, that's why.

And since Social Security will be bankrupt long before they sprout gray hair, why should they even bother to carry it?

Don't tell me when to shift!

November 24, 1991

I recently bought a new pickup truck—to replace the one my dear, darling, allowance-garnisheed-until-the-year-2005 daughter bashed into a tree—and was shocked to discover it came equipped with a back-seat driver.

Technically, it's a dashboard back-seat driver. Since there is no back seat in a pickup truck, Detroit found a way to install this annoyance right in front of my eyes. And if the stupid thing keeps telling me how to drive, it and I may have a session of attitude adjustment. With a tire tool.

This thing is called a "shift indicator." It's a little yellow light, complete with arrow, that comes on whenever some computerized gnome in the bowels of the engine decides it's time to change gears.

I do not need a pest telling me when to shift gears, thank you just the same. I have been driving straight-shift vehicles for 25 years, and not once have I required assistance in knowing when to switch from one gear to another. If you don't believe me, ahem, ask my wife.

It's bad enough this in-dash pest exists at all. What's worse is that it and I do not agree on when to shift gears.

I'm at an intersection and the light turns green. I start out in first, and before I can think about changing to second, the stupid light flashes on. So I shift. Before the engine revs a couple more RPMs, the pest says go to third.

Third? At 15 miles per hour?

Yes, insists the pest, adding that I better not take my foot off the clutch because fourth and fifth gears are waiting in the wings. With any luck, we'll be blazing along at a full 32 miles per hour by then.

I consulted the dealer. Nobody likes that dashboard pest, he told me; customers complain about it all the time. But it is hooked to the engine's computer, and lots of things will go on the fritz if it's disconnected.

The solution? Don't look at the light, the dealer told me.

What? Don't look at it? Excuse me. Is this the same as ignoring a dripping faucet?

Then cover the pest with a small piece of black tape, the guy said.

Wonderful. I spend a mountain of money on a shiny new truck and the first thing I'm supposed to do is wrap it with electrician's tape? Is there any wonder the automobile industry is in a tailspin?

There is another remedy—and I intend to take advantage of it at the first opportunity. Have a service technician reach waaaaay back under the dashboard and pluck the pest's lightbulb. Then the computer can scream, "Shift! Shift! Shift!" to its digitized heart's content, and I won't be distracted.

Actually, I should be thankful for small favors. If I had waited much longer to buy a truck, it might have come equipped with talking tires. Goodyear recently announced it will soon hit the market with tires that have a computer chip "brain" down deep in the rubber. According to a company spokesman, this will enable the tire to "talk" about its performance as the miles melt away.

Hoo boy. I shudder to think about the choruses of back-seat driving advice that'll come forth then:

"Hey, fatso! Didn't you see that curb? How d'you expect me to get 50,000 miles if you keep cutting it so close? I've got tender sidewalls, you know."

Or: "Go easy on the brakes! I can slow down in plenty of time if you'll use some sense with the pedal. No more of those brickwall stops, pal, or you'll be pulling your teeth out of the steering wheel."

The future is frightening. Really. You walk through a dealer's showroom, and all manner of brains, pests, gadgets and widgets start chirping in unison, "This guy's a loser, boss! He's heavy on the gas, doesn't change his oil and never visits a car wash. Besides, word going around here says he's a bad credit risk. Send him to the competition, boss. *Aaiieee!* He's also a tire-kicker! Get him outta here, quick!"

I wonder if my old bicycle still works.

Diaper duty

November 27, 1994

For the second time in as many days, I walked into the men's room of a fast-food restaurant and discovered a "baby changing station."

At least on the second trip I wasn't shocked out of my shoes. The first time it happened, I dashed out of the room and made certain the sign on the door said "Men." It did.

Nor am I alone in this discovery. On my second visit, another man was standing at the sink, washing his hands.

"You aren't gonna believe this," he said, nodding toward The Station. "But when I saw that thing, I went back out to make sure I was in the right room."

I understood completely. One glance at this guy told me he was a fellow IMCIOF—Ignorant Male Closing In On Fifty. There seem to be more of us every day. We are diaper-impaired, being beyond the having-babies stage, but not ready for Depends. Thus, when a diaper-changing device shows up at McDonald's or Wendy's, it catches our attention.

I'm used to seeing lots of strange things in public restrooms. I have read a few clever inscriptions on the walls, along with volumes of trashy, racist, homophobic scrawls, rife with misspelled words. I've been in a couple that were cleaner than the bathroom at my house, but more often have had to hold my breath and hope germs can't jump. At some of the larger interstate rest stops, I've even seen designated diaper-changing areas. But not at the home of McGrease.

It's a sign of the times, of course. More and more fathers, married or otherwise, assist with diapering chores. If my kids were in Huggies instead of college, I would probably use The Station myself.

There being no kid handy for a test, I wasn't able to put The Station through its paces. But from my brief IMCIOF perusal, it consisted of a platform that pulls down from the wall, like a tiny ironing board, where the infant is positioned for the procedure. On the side were little containers of disposable wipes, plus a large container for the, uh, used product.

Quite helpful. And surely more sanitary than flopping Junior down on the sink, where some geezer will set his false teeth 10 minutes later.

Back when I was an IMCIOF-in-training, we changed diapers the old-fashioned way: On the front seat of the car in the parking lot.

This exercise brought daddies and their friends close together. Indeed, they often clunked heads from opposite sides of the car as they groped under the seat for the diaper pin—a quaint item available in antique shops today—that invariably slipped into hiding. You could always tell who found it by the way he screamed.

True, babies that underwent diapering in the parking lot did not look the picture of Gerber perfection. Between a flickering dome light and the curve of the seat, the diaper often wound up positioned, toga-style, between the right shoulder and the left ankle. But what the heck; it worked.

And I'll tell you something else: Moments later, when we marched into the john to wash our hands, we didn't have to run back out and make sure the sign said "Men."

Dial-a-disaster

October 8, 1991

As if we didn't have enough problems with those fine folks at the Internal Revenue Service, have you heard their latest idea? Telephone tax tabulation.

A few days ago, the IRS announced a test plan that will permit taxpayers to file their 1040s by way of Ma Bell. The program works something like this:

Using touch-tone phones, taxpayers punch in their wages, plus their interest payments and the amount of taxes withheld. A few seconds later, so the plan goes, a computer tabulates the tax to be paid or refunded.

This is high-tech, state-of-the-art stuff. According to experts from the IRS, the innovative program will give millions of citizens the opportunity to settle their tax accounts with no more effort than it takes to call their Aunt Effie in Illinois.

Sure, it will. And Ross Perot paints houses on weekends to make ends meet.

You and I both know what's going to happen. Fouled-up forms will clog every telephone circuit of America, exploding in a shower of electronic digits and dollars faster than you can say, "Ain't progress grand."

I shudder to think of the awesome potential for disasters.

A guy in Cincinnati picks up his receiver and attempts to call his fishing buddy in Dayton. He hits the wrong numbers. Big deal; he hangs up and dials again. But the telephone, which doesn't understand what has just taken place, spits out a $19,473,852.49 assessment to some unsuspecting mope in Toledo and demands payment within 30 days.

Or else a woman in Detroit, intent on filing her taxes over the telly, strikes one or two numbers out of sequence and winds up ringing the second floor phone at a firehall in Boston.

Or else—and this is really scary—some teenager in Buffalo dials an 800-number to order a computerized pizza. There's a glitch on the line and, zappo! He wipes out the tax records for everyone named Jones in a 12-county radius, substituting their returns with overcoat orders from Lands End and L.L. Bean.

And think what might happen if you do dial all the numbers correctly and the machine does tabulate your taxes? How are you gonna pay—by stuffing quarters into a pay phone?

My plea to the IRS and Ma Bell is to nip this ugly plan in the bud. American taxpayers have a proud tradition of breaking pencils and wadding paper and kicking furniture across the room when April 15 rolls around. Don't complicate things by making us vent our frustrations with the teeny-tiny buttons of a telephone.

Hmmmm . . . on the other hand, maybe this plan does show some small potential. Think what a wonderful excuse we'll have for failing to pay:

"I tried to call you folks. Honest I did. But all I got was a busy signal."

No more ashtrays

October 26, 1995

I f you have shopped for a new car recently, you've probably noticed something different from just a few years ago. Beside the outrageous price, I mean.

Fewer and fewer models come with cigarette lighters and ashtrays as standard equipment. So unless smokers want to carry a Bic and flick their ashes out the window, they must special-order these items.

Makes sense, I suppose. A study by the Market Opinion Research group showed that four out of five American drivers don't smoke in their cars, nor do they permit passengers to light up. (The fifth, presumably, chain-smokes Camels and crushes them into the carpet.) Thus, car makers have taken the hint and sliced several ounces of metal from each unit.

Naturally, a change like this will send reverberations throughout all of society. Particularly the movie industry.

From "Thunder Road" to spy mystery thrillers, one of Hollywood's patented high-speed-chase tricks is to have the good guy pull alongside the bad guy, flip a cigarette out his window and into the face of the bad guy. The bad guy then screams, releases the steering wheel, grabs his face and veers off a cliff.

What goobers those bad guys are. You'd think they would learn to roll up their windows when the good guy pulls alongside them and draws deeply on his cigarette. Or at least keep saying to themselves, "Whatever happens, don't let go of the steering wheel, you idiot! Don't let go of the wheel!" But no. Right off the rocks they sail.

Even if they don't smoke, Americans are going to miss their

automobile ashtrays. They're a convenient place to keep change, spare keys, paper clips, pencils, pens, note paper, lottery tickets, ATM stubs, combs, hairpins, as well as packets of fast-food salt and ketchup.

What will eventually wind up in their place? Only heaven and automobile designers know.

Maybe a slot for holding floppy discs for a laptop computer. Or something for cellular telephones. Perhaps a complete toiletry kit. Maybe a lunch counter. As many people as I see racing along the interstate, yammering on the phone, eating and brushing their hair at the same time, I wonder if each vehicle shouldn't come standard-equipped with a deli, a barber shop and a full-service drug counter.

But you can't fight trends. Our all-knowing car manufacturers have given ashtrays the pink slip, and that is the end of that. At the very least, we'll all breathe easier, even though this will proba-bly mean a few billion more cigarette butts to litter the pavement each year.

Still, as these automotive repositories fade from the scene, part of the golden age of motoring will fade with them. And part of Americana as well.

For the life of me, I can't imagine a good guy in a high-speed chase throwing his hairbrush through the car window at the bad guy. Even if the bad guy takes his hands off the steering wheel to catch it and crashes off a cliff, it just won't be the same.

No greeting card for Goldie

September 2, 1994

I consider myself a caring pet owner. I feed my dog high-quali-ty chow—although, wuss that she is, Goldie backs off at the slightest nudge and lets any dog, cat or mouse in the neigh-borhood eat its fill before taking another bite.

I see to it that she gets bathed, sprayed and inoculated at regu-lar intervals. I had her plumbing fixed so unwanted puppies aren't running all over creation. I scratch Goldie's ears and pat her belly and occasionally, when no one else is listening, I say cutesy things to her like dog owners are wont to do.

I will not, however, send her a greeting card. Not even on her birthday, assuming I could remember what day she was born. Or whelped, as the case may be.

If pet owners all over America will similarly refrain, perhaps the Hallmark Corp. will drop its latest project and stick to Valentine's, Christmas cards and get-well wishes. For humans.

Not only has the company unveiled a line of greetings from owners to pets (when Snookums gets spayed, for instance), there's also a selection that pets can give to their owners. As in "Happy Birthday to My Person."

Don't laugh. Terry Madison of Linda's Hallmark on Chapman Highway told me people occasionally inquire about pet cards. Not long ago, she said someone whose dog had a litter of puppies wanted to send "Congratulations, Grandmaw" greetings to the mother of the blushing bitch.

On the other side of the coin, Carol Ann Norton of Carol Ann's Hallmark in Suburban Center called cards for pets "the stupidest thing I've ever heard."

Oh, I wouldn't go that far. Otherwise-normal people will go to much greater lengths to spend their money when precious panting pets are involved. In fact, they don't have to be panting. Does the term "pet rock" ring a bell?

Please understand. I know all about the emotional attachment between humans and animals. I have wept myownself while digging dog graves. Furthermore, I am convinced some pets have an extraordinary ability to communicate with humans—and vice versa.

Jody and Betsy McKenry once had a black Lab named Pepper that would sit up and watch while humans were talking. Her head moved back and forth as conversation was exchanged, like she was following a tennis match. Her facial expressions reflected the mood of the story being told: surprise, laughter, anger, whatever. It was almost to the point that the McKenrys had to spell out words when it was time to go to the v-e-t for s-h-o-t-s.

Even so, I never bought Pepper a greeting card and have no

intention of doing so for any other dog. I'm afraid they'd take one look at my selection and say, "Woof-woof-woof!"

Which is pooch for, "Hey, stupid! Do you actually think I can r-e-a-d?"

Putting on the botanical brakes

September 22, 1994

There's big news on the botanical front. Researchers say they have discovered how to boost plant production by manipulating a gene that controls the growth hormone. If this is true, it could lead to bumper crops of grain, larger trees and bigger and more beautiful flowers.

This amazing breakthrough was announced in the professional journal Science.

"When I think of the uses, it's fantastic," said Jedrzej Szerszen (yes, that's his real name) of Michigan State University, one of the discoverers of the gene. "It's exciting," added Dr. Jerry Cohen of the U.S. Department of Agriculture.

Yes, I suppose it is. This could mean more food to feed hungry people, without the evil side effects of pesticides and fertilizers. I'd much rather hear about the development of whopper wheat and magnum mums instead of some super-destructo weapons system that can melt the world into radioactive goo.

And just think of the changes this will make at county fairs! Farmers vying for a blue ribbon will have to bring in their ears of corn on flatbed trucks. Judges will need step ladders to inspect the melons—and if they want to sample a slice, they'll have to crank up the ol' chainsaw.

What scares me, though, is this: What happens after the gene genie gets out of the bottle? Will plants take off on a tear, growing and grappling, creeping and climbing, until they choke humans into extinction?

I voice this concern because I am a native Southerner, and I know what can happen when certain plants—kudzu, honeysuckle and poison ivy pop into mind—go from the cute little baby stage to teenaged hellions. In a wet, hot summer, this usually occurs in, oh, about three days.

You'll be standing beside a tract of well-groomed real estate, minding your own business, when suddenly a tentacle of kudzu grabs you by the leg. You are doomed. Before you can scream, "Somebody grab the 2-4-D!" thick green ropes lash around your body like a bullwhip. And with a maniacal vegetative scream, kudzu claims yet another victim.

Well, maybe it doesn't happen *that* quickly. But if you've ever done hand-to-stem combat with these plants, you know what I'm talking about.

As far as I'm concerned, this gene development business needs to be a two-way street, right from the start. For every growth-spurt secret the scientists unlock, they have to discover a way to retard plant proliferation.

In fact, I'd love to see researchers come up with a system to make the growth genes in plants stop or start on command. This is the answer to every homeowner's prayers.

You plant a tree next to the front door, give it a couple of years to fill out and then—*screech!*—you put on the botanical brakes. No more roots to crack the sidewalk. No more broken branches in the gutters.

Or as soon as the grass greens up nice and pretty in the spring, you give it one cutting and—*zap!*—no more growth until next year. No more weeds. No more raking.

You reckon it's too early to sell my lawnmower?

CHAPTER NINE

Clothes break the man

There are several advantages for refusing to be a slave to fashion.

You save a ton of money, not to mention vast amounts of closet space, and don't have to clutter your mind trying to remember what the current rage happens to be.

Of course, there are risks associated with this approach. Once—I swear this is true—I showed up at a homeless shelter to help serve supper. At the front desk, I asked directions to the kitchen.

The guy looked me up and down and said, "I'm sorry, sir, but you'll have to wait outside with everyone else. We won't start feeding for another half an hour."

I suppose this blows any chance I might have of appearing on the cover of Gentleman's Quarterly.

Clodhoppers on campus

July 28, 1994

E ven though her college classes don't resume for nearly a month, my daughter did some back-to-school shopping for footwear the other day.

She did not buy sneakers. Or sandals. Or loafers. Or high heels. Instead, she bought a pair of work boots.

I am as serious as a heart attack. My she-child came home with a pair of the heaviest, clunkiest, lug-soled, leather clodhoppers this side of Jed Clampett.

"Aren't they simply adorable?" Megan bubbled.

Hardly. There are at least a dozen adjectives that accurately describe work boots—sturdy, functional, durable, tough and rugged—but adorable isn't one of them.

"A chainsaw isn't adorable," I said. "Neither is a shovel or a screwdriver. They are tools. They aren't supposed to make a fashion statement. Same with work boots. They are for wearing to a construction site, not English class."

I knew it was useless to argue. Once the gods bestow fashion status on any article of clothing, it becomes the rage, and no amount of logic is permitted to enter the fray.

That's why we have suffered through the horrors of leisure suits and double-knit bellbottom trousers. If sackcloth and ashes suddenly get the fashion nod, that's what everyone who is anyone will be wearing.

There are variations to the rule, of course. Sometimes illogical fashion dictums will merely alter the way an item of clothing is to be worn.

A few years ago, baseball caps were standard issue among

males. They had a wide bill in front that was exceedingly useful for blocking the sun.

Then young men got the notion that caps should be worn backwards. These same young men suffer facial sunburn and squint a lot these days, but that's the price they pay for dressing to the nines.

There's another quirk about fashion: Even the most unlikely candidates can be trendsetters.

Stan DeLozier, a colleague of mine at The News-Sentinel, started wearing his National Guard combat boots to the office a few years ago. It didn't matter if he was dressed in khaki slacks and a golf shirt or a button-down and necktie, Stan always laced up his government-issue boots. We teased him unmercifully.

Then the inevitable occurred. Young women adopted combat boots as high fashion. You see them on female feet everywhere these days—high school and college campuses to athletic events to restaurants and bars.

Stan takes credit for starting a footwear revolution, but I disagree. I think he happened to be wearing the right item at the right time; or wrong, as the case may be. Whatever the reason, Stan has quit wearing combat boots. He has gone back to loafers, which more accurately describes his work habits.

I, myownself, am waiting until hip boots come into style. Between what I own for duck hunting and trout fishing, there are seven pairs hanging in my garage, one for every day of the week.

We role-models-in-waiting take our responsibilities seriously.

Beach bulges

August 4, 1992

The fashion industry—which suffered severe head injuries approximately 450 years ago and never fully recovered—is pleased to announce a revolutionary concept for the woman who doesn't have everything.

It's an "air" bikini, featuring tiny rubber bladders hidden in the top. You simply pump up the, uh, lobes and—*tah-dah!*—instant Partonism. No surgery, no tissue paper, no strenuous exercises counted to the beat of "We Must, We Must, We Must Increase Our Busts."

This thing has a lot in common with pump-up athletic shoes, except golfer John Daly will probably not be chosen as spokesman. Wearers simply activate the ol' air chamber and, as promotional material by the company says, "Fill the void!"

A company called Cole of California has just introduced this $72 trinket. Named "Top Secret," it's not expected to be in the hands, or whatever, of consumers until next swimming season.

In the meantime, perhaps someone will answer these questions: Why design a bikini that gives the illusion of adding flesh? Instead, why not invent one that takes away?

As a longtime swimmer and boater, I have seen my share of bikini-style suits, both of the male and female variety. Some people, because of heredity, exercise, diet or a combination of all three, are built to wear them. Right off the bat, I'd say a good .000000000006 percent of American adults fall into that category.

The rest of us have no business whatsoever walking within 150 yards of these aquatic postage stamps, let alone actually wearing them in public. And yet, people do.

Men with Michelin bellies squirm into those itty-bitty, triangular bikini briefs and strut around the pool like teenagers.

Women with 25 years worth of cheeseburgers protruding Down Yonder, plus a matched pair of 18-pound country hams Up Yonder, bind all that acreage with a two-piece tow rope and call it a bikini.

Have these people never heard of that wondrous wardrobe device called a mirror? Have they no shame? Have they no spouses or friends to gently take them aside and say, "Holy @#$%!, Thunder Thighs! You remind me of a pregnant walrus! Is that thing as uncomfortable as it looks? Don't you hear those people across the pool laughing themselves silly? And, hey! Don't sit there! You throw too much shade, and I'm trying to get a tan."

Apparently not.

Which means the "Top Secret" will probably earn millions of dollars for its designers and inflict even more visual pollution upon

America's lakes, rivers, streams and beaches.

Ah, but if the fashion people want to make some really serious money, as in beellions and beellions, they'll design a deflating style of bathing suit. One that you put on and push a nozzle and— *woooooosh!*—20 pounds of unsightly overhang fizzles into thin air.

Call it "Hidden Assets." I bet they'd sell 50 million the first day.

A pain in the B.V.D.'s

February 8, 1990

There is a special place in hell for the person(s) who invented plastic clothing tag holders.

Maybe "clothing tag holder" isn't the proper name for it, but you know what I'm talking about.

It's that sliver of plastic thread with a fat T at both ends. One T is embedded in the fabric of the clothing itself. The other T holds the price tag in place. Surely you have seen one.

One, my foot. You've seen hundreds of the awful things, and you probably hate them as much as I do.

I can understand how clothing manufacturers are attracted to these little do-jiggies. Once implanted, they can keep a price tag in place through fires, earthquakes, floods, after-Christmas sales and other natural disasters.

That's the problem. They hold on too long. After they've served their purpose, they refuse to go away. Instead, they stick around and become pests. Didn't kudzu start out this way?

The first time I tried to remove one of these loathsome devices, I yanked a large pigtail of yarn from the sleeve of a brand new sweater.

Silly me. I figured all I had to do was pluck the thing out and throw it away. How was I to know it was rooted deeper than a mature California redwood?

So I tried cutting it.

One snip with fingernail clippers and the tag fell away. But that only compounded the problem.

You see, one of the T's was still buried deep inside my sweater. The other dropped silently to the floor where it remained—upright and invisible—until I walked barefoot through the room two days later.

Odd, now that I think back on it. I had no idea I could jump so high.

If tag holders only came with new clothes I could cope; I don't buy much clothing. But this pox has infiltrated every sector of industry and commerce. It doesn't matter if you purchase a hammer, an outboard motor, a dozen pencils or a Trident missile, that stupid plastic thread comes with the deal.

Even once-worn clothing isn't spared. If you've sent anything to a commercial laundry recently, you know what I mean.

These days, the people at laundries don't identify your clothing with a marking pen or colored safety pin. They use those cussed plastic ribbons, which means you can be subjected to fits of rage on a weekly basis.

No matter how hard I try, I can't keep from dropping one of the ends when I remove them from freshly laundered shirts. Hours or days later, I discover it inside my shoes, buried in the sheets, or on top of my dresser. I'm starting to think the evil things are breeding—you know, like one-of-a-pair socks that show up in the washing machine.

I was walking down Gay Street the other day when I discovered their latest hiding place. At the moment of this revelation, however, I wasn't thinking great thoughts of discovery. I was thinking I had just been bitten on the buns by a poisonous spider.

A subtle *"yeee-iiii!"* issued from my lips as I sprang two stories into the air.

Falling back to the pavement, I limped to the office, confident I was maimed for life. I dragged myself into the men's room and made a hasty inspection. (In a stall, of course. Even when a venomous spider has just sunk its 4-inch fangs into one's flesh, one should have the decency to survey the damage behind closed doors.)

To my great surprise and relief, there was no spider in my undies. There was, however, a piece of laundry tag holder.

Apparently it had fallen from my starched shirt that morning and stowed away for several hours. Then it jabbed me in the tush like 40-c.c.s of penicillin.

If the people responsible for visiting these thingamajigs upon society ever run afoul of the law, they'd better hope I'm not sitting on the jury.

Taking a powder

February 16, 1995

A businessman cornered me the other day and started droning on about interest rates, tax rates, inflation rates, blah-blah-we're-going-to-hell-in-a-handbasket-blah-blah-blah. I was attempting to recuse myself from his monologue when my eyes suddenly focused on something on the collar of his white dress shirt.

Makeup.

No, not a smudge from his wife or some honkey-tonk honey.

This wasn't a smudge at all. It was a thin, steady line of makeup that arced from either side of his tie and ran alongside his neck.

"Holy eyeliner!" I thought to myself. "This guy has painted his face!"

I peered closer, studying his cheeks, ears and forehead as he rambled on. No question about it. He was dolled up slicker than Barbie.

Normally, I would have been curious enough and nosy enough to inquire. But I wanted to get shed of this goof as quickly as possible; he could have had a $100 bill pasted on his forehead and I wouldn't have offered to say a word. He finally exhausted his inventory of gloom and doom and moved on.

So it's come to this, has it?

"Yes, I do sell a little bit of makeup to men," said Courtney Julius of The Body Shop on Kingston Pike. "Most of the time, it's a concealer. Younger men use it to hide skin blemishes. Older men want it to cover the dark circles under their eyes."

Are we talking the wave of the future?

"I doubt it," Julius answered. "Women have been using makeup forever and ever, but most men aren't into it. I don't think the average guy will be buying it."

June Montgomery of the Merle Norman Cosmetic Studio in Bearden Shopping Center disagrees.

"I think we'll see more of it," she told me. "More men are becoming conscious of the need to take care of their skin. Many of them are already using their wives' moisturizers."

Hoo-boy. We should have seen this coming 25 years ago when men's hairstyles began creeping over the ears and down the neck. It seemed so innocent at the time, just a tiny bit of loosening of the ol' starched collar. What harm could it cause?

We found out 10 years later when men's clothing designers introduced those hideous stack-heeled shoes. Congress should have intervened immediately.

But no. Nothing happened. We sat around and twiddled our thumbs. Next thing you knew, men were wearing earrings.

Some men, I should say. The closest I ever came to having my ears pierced—and other parts, for that matter—was the time three buddies and I were riding in a station wagon en route to a day of quail hunting. We got broadsided by another vehicle at 50 mph, and I was knocked into the back compartment on top of three very scared, very angry bird dogs who vented both their fear and their anger, repeatedly, on my chubby little body.

As for makeup? You gotta be kidding.

Right now, this definitely-not-with-it guy has an overwhelming urge to go splash on some Old Spice.

Picture day for geezers

January 31, 1992

P icture day recently was held at The News-Sentinel, giving the beautiful people a chance to make fun of my clothing. Again.

We have picture day every few years, or whenever the graphics experts discover some hilarious new way to make writers look ridiculous in print. It's just like picture day you remember from elementary school.

A note goes on the bulletin board announcing when the dread event will be held. Everyone is supposed to dress up, which is a direct violation of truth in advertising because nobody around this newspaper puts on the dog unless there's a funeral, a wedding or a summons to court. But on picture day, we all comb our hair and dig out coats and ties and desperately try to avoid catsup until the deed is done.

I wore what I always wear on picture day. A blue blazer. A blue, button-down-collar, oxford-cloth shirt. A striped tie.

I also wore pants and shoes, but it really wasn't necessary because the photographer never shoots anything but head and shoulders. We're like TV newscasters in that regard. Don't you ever watch Dan Rather or Peter Jennings and wonder if they're wearing anything besides undies?

Anyhow, as soon as I entered the newsroom, beautiful people started laughing. They called me cruel names and asked what was happening at the retirement home.

Why such abuse? Because stupid neckties are the rage these days, and I refuse to wear them.

You know the ties I'm talking about. The ones with flower designs and swirls of blue, yellow, red, orange, brown, green and black all slapped together. They look like a bruise.

Bruise ties are uglier than a four-day hangover and, hopefully, will soon fade from the scene. If not, no problem. It's more comfortable and economical to let fashion go its merry way.

I tried to be cool once. Oh, how I tried. When pleated pants came back in style—only old men wore them when I was a boy—I went to a clothing store and tried a pair on. One glance in the mirror and I suddenly remembered it was skinny old men who used to wear them. When you've got a gut like mine, pleats give you that Camel Tent and Awning profile.

New belt styles? That's another no-no.

You know how young men hitch up their pants these days? They buy an extra-long belt and let the tag end hang waaaaaaay down their left leg.

I could do that, too. I'd just need an industrial-length belt. At least 15 cows would have to be slaughtered for such an expanse of leather, and I don't want that on my conscience.

The beautiful people also laugh at my blue jeans. That's because my jeans aren't stone-washed or acid-rinsed or whatever. Instead, they are plain blue jeans, suitable for wear with cowboy boots, which is yet another of Venob's Fine Fashions. Along with velour sweaters.

I'll tell you just how bad it is. My daughter, a beautiful person in training, recently told me that the way I dress reminds her of the old coots she and her friends make fun of at the mall.

Geezerdom! After all these years of practice, I've finally reached the pinnacle of success.

A trying-on ordeal

June 20, 1995

I don't know whether or not O. J. Simpson was faking when he struggled desperately to put on those bloody gloves in the courtroom.

But one thing's for certain: It's embarrassing as whiz to have to try on any kind of clothing in public.

The gloves in question were the ones found at the Nicole Brown-Ronald Goldman murder scene, as well as at Simpson's house. They were important pieces of evidence against Simpson. When the prosecution asked him to try 'em on, he jerked and yanked and said in frustration to the jury, "They're too small."

Maybe. Maybe not.

The next day, a clothing expert examined the gloves and said they had shrunk from their original size. He insisted they would have fit Simpson at one time.

In any event, for once I couldn't help but feel sorry for The Juice. Maybe it's a man thing, or maybe it's just a quirk of mine, but trying on ANYthing while other people are watching makes me uncomfortable.

Surely it goes back to birthday parties in the formative years. You rip into a package that looks for all the world like a set of Gene Autry six-shooters. Or maybe a tackle box or a new seat for your bicycle.

But when the box opens—*arrrgh!*—it's a pair of pants.

"Oh, how nice!" somebody's mother coos. "Why don't you go try them on!"

Yeah, right. You'd rather die a dozen deaths.

But there is no escaping the task. As your buddies snicker devilishly, you slink into the next room and remove your comfortable, worn-out-at-the-knees jeans and pull the stiff, new pair into place.

Even worse, you are then forced to parade around in the hateful things in front of Gawd and half the neighborhood, the legs as unyielding as if they'd been splinted with 2-by-4s, while every mother in the joint tugs at the baggy areas and says, "Oh, don't worry. He'll grow into them."

It doesn't get better in adulthood. Go to a men's clothing store and see for yourself.

They make you stand in front of a mirror that has approximately 214 panels on it and shows your bulging image not only from the front, but also the back and both sides. At the same time, coveys of clerks with measuring tapes, straight pins and chalk are tugging and pulling and announcing to everyone in six adjoining counties, "Oh, don't worry. We can let it out."

Pioneers in the mail-order clothing business capitalized on this gender phenomenon, and now the men of America spend jillions of dollars a year trying on duds in the privacy of their own homes.

We never get the correct size on the first couple of orders, of course. Thus, we wind up spending half again as much on postage as we would if we'd just gone to the store in the first place and made our purchase over the counter.

But trust someone who knows. It's a small price to pay for dignity.

The seasonal sweater exchange

November 18, 1994

I did a stupid thing the other day. I took my sweaters out of storage in the garage and switched them with the T-shirts and shorts in my clothes drawer.

It's not the first time I've performed this routine. I do it every fall. And then in the spring, I reverse the process; the T-shirts and shorts come out of storage in the garage and get switched with the sweaters in my clothes drawer.

I've never understood why I bother with this seasonal exercise. Tradition, I suppose. It's one of those parental admonitions branded into the brain at an early age—along with wear clean undies in case you have a wreck, return borrowed items, and say please and thank you—and never goes away.

What's so stupid is that I rarely wear sweaters.

I've never taken an official count, but I'll bet between November and March, the total number of days I put on a sweater could be tallied on two hands.

The main reason is I'm too hot-natured. I can erupt into a rain forest of perspiration on the coldest day of the year.

Nonetheless, I fall victim to my own ignorance several times each winter.

I'll peek out the window at dawn, and the world will be sheathed in a thick layer of frost. Gray skies. Breeze out of the north. Perfect sweater weather.

Trouble is, the sweater weather stays outside. As soon as I get to the office, where the temperature is reminiscent of Miami in July, I turn into a pool of melted butter.

It would be different if I spent most of my time outdoors. That's where a sweater earns its keep.

But that brings up another quandary: Who, besides a model for L.L. Bean, would go outside and cut firewood or shovel snow while wearing a good sweater?

Thus, I wind up saving my sweaters for more dress-up occasions. Indoors, of course. Where I drown in sweat.

Some people are cold-natured. They can be mummified in yards of wool, cotton, acrylic or any other fabric and appear the epitome of comfort.

Not me. I look like Rodney Dangerfield under intense police questioning.

I'll tell you another reason why I tend to shy away from sweaters: No matter what you may have heard or read or thought to the contrary, a rumpled, loose-fitting sweater does not camouflage a jelly belly.

Trust your Uncle Rotundity on this matter. He has glanced into a mirror a time or three and seen his shame on public display. A bulbous belly is a bulbous belly, regardless if it is shielded by a golf shirt, a dress shirt or a sweater. Except that a sweater, in this circumstance, tends to take on the proportions of a pup tent.

I have long-since resigned myself to my fate. Just as I walk through the stupid clothing drawer exchange twice a year, I will forget this column in a few weeks and climb into a sweater. And spend the entire afternoon moping my brow.

Oddly enough, I have never noticed so much as a droplet of sweat, let alone a hint of jelly belly, on those models for L.L. Bean.

Good grief, Lord Sieff!

November 28, 1993

There is cause for great happiness this Christmas shopping season: Lord Sieff's underwear is not available on the Knoxville market.

I have come to this joyous conclusion after checking three men's clothing shops. At each location, I got the same reply. "Never heard of Lord Sieff."

Wonderful. We can only hope it stays that way. But it probably won't.

Lord Sieff is an English brand of clothing. Given the strong tradition of British influence here in the colonies, I fear it is only a matter of time before the invasion occurs.

I learned about Lord Sieff's underwear a couple of days ago in a column from the London (not Kentucky) Times. It described the vast popularity of this new rage in men's underclothing. At Kensington High Street's Marks and Sparks store, one clerk said, "We've sold thousands."

What's is so horribly wrong with these undies?

Two things.

First, they look like a man's swimming suit from the 1920s. They are a one-piece affair with a tank top and knicker-style leggings that run down to just above the knee. These are form-fitting drawers, like an aerobics workout suit.

That's bad enough. As an American male with over four decades of underwear experience, I speak with authority when I say men want boxers or briefs beneath their britches, not something Gramps wore for a dip in the creek.

But by far, the more frightening point of criticism is that these puppies have a major design flaw, one that men are sure to discover shortly after their third cup of coffee.

There ain't no way to do Number One.

Or, as London Times columnist A.A. Gill so beautifully put it, "There's no hole, slit, vent or aperture for thingy, the old man."

Yes. Lord Sieff's undies have to be taken off at the shoulders and then peeled all the way down before Number One can be accomplished. At least that's the case for 99.9 percent of maledom. I once saw a duck hunter—he was wearing chest-high waders and standing in waist-deep water at the time—perform Number One with nary a mistake, but the feat required a combination of anatomy, acrobatics and accuracy achievable by surely no more than two men in 20 million.

I feel certain a radical feminist is behind this madness. Probably a female clothing designer who has never forgiven men for making bras that snap in the rear. This is her idea of revenge.

It could be worse. Given the savage, anti-male events that occurred this year, the introduction of underwear without a porthole is the least of men's worries.

Surely everyone in America knows the pitiful situation of John Bobbitt, whose angry wife sliced off his thingy. Then a few days ago in Los Angeles, a 39-year-old man named James Macias underwent involuntary castration at the scissors-wielding hands of his wife.

If the worst thing your bride does is order you a pair of Lord Sieff undies from London, count your lucky stars. Among other thingies.

A royal pad in the butt

September 3, 1995

It is fitting that in 1995, the 75th anniversary of women's suffrage, men are finally getting equal rights in the clothing department.

We're being encouraged to wear falsies.

No, not *that* kind of falsies. I'm talking about something a bit farther to the south.

Don't take my word for it. Look over my shoulder as I read the latest sartorial news from Rush Industries of New York, maker of "Super Shaper" underwear.

"It's the dawn of a new era, when men can cosmetically enhance their physical appearance as women have done for centuries," the report begins. "Men no longer have to be satisfied with what nature provided. By wearing Super Shaper briefs, men can achieve eye-catching buttocks instantly."

That's right, lads. Junk the Nautilus machine and burn your health club card. Toss those expensive running shoes into the Goodwill bin, ice down another six-pack, and order an extra-large pizza. If you don't have the patience to develop buns of steel the sweaty way, just cough up $24.95 and own the tush you've always coveted.

The report goes on: "This innovative garment is designed with special pads to discreetly build up the bottom and has center-stitched seams for 'eye-popping' cleavage, along with a bottom band to achieve perfectly proportioned buttocks. Totally undetectable. No ride-up crotch. No binds. No pinches. Only you will know the Hollywood secret of looking like a hunk."

That's not all. For an extra five bucks, you can buy a "specially contoured endowment pad" that snaps in place on the front.

(Which reminds me of an utterly tasteless story about the country boy who decided to impress the women by sticking a large Irish potato inside his undergarments, just like he'd heard down at the pool hall, but the gimmick didn't work for him because he put it in the back. But the story's so tasteless, I don't believe I'll tell it.)

This is progress? Women used to admire men for our brains, our quick wit, our cool reserve in the face of a crisis. Now, we've been reduced to nothing but a piece of raw meat.

Ooooh, I feel so violated! I want to run home and take a bath.

We should have seen it coming, I suppose. Once women started wearing pants and neckties into the corporate board room, it was only a matter of time before men started prancing around in falsies. Next thing you know, we'll be dabbing on lipstick, and they'll be shopping for power tools and chewing tobacco.

John Wayne is surely spinning in his grave at the very thought of it all. If he were still around, by golly, he'd—

Wait a minute! Now that I mention it, The Duke did have a fancy rear end, didn't he? The way he sauntered along at an angle, swinging those arms, slinging those hips from side to side, his butt poked out like a $4 ham hock. Gasp! You don't think he wore Super Shapers, do you?

I don't want to know.

Don't issue the skirts

September 6, 1994

About 20 years ago, men began wearing shoes with stacked heels. "Hoo-boy," I said at the time. "What'll be next? Earrings?"

About 15 years ago, men began wearing earrings. "Hoo-boy," I said at the time. "What'll be next? Skirts?"

About two weeks ago, I saw a fashion story that described the growing popularity of men's skirts. I was too stunned to say anything.

Thankfully, this bold new design has not taken the local market by storm.

"We don't have men's skirts," said Michelle Edgens of The Gap. "I'd say Atlanta is the closest you'll find them."

A similar response came from Matt McClellan of M.S. McClellan & Co.: "We haven't had any requests. I don't expect we will."

Ditto from Kevin Matthews of J. Riggings: "Nobody has asked for them, and I don't foresee us carrying any."

But you never know about the whims of fashion. If you doubt me, let the words "leisure suit" roll around in your mouth for a moment, and see if you don't break out in hives.

"I have seen several articles about skirts in men's fashion magazines," said Mike Grebe of Attitudes. "Apparently, this is what's happening in Italy. I doubt you'll see much of it around here, though. Our company is bringing in some different fashions, not the same basic stuff Knoxville is used to. But skirts are not on the agenda."

On the other hand, some young men already are buying women's skirts at Merry Go Round, "if they're skinny enough to fit into them," said Karen Waites.

"We've sold them for a couple of years," she added. "It's mainly the teenage and college group."

Good. That means that I—and other members of the Over 40 But Not Quite Over the Hill Gang—won't have to worry about chasing the latest style. As if we ever did.

What we do is wait for style to come to us, which happens from time to time. Whenever blue jeans and cotton shirts surge to the top of the fashion charts, we dress to the nines. Otherwise, we simply wear our blue jeans and cotton shirts and get laughed at by the beautiful people.

I'm anxiously waiting for the rebirth of another Over 40 But Not Quite Over the Hill Gang favorite. Coaches' shorts.

Coaches' shorts are the only form of polyester suitable for mankind. They have wide elastic waistbands that yield to the mature figure, particularly if the figure is growing more mature, bite by bite, under the influence of barbecued ribs, baked beans, cole slaw and beer.

Coaches' shorts can be washed approximately 10,587 times and show no sign of shrinkage. Best of all, they contain pockets, fore and aft, for storing knives, spare change, chewing tobacco, handkerchief, toothpicks, car keys, billfold and notes from our wives to please stop at the store and pick up some bread, milk, cereal and eggs, which we always forget until we get home.

Where would men keep these important items if we had to wear skirts?

In our pantyhose?